RULING PASSIONS

WITHDRAWN

RULING PASSIONS

Sexual violence, reputation and the law

Sue Lees

Open University Press
Buckingham • Philadephia

Open University Press
Celtic Court
22 Ballmoor
Buckingham
MK18 1XW

and
1900 Frost Road, Suite 101
Bristol, PA 19007, USA

First Published 1997

A catalogue record of this book is available from the British Library

ISBN 0–335–19613–6 (pbk)   0–335–19614–4 (hbk)

Library of Congress Cataloging-in-Publication Data
Ruling passions: sexual violence, reputation, and the law / [edited
  by] Sue Lees.
       p. cm.
    Includes bibliographical references and index.
    ISBN 0–335–19614–4 (hb). — ISBN 0–335–19613–6 (pb)
    1. Women—Crimes against—Great Britain. 2. Violent crimes—Great
Britain. 3. Sex discrimination in criminal justice administration—
Great Britain. 4. Sex discrimination against women—Great Britain.
5. Sex role—Great Britain. I. Lees, Sue.
HV6250.4.W65R85 1996
364′.082—dc20   96–19876
                                                                        CIP

Typeset by Graphicraft Typesetters Ltd, Hong Kong
Printed in Great Britain by Biddles Ltd, Guildford and King's Lynn

Contents

Acknowledgements

The author and publishers wish to thank the following for permission to use copyright material: Sage publications for 'The policing of girls in every-day life: sexual reputation, morality and the social control of girls', in M. Cain (ed.) (1989) *Growing Up Good*, pp. 19–37; Carfax Publications for 'Talking about sex in sex education', in *Gender and Education* (1994) Vol. 6(3), pp. 281–92; reprinted from *Women's Studies International Forum*, 'Judicial rape' (1993) Vol. 16, pp. 11–36 with kind permission from Elsevier Science Ltd, The Boulevard, Langford Lane, Kidlington OX5 IGB, UK; Routledge publications and Jeanne Gregory for permission to reprint 'In search of gender justice: sexual assault and the criminal justice system' written with J. Gregory in *Feminist Review* (1994) No. 48, pp. 80–93; Open University Press, Buckingham for 'Lawyers' work as constitutive of gender relations' (in this book entitled 'Men getting away with murder'), in M. Cain and C. Harrington (eds) (1994) *Lawyers in a Postmodern World*, pp. 124–55; and to Open University Press for permission to reprint 'Naggers, whores and libbers: provoking men to kill', in J. Radford and D. Russell (eds) (1992) *Femicide: The Politics of Woman Killing*, pp. 267–89.

Many have contributed to this book over the years. Caryll Faraldi, a freelance journalist gave invaluable help taking transcripts of murder trials at the Old Bailey and David St George, Press Officer at the Old Bailey was always helpful. I am immensely grateful to Jeanne Gregory who collabor-ated with me on the research into police recording practices, and made invaluable comments on several chapters, and to Lynn Ferguson, Producer of *Dispatches's Getting Away with Rape* and *Male Rape*, and Channel 4's 'Till Death Do Us Part. In particular I would like to thank Lynn for her contribution to the analysis contained in Chapter 5 on male rape. I am also grateful to David Lloyd, commissioning editor of Channel 4. Thanks too to Maureen Cain who encouraged me to start writing many years ago, to Celia Cowie who collaborated with the research on young women, to Eileen McColgan and Phil Rumney who both contributed to the chapter on marital rape, and to Jill Radford and Rights of Women for advice. I am also indebted to John Lea for his support and help, in particular with word processing. Finally, many thanks to Jacinta Evans for suggesting this book and for her constant encouragement.

Introduction

This collection of essays draws together some previously published papers that have been updated along with three additions. Their main aim is to explore the gendered characteristics of the processes of power underlying the constructions of masculinity and femininity within a number of different social contexts such as the school, where adult identities are developed and the judicial system, where the law regulates the limits of acceptable behaviour. The essays address Heidensohn's (1985: 108) injunction to address 'the production of conformity' and chart the way that social, legal and institutional processes serve to legitimate male domination and possessiveness, and a particular form of femininity which is geared to the production of conformity to patriarchal society.

Adrian Howe (1994) pointed to two distinct projects within criminology: a masculinist one of analysing the emergence of punishment regimes in the contest of the state's power to punish, and a feminist one of mapping the differential impact of disciplinary power on lived female bodies. The following chapters indicate that these two projects, of analysing the emergence of punishment regimes and the control of disciplinary power on human bodies, run parallel to each other and are interrelated. The state's failure to punish male violence against women runs parallel to the way aggressive masculinity is constituted through the social processes by which male bodies are disciplined through sport and within other male institutions as described by Connell (1995) and Mac an Ghaill (1991, 1994). Likewise, the double standard of sexual reputation acts both as a form of disciplinary power over women's bodies, constricting their independence; and, as the basis for assessing a woman's credibility in legal trials, it serves as an institutionalized norm within the legal system to legitimate male violence in the name of scientific objectivity, impartiality, and neutrality. I show how these male norms are institutionalized at every stage of the criminal justice system although they may not always be consistent or coherent. The law ostensibly constrains male violence against women but in substance allows such violence to continue (see MacKinnon 1987, 1989; Smart 1990).

Constructions of masculinity and femininity are dynamic. They vary from one society to another and have evolved historically. There is a sense, however, in which they are remarkably impervious to change. These essays explore the processes (or what Foucault referred to as disciplinary procedures) by which conventional femininity is constituted and reconstituted, developed and resisted, in the everyday life of young men and women. We need to examine the way gender is situationally structured (depending too on certain differences of race, class and social orientation) in order to understand the relationship between gender, power and social structure (see Connell 1987, 1995; Messerschmidt 1995). Femininities must be viewed as structured action in which women are positioned differently.

Methodology

How young women and men develop a gendered subjectivity is dependent on language. Language, belief systems and social relations are all interrelated. Language reflects a type of power which limits and constrains modes of expression and belief. All forms of talk invoke some constraints. Language also plays a role in limiting discourses. According to Bronwyn Davies (1989: 1), an Australian researcher, who studied the development of discourses in preschool children:

> In learning the language they learn to constitute themselves and others as unitary beings, as capable of coherent thought, as gendered and as one who is in a particular relation to others. Language is both a resource and a constraint. It makes social personal being possible, but it also limits the available forms of being to those which make sense within the terms provided by the language.

In passing language on to children we also pass on a relative entrapment in the social order, including those elements of the social order we might well want to move beyond. These essays explore how the discourse of female reputation acts as a material practice which constricts women's independence and acts as a form of power and domination over emotions and passions. The discourse of female sexual reputation (by which women are categorized in terms of the virgin/whore dichotomy) is the main criterion on which female identity is assessed in adolescence and is also reflected in legal discourses regarding a woman's credibility when appearing as a complainant in rape trials.

During the past 15 years I have carried out four research projects, varying in size and duration: the first, funded by the Inner London Education Authority, involved interviews and group discussions with 100 15–16-year-old young women (and some 30 young men) in three London comprehensive schools conducted between 1981–85; the second involved taking transcripts of rape and homicide trials at the Old Bailey and some other Crown Courts in the late 1980s and analysing the contents. This research, comprising here of an analysis of the representation of the body in rape trials, is drawn from my own transcripts of rape trials in 1988 and 1989 and provided the stimulus for two Channel 4 television documentaries shown in 1993 and 1994. Additional material from research conducted in conjunction with a Channel 4 *Dispatches* programme shown in 1994 is included. The third project, carried out with Jeanne Gregory in 1991–93, involved an analysis of police reporting of sexual assault cases and interviews with women who reported sexual assault. This was funded by the Crime Prevention Unit of Islington council under the auspices of the Department of the Environment (see Gregory and Lees 1996). Fourth, two further chapters investigate first the link between marital rape and murder through documentary analysis of Court of Appeal reports and second, explanations for sexual assaults on men undertaken in conjunction with another television *Dispatches* programme shown in May 1995.

The construction of sexuality

In the research I undertook on adolescent girls, the subject of the first two chapters, I found that the construction of female sexuality involved the construction of a difference between slags (whores, promiscuous girls) and drags (marriageable respectable girls). Sexuality is not natural for women but only resides in the slag. A girl who enjoys sex is therefore potentially deemed to be promiscuous and a slag.

The actions and evaluations and labelling of one another by girls and of girls by boys is indicative of the operation of a particular discourse about sexuality and moral worth. The language of slag is not exercised by boys over girls, rather both sexes inhabit a world structured by the language quite irrespective of who speaks to or about whom. The double standard of morality is so embedded in language and in the conceptions of masculinity and femininity that girls rarely contest them although they are preoccupied in their talk about boys and with the injustice of the way in which they are controlled by boys.

The criteria for assessing reputation, from appearance (such as wearing your skirt too short or your top too low) to acting independently (such as going places on your own or being a single mum) are ambiguous. The lack of specific content of the term slag means that girls are in a permanent state of vulnerability. The terms are so taken for granted that few girls know how to deal with them. Their only defence is to deny the truth of the allegation or to revert to the protection of a boyfriend by getting attached. As Cain (1989) points out, the solidarity and collective denial of the validity of these boyish criteria has not even occurred to them. They accept the criteria and end up assisting the boys in the policing of other girls: 'They are as likely to call other girls slags as the boys. They become God's police in North London' (Summers 1975).

It is therefore difficult for girls to contest insults. Their subjectivity, their experience of sexual desire and love, their very emotions are structured by language. How sexuality is talked about, thought about, displayed and structured is a crucial aspect of social life. The importance placed on their sexual reputation acts as a constraint on female independence and desire. Young women have no language to draw on to talk about their desire (what Fine 1988 refers to as the missing discourse of desire) and the double standard embedded in the taken for granted patterns of male and female sexuality are assumed to be natural.

In a similar way boys too police each other. Donna Eder (1995), in a fascinating study of the social relations of boys and girls in an Australian secondary school, found that great importance was placed on men being aggressive and tough and that the boys conveyed the importance of toughness through ritual insults. Many of the names the boys used to insult each other implied some form of weakness such as wimp or squirt. Other names such as pussy, girl, fag and queer associated lack of toughness with femininity or homosexuality. She quotes a number of studies which indicate that boys police masculinity in each other's peer groups. Boys enhanced their masculinity by throwing homosexual insults at boys who failed to engage in stereotypical masculine behaviour. One of the boys I interviewed who preferred the company of girls was similarly stereotyped as gay despite his clear heterosexual orientation. Beynon (1989) found similar insults in everyday use at a tough comprehensive school in England.

Therefore language (or the discourse of female reputation in particular) acts as a material practice with its own determinate effects, acting as a form of control over their emotions and passions and steering girls into subordinate relationships with men. Marriage or becoming attached, adopting the conventional role of a wife, as we shall see, is the only sure way to redeem your reputation.

The type of analysis undertaken could be described as discourse analysis which can be understood as 'a particular way of analysing how ideas, or ideology function as a system of power and domination'. We investigated the way young men and women talked about their lives and the myriad of conversations and actions which daily constitute them. Verbal sexual abuse (in Britain by the use of the term slag derived from the slagheap, a term used to describe the coal dust which is discarded) acts as a moral censure. Being called a slag, redeeming oneself in certain ways (getting a steady boyfriend), discussing whether one's friends are slags, blaming the girl for precipitating rape, for putting up with sexual violence – this is the practice of the language of sexual power, not a reflection of some other process hidden from view. The effectiveness of slag rests on its uncontested nature as a category, its elusiveness and its denigratory force. Desire is shaped through such regimes of truth which make particular desires seem correct and inevitable and others appear to be harmful or disreputable.

The effect of insults on young women's lives show there are real penalties for breaches of social behaviour and no girl can afford to disregard them. As Maureen Cain (1990: 7) writes:

> There are real rewards for conventional living, and real penalties for eschewing it. It is therefore necessary for researchers to recognise these realities and the discourse of sexually appropriate behaviour which expresses and constitutes them ... it is clear that discourses can be used to authorise and justify painful and even penal practices, and that sometimes the use of language can constitute a pain itself.

These penalties lead girls to become implicated, albeit unconsciously, in the enforcement of patriarchal control in a similar way that, for example, mothers in some societies become implicated in enforcing genital mutilation on their daughters. This is a more extreme way of controlling female sexuality, safeguarding a woman's virginity until marriage, protecting woman's honour and enhancing men's pleasure in intercourse (Hicks 1993: 73–8).

I am reminded of the concept of 'power' as 'self carried' which has been elaborated by Foucault (1990), a power of male dominance which is not exercised by boys over girls, but which girls carry with them and which permeates their lives and their recreations. Using the analogy of the panopticon, where individuals can all be seen from a central tower but do not know when they are being surveilled, Foucault (1991: 200–2) describes how each individual ends up interiorizing this inspecting gaze to the point where he is his own overseer. This induces a state of conscious and permanent visibility that assures the automatic functioning of power.

The discussion of power does not relate to whether girls are concentrated in certain roles rather than others, but can be seen as a field of force in which men and women are equally trapped rather than being exercised by men over women. It can perhaps be seen as an example of how Foucault (1991: 298) conceived that the great carceral network reaches all the disciplinary mechanisms that function throughout society including as Howe (1994: 190) suggests 'the moral censures of girls' sexuality'.

What Foucault fails to explain is why discourses are so systematically produced in male interests and why his denial of power as a possession is so difficult to reconcile with feminist calls for subverting and contesting male power. The reality of male power is difficult to ignore. As Ramazanoglu and Holland (1993: 244) point out,

> If men demand sexual intercourse but refuse to wear condoms; if young women fake orgasms to keep their men happy and so ensure a continued relationship; if women silence their own desires by defining 'sex' as his penetration, his orgasm, his satisfaction, explanations are needed of how power is being exercised, how men get and keep control and what, if anything, should be resisted.

The meaning of sexual violence

Since the 1970s feminists have challenged all kinds of myths about sexuality and sexual violence: the myth that rape was an expression of sexual desire rather than of sexual power and violence; the myth that rape was due to an irresistible urge of male desire, or a question of men 'misreading signals' in a sexual negotiation rather than a violent sexual assault; or the myth that the typical rapist is a stranger or black. Whereas rape is seen by the courts as an act motivated by sexual urges or passions, feminists argued that it should be seen as an act of violence and humiliation (see Brownmiller 1976). Zsuzsanna Adler (1987: 11), who carried out the first study of British rape trials in the early 1980s, suggested that 'so long as rape is seen as an act of sexuality rather than aggression and hostility, it will continue to be interpreted as predominantly pleasurable to both parties rather than harmful to the victim'. The refusal to link the crime to sex by feminists can be seen as a reaction to claims that rape was the inevitable result of innate male aggression coupled with an uncontrollable sexual need. Carol Smart, Professor of Sociology at Leeds University (1989), identified a drawback in calling rape violence as avoiding challenging male sexuality when 'male sexuality and its prerogatives are precisely what rape and rape trials are all about'. If rape is to be seen as a sexual crime, this does not mean that it is an expression of sexual desire. Rather it should be seen as the use of sexuality to express issues of power and domination.

Embedded in the idea of male sexuality as natural and therefore uncontrollable is the idea that women are responsible for tempting men and, by the way they dress or behave, leading them on into uncontrollable rape and violence. This means that quite reasonable behaviour on the part of the woman can be interpreted by the court as provocative to the rapist, and clothing which women may wear merely to keep up with the latest fashion may be said in court to 'invite' the man to make a sexual assault.

This is one of the core issues of rape trials as it raises the question of what characterizes consensual sexual intercourse and how it can be distinguished from rape. The law provides no positive definition of consensual sex. Moreover the picture that emerges from rape trials implicit in the arguments presented by defence counsels of why the alleged rape was really 'only normal sex', is that normal sex is far removed from mutually negotiated, mutually satisfactory sex between equals. Rather the legal view of 'normal sex' encompasses a male view of women acquiescing to sexual use by men. Mutual negotiation is not a test of normality (see Jamieson 1994). How we conceptualize consensual sexuality is therefore a core issue in social life and the law.

Research into disciplinary processes in adolescence

Chapters 1 and 2 are based on the research on adolescent young men and women. Until the 1980s, sociological research on youth was limited by two main shortcomings. First, it was almost exclusively concerned with boys. Images of youth that emerged from poetry, literature, psychology, education and sociology were of male adolescents and rarely included girls. A second weakness was the almost total lack of an analysis of gender relations. Rather than examining the savage chauvinism of male youth culture, texts often reflected a celebration of masculinity depicting rock bands, drug culture, hippies and skinheads, romantically disregarding the sexism embedded in many practices. Until the 1980s the emphasis was on class differences, with little discussion of gender dominance and subordination, of the construction of masculinities and femininities, or the effect of these constructions on the development of identities. Psychological studies of girls were equally limited in so far as they neglected to address gender subordination and tended to regard non-conformity to traditional sex roles as some kind of deviance.

It was within this context that I set out, with Celia Cowie, a researcher, to investigate the experience of ordinary young women in three comprehensive schools in London. We spent the first year negotiating with schools and having endless discussions about the methodology. One burning issue was whether to include young women from different ethnic groups or whether the samples would be too small to be useful. We decided to ask young women to form their own groups for discussions and therefore our final sample included a full range of the diverse ethnic backgrounds represented in London schools.

In the research on adolescents we used individual and group interviews to explore how they saw their lives in their own terms rather than by asking preconceived questions. We decided to do this by eliciting the terms on which they describe and handle their world. The method was non-directive although we investigated five main areas: what the girls thought about school, friendship, boys, sexuality and their expectations of the future. The aim was to explore the various discourses through which they described their experiences. For example, it was more important to understand how girls talked about sex than to find out about the prevalence of, say, pre-marital sexual relations. What we found of particular significance was the operation of an ideology that transforms the experience of unfair relations between the sexes into an acceptance of those relations as natural. It is somehow wrong and nasty for a girl to invite sexual activity but natural for the boy to be after it, to attempt to pester you into it, to tell if you do and to fabricate its occurrence if you don't.

The research bridges the gap between discourse and empirical research in linking the ideological and material facets of women's lives and expos-ing the complex and contradictory disciplinary processes that constrict their experience. We took transcripts of all the interviews and group dis-cussions and by examining the transcripts tried to tease out exactly how certain concepts – particularly sexual insults such as slag, cow and poof – were used. This can be seen as a way of exploring 'the making and remak-ing of conventions in social practice itself' (see Connell 1995: 35). Looking across at the transcripts enabled the girls' responses to be followed up, and allowed them to be more specific and more revealing of both intimate material and the connections across material that indicate the social con-text of those feelings, beliefs and ideas. We were thus able to examine the communalities of the girls' lives and the way in which their individual experiences were socially structured. This comprises an analysis at the level of language and is a way of observing how constructions of masculinity and femininity are dynamic. They are under a continual process of integration and contestation.

Given the strictures against the researcher making any positive critical intervention in order to avoid bias, it was difficult at times to know how far to question the girls' ideas. A useful technique was to ask girls to give examples to illustrate exactly what they meant by what they said. So if they referred to the word 'slag', I would question them about when the term might be used, or what happened if a boy boasted he had had two girls. Another useful strategy was to ask girls to discuss in a group what a girl's reputation rested on and whether violence ever occurred. Girls often disagreed with each other, and discussions were dynamic and often heated. My approach could be described as one of conscious partiality (Mies 1983: 122), where the researcher identifies her own experience, in this case of the contradictory nature of growing up in a patriarchal society, with girls or women who are the participants.

Girls are not passive victims. Femininities are polarized around accom-modation or resistance to male dominance (Connell 1987) as I show in discussing the various ways girls deal with the double standard. Yet this can be a contradictory phenomenon. It is difficult for girls to reject many of the characteristics of conventional femininity. As Messerschmidt (1995) reveals in his study, African American girl gangs in the United States were deeply implicated in crime and violence yet heterosexual monogamy for girls was taken for granted. However it was considered unnatural for boys to refuse offers of sex. 'Bad girl femininity', as he depicts it, consists of a combination of conventional and atypical gender practices (such as violence); each practice being justified by appropriate circumstances.

In Chapter 2, the implications of this research for formulating sex education policies is developed. Sex education is often embarked on without an adequate understanding of the social context of sexuality and of the significance of changes in sexual practice that have occurred over the past few decades. The reasons for the difficulty men and women have with communicating with each other are discussed and the need to develop ways in which the power relations between boys and girls can be addressed and the derogatory way menstruation, pregnancy and girls are perceived by boys can be challenged.

Research and the law

Much feminist criminology has been concerned with explaining the polarity between male and female crime rates with reference to the way feminine and masculine identities are constituted and regulated by the law. Women commit crime rarely and research has shown that imprisonment is more likely to be due to their sexual status and non-conformity to the traditional feminine role than to the gravity of the offence committed. Pat Carlen (1983: 4) found that most of the women she interviewed in prison had committed only very minor offences and questioned whether the modern prison was necessarily about crime and punishment at all. Single parents, African Caribbean women, separated or divorced women, or women who do not fill the appropriate female roles are more likely to go to prison than women who portray conventional feminine characteristics (see Carlen 1985; Carlen and Worral 1987; Hudson 1987: 119–21).

When women appear in the courts it is more likely to be as complainants in cases involving interpersonal violence than as suspects of crime. Even in regard to murder, few women kill and those who do have often been subjected to years of previous violence from their partners. Yet these essays vividly show that not only are women's complaints of assault persistently dismissed or minimized, but women are portrayed as liars, slags, whores, vengeful, spiteful, dangerous, uncontrollable and unscrupulous harridans.

bell hooks, the American feminist writer, makes the perceptive point that women are expected to keep quiet about rape. Women who are brave enough to speak out should not, therefore, be labelled 'victims' but should be seen as rebels who are unprepared to remain silent. By reporting assaults to the police, hooks (1989) argues, they become targets of punishment themselves for the transgression of speaking out. Even when convictions ensue, the length of cross-examination is quite out of proportion as illustrated by two recent cases. In 1996 Julia Walton gave up her anonymity to protest at the way she had been cross-examined for six days by her assailant, Ralston Edwards after he had discharged his defence barrister. He had worn the same clothes as when he had repeatedly raped her (*Daily Telegraph*, 23 August 1996). Shortly after, a Japanese woman who had been gang raped by five attackers was subjected to 12 days of cross-examination (*The Guardian*, 7 September 1996).

The sexism of the judicial system takes many forms, from legal constructions (such as concepts of rationality), as has been documented by feminist philosophers' critique of the neutrality of the law, to the attitudes of lawyers, and the intricate and ostensibly 'neutral' rules of evidence and court procedures, as outlined in this book (see MacKinnon 1989; Smart 1995). The law is not simply patriarchal but bourgeois, discriminating against poorer and black men as well as women (Naffine 1990). Nonetheless, in regard to sexual crimes, most men, whatever their social class or racial origin are likely to be acquitted. Some barristers share views that many rapists appear to have regarding the promiscuity of women. David Lederman, defence barrister in one of the trials monitored at the Old Bailey, the Central Criminal Court (interviewed for the *Dispatches* documentary, *Getting Away with Rape*, shown in 1994) explained the man he was defending, who had been reported by no less than eight independent women for rape in the following terms:

> What 18–20-year-old girl who's gone to a discotheque and within five minutes is going for a drive with a man she'd never met before, what has she got in the back of her mind? I mean, is she really going for a drive in order to discuss the Liberal Democrat next election manifesto in relation to local government elections, or is she going in the car with, in the back of her mind the thought that she quite fancies him, he quite fancies her and something exciting might happen?

He dismisses the woman's account of a terrifying drive at high speed at the dead of night, and of being raped and buggered and her fear of being killed. Instead he dismisses her story as false allegations.

It may well be that there is a convergence of views among men (and women) who represent the most dominant form of masculinity, such as judges and barristers, and some men who resort to enhancing their masculine identity through violence when other means, such as paid work, are absent. Certainly, as we shall see, some judges appear to express sympathy for men who have killed their wives in horrific circumstances, and the tactics used by some barristers to defend men accused of rape indicate a significant degree of empathy verging on condolence. Such attitudes mirror

Pat Carlen's (1983) fascinating scrutiny of the views of Scottish sheriffs about the criteria by which they decide whether women should be sent to prison, where emphasis on conformity to conventional femininity was crucial. In a similar way, according to Dobash *et al.* (1986) a successful outcome of therapy for women prisoners is judged by the characteristics of the good woman (dependence, compliance and caring for others rather than themselves).

Methodology of research on the judicial system

There is a paucity of research into the conduct of judicial trials. Many obstacles exist: gaining access is the greatest hurdle which requires time, patience and a great deal of determination. It took me two years to obtain a pass from the Department of Public Prosecutions which gave me access to the press seats at the Old Bailey, the Central Criminal Court, in order to be able to observe Crown Court trials. From the public galleries it was impossible to hear sufficiently well to take transcripts of trials and it was also very difficult to find out what court trials of a particular kind were to be heard. On occasion trials are shifted from one court to another which means that it is essential to have access to the listings office. Gradually by getting to know journalists attached to the Crown Court and the court officials it became easier to find out exactly when trials were to be heard. I also was lucky to gain access to police records, many of which I examined in the vaults of the Old Bailey, a ghostly place to read such trials. The research involved taking transcripts of trials, documentary analysis of records of reports of rape and sexual assaults, and analysing the transcripts and interviews with various professionals.

One of the most disturbing aspects of sitting in on rape trials was my growing awareness that for all the apparent rationality of the proceedings, the ambivalence of male attitudes towards rape colours everything. Outside the courts, in the listings office at the Old Bailey, I looked at the notice board which contains details of cases coming up. Someone had written in pencil under the charge Attempted Rape the word, 'Shame'. Shame, that is, that he had not succeeded.

Chapter 3 reports on this research, which formed the basis of articles I wrote for the *New Statesman and Society* (Lees 1989a, 1989b) and which led to a lively controversy in the letter pages lasting several weeks. These articles came to the notice of Lynn Ferguson, an independent TV producer, who contacted me shortly afterwards with the idea of making a programme to highlight the deficiencies in the judicial treatment of rape and sexual assault. It was not until three years later that we went together to meet David Lloyd, commissioning editor for Channel 4 *Dispatches*, who agreed to support the programme and subsidized a year's background research into the experiences of women who had been raped.

The TV consultancy research conducted with *Dispatches* provided a unique opportunity and funding so that we were able to monitor all rape trials at the Old Bailey over a four month period as well as covering 11 trials at Nottingham Crown Court and another smaller Crown Court. The television team, consisting of three researchers, a producer, a reporter and several others, were extraordinarily committed and worked day and night. There is always a risk in undertaking television research that confidentiality will not be respected or that the aims of the programme will clash with the aims of research. However Lynn Ferguson is an unusual TV producer who was totally dependable and always left it up to any woman to decide what she was or was not prepared to say on screen. Working with her was both stimulating and exacting.

Using the same method that I had first devised of taking verbatim records of rape trials, the *Dispatches* researchers took records of rape trials taking place over a four month period at the Central Criminal Court where there was any degree of acquaintance between the defendant and complainant. All the cases that occurred during this period were monitored. We also obtained official transcripts of the main cases that were investigated, some at other Crown Courts. Interviews were held with complainants and numerous others, ranging from judges to forensic scientists. The programme was screened in February 1994 and won the Royal Television prize for the best home documentary for 1994.

Drawing on this research, Chapter 4 analyses the way the body is represented in rape trials as both a site of contestation and how it functions as a medium of social control. This is analogous to Foucault's notion of power, which is produced in social relations that works through the production of docile bodies. Power is not a possession, as radical feminists have argued, but is seen as embedded in the discourses of medicine, law, psychology and the social sciences. This chapter also explores rape trials in the context of Foucault's notion of the changing nature of punishment in the modern era where I suggest that rape trials retain some elements of the feudal notion of punishment as a spectacle of degradation of the body, as reflected in torture, but visited on the victim rather than the offender. The increasing emphasis on the importance of sexual reputation coincided with the growing independence of women in the eighteenth and nineteenth centuries as portrayed by Anna Clark (1987). I explore the way even today, the 'discourse of female chastity' is not only reflected in the cross-examination of the victim in regard to activities such as drinking, but also in regard to the physiological processes of the female body, from menstruation to the medical scrutiny of assumed bodily signs of consent and 'appropriate' psychological reactions to assault.

Chapter 5 is also based on consultancy research undertaken with Lynn Ferguson, who was the director of the Channel 4 *Dispatches* programme on male rape (male sexual assaults on men) shown on 17 May 1995 following the widening of the definition of rape to include non-consensual anal penetration in the Criminal Justice and Public Order Act 1994. It is one of the first attempts to investigate the hidden problem of sexual assaults on men (see also McMullen 1990; Mezey and King 1992).

The relation of male and female rape is explored in relation to Connell's view (1995) that masculinity should not be seen as an undifferentiated category but is comprised of many diverse forms. Drawing on the concept of hegemony derived from Antonio Gramsci's analysis of class relations, it refers to the cultural dynamic by which a group claims and sustains a leading position in social life. Connell *et al.* refer to the most ascendant or dominant form in western industrialized capitalist societies as hegemonic masculinity, which is defined in relation not only to the sub-ordination of women but also to other subordinated marginalized masculinities. The enforcement and enhancement of hegemonic masculinity is characterized by an aggressive and macho form achieved through the subordination of women and men who are seen as homosexual or feminine (as marginalized). This chapter shows how this seems to be the most feasible explanation for why sexual assaults on men are predominantly perpetrated by men who regard themselves as heterosexual in sexual orientation. It also explains why male rape so often takes place in all-male institutions such as prisons and the army. By sexually humiliating men who do not appear to live up to the dominant form of masculinity, the perpetrator's own masculinity is enhanced.

Chapter 6 investigates why the marital rape exemption has taken so long to abolish. When laws giving substantial rights to the joint property on divorce had long been in force, the rape immunity law survived precisely because its abolition challenged the view of women as the possessions and passive objects of their husband's desires. Its abolition carries the clear implication that women now have a right to self-determination and that acceptable forms of sexuality require the presence of mutual desire. Yet consent is still absent from the definition of rape as interpreted in the present law.

In this chapter Court of Appeal cases of marital rape heard between 1991 and 1995 following the abolition of the marital rape exclusion in 1991 are reviewed. Marital rape is still not regarded as 'real' rape, sentences are awarded at the lower end of the scale and 50 per cent of the sentences reaching appeal were reduced even further.

This chapter can be seen as a bridge between the chapters referring to rape and those relating to wife killing. Research reviewed here indicates there is a close connection between reported marital rape and murder, and both are likely to occur where the marriage is breaking down or after separation and divorce. Most of such cases involve women who are desperately trying to escape from their husband's violence and where the woman's life may even be at risk. Contrary to judges' opinions, rape by a past or present lover is often more serious than that by a stranger. Wife and lover killings account for 45 per cent of homicides involving female victims. The research indicates that the threat to women's lives involved in cases of marital rape are still not taken seriously by the courts apart from cases involving weapons or severe injuries.

Chapters 7 and 8 should be read together as they are based on research conducted into 30 homicide trials at the Old Bailey, the Central Criminal Court, newspaper reports and judicial interpretations. These two chapters examine the ease with which men appear to be successful in pleading manslaughter (on the grounds of diminished responsibility or provocation) when accused of murdering their wives. The double standard operates in such a way that some judges appear to regard it as 'common sense' for men who kill their wives to be treated more leniently than wives who kill husbands. They rarely take into consideration the different circumstances under which men and women kill.

The first chapter charts how older forms of arbitrariness regarding, for example, the unreliability of women as witnesses, that have survived the growth of civil and legal rights, can find their point of re-entry into the modern legal system through the discretionary spaces embedded in the law, not least those involved in pleas of mitigating circumstances. The relationship between moral responsibility and defences of murder are discussed with reference to feminist critiques of concepts of the 'reasonable' man, the benchmark on which juries are instructed to decide culpability.

Chapter 8 draws on the transcripts of trials taken at the Old Bailey and various newspaper reports. Comparisons are made between the use of provocation as a defence by women who have killed their husbands or lovers, a topic which has been much debated (see Radford 1993), and by men who have killed their wives. These cases indicate how the acts of men and women are subject to a different set of legal expectations and standards.

These two chapters provided the background of another Channel 4 documentary, *Till Death Do Us Part*, on men who kill their wives, also directed by Lynn Ferguson. Research undertaken for this programme indicated that 60 per cent of men accused of killing their wives successfully pleaded diminished responsibility and were sentenced to an average of only four years imprisonment (Channel 4 1995). In monitoring all charges of murder over a four month period, the television researchers found that for domestic murders, the defence of 'diminished responsibility' formed the basis for the acceptance of manslaughter pleas by the Crown Prosecution Service (CPS) in 32 per cent of 'domestic' killings. In such cases, as illustrated in the Collins case described in Chapter 6, the defendant did not even have to stand trial.

In Chapter 9, which was written with Jeanne Gregory, Professor of Gender Studies at Middlesex University, we review various feminist approaches to challenging the law, outlining the constraints and limitations of such attempts. As Carol Smart (1989) has argued, hard-fought struggles to achieve legal reforms have often been translated into measures that only slightly improve the position of women.

In this chapter we review research into police recording practices and multiagency approaches to the problem of sexual assault. This research, although modest, was one of the first investigations into police practices in which access to police files was negotiated, and where it was possible to follow up complainants who had reported sexual assault to the police.

The fact that they were given access to police records represents a considerable breakthrough in the secrecy in which many judicial processes are shrouded. It took us two years of negotiation, involving contacting Scotland Yard, a number of interviews with local police chief superintendents and meetings with Islington Council Crime and Prevention Unit Support committee.

Police record forms of all cases of sexual assault reported between September 1988 and September 1990 at two London police stations were analysed. The research was funded by the Department of the Environment through the Islington Crime Prevention Unit and included interviews with 28 women who reported rape to the police, and agencies such as Victim Support, Rape Crisis and child protection teams as well as the Crown Prosecution Service. This chapter describes the achievement and limitation of researching into the judicial system.

Reforming the judicial system

There is evidence that the way the judicial system deals with sexual assault has deteriorated over recent years. It is now a disaster area. The conviction rate has dropped dramatically. In 1980 37 per cent of reported rapes in England and Wales resulted in a conviction, but by 1994 this had dropped to 8.4 per cent. There are several possible reasons for this dramatic drop. The CPS is underfunded and has been pressurized to cut the rising costs of trials as crime has risen. The proportion of cases overall not proceeding to court has increased from 7 to 33 per cent. The CPS performance indicators limit flexibility and encourage prosecutors to drop cases rather than risk an acquittal (see Rose 1996).

As McBarnet (1981) convincingly argues, there is a need to investigate not only the 'front men' of the legal system, like the police, but also the 'judicial and political élites' who make the law. This should include studies of sentencing policies (Box-Grainger 1986; Moxon 1988) and the impact of such policies on attrition rates. Additionally, a package of reforms is needed to create a fairer judicial system. New South Wales, Australia introduced such a package in the Crimes (Sexual Assault) Amendment Act (1981), which has led to a significantly higher proportion of cases going to trial and a higher conviction rate of 82 per cent (see Allen 1990: 231).

The research reported here indicates that the judiciary has become more entrenched than ever in denying and minimizing the abusive way that some men treat women, whether wives, lovers or acquaintances. Women complainants in rape and some murder trials are put 'on trial' and their credibility is judged by totally unfair and sexist criteria. The Court of Appeal still regards rape of wives as not 'real rape', and appears to be impervious to the stalking and persecution that some wives are subjected to from over-possessive husbands and partners. Men who kill their wives under such circumstances are often regarded with sympathy and given low sentences.

Far from living in a postfeminist era, and in spite of improvements in the way the police treat complainants, violence against women is still condoned by the judicial system. The personal and social costs of violence are immense (see Labour Party 1995). It is time for a radical overhaul of the system.

CHAPTER 1

The policing of girls in everyday life: sexual reputation, morality and the social control of girls

It's a vicious circle. If you don't like them they'll call you a tight bitch. If you go with them then they'll call you a slag afterwards.

A woman's sexuality is central to the way she is judged and seen both in everyday life and by the courts and welfare and law enforcement agencies. The denial of non-gendered subjectivity (treating women as human beings rather than as sex objects) is the major barrier to women's equality. To speak of a woman's reputation is to invoke her sexual behaviour, but to speak of a man's reputation is to refer to his personality, exploits and his standing in the community. For men sexual reputation is, in the main, separated from the evaluation of moral behaviour and regarded as private and incidental.

The policing of women through sexual reputation starts in adolescence, where a girl's sexual reputation is a constant source of debate and gossip between boys and girls, as well as between teachers and social workers. A girl's standing can be destroyed by insinuation about her sexual morality. A boy's reputation in contrast is usually enhanced by his sexual exploits.

When we set out in the early 1980s to talk to 15–16-year-old young women from different social classes and ethnic groups about their views of school, friendship, marriage, and the future, we did not intend to focus particularly on sexuality and gender relations. It was the girls' concern about their sexual reputations (epitomized by the ubiquitous use of the term 'slag' both by girls and boys) that led us to consider how sexual relations were socially structured. This made us increasingly aware of how frequently girls were the target of abuse from boys and other girls and to examine the way that the term 'slag' (implying sexual promiscuity), was used. The emphasis in youth culture studies on class has deflected attention away from the power imbalance between boys and girls, so that few studies have questioned the taken for granted subordination of girls by the structuring of gender relations.

The chapter is based on a three year research project in three London comprehensive schools carried out in the early 1980s.[1] A hundred 15–16-year-old young women from varied social class and ethnic groups were interviewed singly, in pairs, or in group discussions. The first two schools were mixed: both had women headteachers and were attempting to put into force an equal opportunities programme. The schools differed in their intake. One was predominantly white working class; another had a high proportion of different ethnic groups. Most of the children had been brought up in the area. The third school was a single-sex school with a mainly middle-class intake where the fieldwork was carried out a year later when the need to investigate the significance of social class differences became evident. Thirty young men were also interviewed from two other schools.

The research objective was to explore the subjective world of adolescent young women. I wanted to elicit the terms with which they describe and handle their world and to follow up the meanings through which they relate to the world, meanings both individually held and collectively shared. Such an objective required a qualitative method allowing the research to be sensitive to the girls' experience of the world. All the discussions and interviews were taperecorded and later transcribed. The design of the research involved analysing the transcriptions according to a schedule developed for the purpose. By focusing on the terms girls used to describe five aspects of their lives – schools, friendship, boys, sexuality and their expectations for the future – light was thrown on how those individual experiences are socially structured. Full reports of the research has now been published (Lees 1986, 1993a).

The structure of sexual relations and the concept of reputation

Boys and girls talk about sexuality in quite different ways. It is possible to delineate three main differences. First, while a boy's sexual reputation is enhanced by experience, a girl's is negated. Boys will brag to others about how many girls they have 'made', but a girl's reputation is under threat, not merely if she is known to have had sex with anyone other than her steady boyfriend, but for a whole range of other behaviour that has little to do with actual sex. Second, a boy's reputation and standing in the world is not predominantly determined by his sexual status or conquests. More important is his sporting prowess, his ability to 'take the mickey' or make people laugh. For a girl, the defence of her sexual reputation is crucial to her standing both with boys and girls, certainly around the age of 15 or so. The emphasis on the importance of sex to a girl's reputation is shown by a whole battery of insults which are in everyday use among young people. Finally, for boys sexism appears to be very important in male bonding, in

as much as denigration of girls and women is a crucial ingredient of camaraderie in male circles. The masculine tradition of drinking and making
coarse jokes usually focuses on the 'dumb sex object', the 'nagging wife' or
the 'filthy whore'. This is not the case for girls. As one girl told me, 'One
thing I noticed is that there are not many names you can call a boy. But
if you call a girl a name, there's a load of them. You might make a diction-
ary out of the names you can call a girl.'

The vocabulary of abuse

This lack of symmetry between the variety of names to call a girl and the
lack of names to call boys is the starting-point for an understanding of the
role of verbal abuse focusing on sexuality in reproducing, among girls, an
orientation towards the existing structures of patriarchal sex–gender relationships. The word which illustrates this asymmetry more clearly than
any other term is 'slag'. There is no equivalent to slag in the vocabulary of
terms available to be directed at boys. Derogatory words for boys such as
prick or wally are much milder than slag in that they do not refer to the
boy's social identity. To call a boy a poof is derogatory but this term is
not so much used as a term of abuse by girls of boys. As a term used between boys, it implies a lack of guts or femininity, which of itself connotes,
in our culture, weakness, softness and inferiority. There is no derogatory
word for active male sexuality. The promiscuous Don Juan or the rake may
be rebuffed, as in Mozart's opera, but his reputation is enhanced.

The potency of slag lies in the wide range of circumstances in which it
can be used. It is this characteristic that illustrates its functioning as a form
of generalized social control, along the lines of gender rather than class,
steering girls, in terms of both their actions and their aspirations, into the
existing structures of gender relations.

The first thing that is striking about the use of the term slag is the
difficulty of getting any clear definition of what it implies from those who
use it. This is true both for girls and boys. Take this girl's description of
what she calls a 'proper slag': 'I do know one or two slags. I must admit
they're not proper slags'. When asked to describe what *a proper slag is* she
says:

> Available aren't they? Just like Jenny, always on the look out for
> boys, non-stop. You may not know her but you always see her and
> every time you see her she's got a different fella with her, you get to
> think she's a slag, don't you? She's got a different fella every minute
> of the day.
> *So it is just talking to different boys?*
> You see them, some of them, they look as innocent as anything, but
> I know what they're like.

The implication here is that the girl who is called a slag sleeps around but this is by no means clear, and the insult often bears no relation at all to a girl's sexual behaviour. Boys are no clearer when it comes to defining what the characteristics used to define a girl as a slag are, which is why they disagree as to who is or is not a slag. In their book about boys, *Knuckle Sandwich*, researchers found:

> The boys classified all the girls into two categories: the slags who'd go with anyone and everyone (they were alright for a quick screw, but you'd never get serious about it) and the drags who didn't but whom you might one day think about going steady with. Different cliques of boys put different girls in each of the two categories.
>
> (Robbins and Cohen 1978: 58)

So while everyone apparently knows a slag and stereotypes her as someone who sleeps around, this stereotype bears no relation to the girls to whom the term is applied.

An alternative to asking those who use a term to define it, is to observe carefully the rules whereby the term is used. A look at the actual usage of slag reveals a wide variety of situations or aspects of behaviour to which the term can be applied, many of which are not related to a girl's actual sexual behaviour or to any clearly defined notion of sleeping around. A constant sliding occurs between slag as a term of joking, as bitchy abuse, as a threat and as a label. At one moment a girl can be fanciable and the next 'a bit of a slag' or even – the other side of the coin – written off as 'too tight'. The girls tread a very narrow line. They must not end up being called a slag. But equally they do not want to be thought unapproachable, sexually cold, a 'tight bitch'.

How 'slag' is used

This constant sliding means that any girl is always available to the designation slag in any number of ways. Appearance is crucial: by wearing too much makeup; by having your slit skirt too slit; by not combing your hair; by wearing jeans to dances or high heels to school; by having your trousers too tight or your tops too low. As one girl said, 'sexual clothes' designate. Is it any wonder when girls have to learn to make fine discriminations about appearances that they spend so much time deciding what to wear? Who you mix with also counts:

> I prefer to hang around with someone who's a bit decent, 'cos I mean if you walk down the street with someone who dresses weird you get a bad reputation yourself. Also if you looked a right state, you'd get a bad reputation. Look at her y'know.

Looking weird often means dressing differently from your own group.

Behaviour towards boys is, of course, the riskiest terrain. You must not hang around too much waiting for boys to come out (but all girls must hang around sufficiently); must not talk or be friendly with too many boys or too many boys too quickly, or even more than one boy in a group; you must not just find yourself ditched.

Almost everything plays a part in the constant assessment of reputation, including the way you speak:

> If we got a loud mouth, when we do the same they [the boys] do, they call us a slag, or 'got a mouth like the Blackwall tunnel'. But the boys don't get called that, when they go and talk. They think they're cool and hard and all the rest of it 'cos they can slag a teacher off.
> *Who would be calling you a slag then?*
> The boys. They think, oh you got a mouth like an oar, you're all right down the fish market . . . They think you've come from a slum sort of area.

Thus slag can just as easily be applied to a girl who dresses or talks in a certain way, or is seen talking to two boys or with someone else's boyfriend. The point is that irrespective of whether, in a particular case, the use of the term slag is applied explicitly to sexual behaviour, since a girl's reputation is defined in terms of her sexuality, all kinds of social behaviour by girls have a potent sexual significance.

Exercising control

Perhaps the key to an understanding of slag is its functioning as a mechanism which controls the activity and social reputations of girls to the advantage of boys. The taken for granted insolence of boys is evident in many accounts:

> Like this boy was calling me a bitch. I don't know what he was calling me a bitch for. He was picking on me. 'You bitch', he goes. He knew my name. He just wanted to make fun or something 'cos he had some friends round there. He comes up to me and he says, 'Hello sexy'. I goes, 'Who are you talking to?' 'You' . . . I was scared and 'cos my friends were there we just walked off. So stupid, fancy calling someone a sexy bitch.

Girls were preoccupied with what might happen after being dropped by a boy: 'Then the next thing he'll be going around saying "I've had her, you want to try her, go and ask her out, she's bound to say yeah"'. Another girl said:

Some boys are like that, they go round saying, 'I've had her'. And then they pack you in and their mate will go out with you. And you're thinking that they're going out with you 'cos they like you. But they're not. They're going out to use you. The next you know you're being called names – like writing on the wall, 'I've had it with so and so. I did her in three days. And I've done her twelve times in a week.'

It may not be a question of the girl actually having slept with a boy, she may land herself with a reputation as a result of going out with one boy, then being dropped and going out with one of his friends. The consequences for a girl are quite different from those for a boy: 'When there're boys talking and you've been out with more than two you're known as the crisp that they're passing around . . . The boy's all right but the girl's a bit of scum'.

If a boy takes you out or boasts that he has slept with more than one girl he is more than all right, his reputation is enhanced: 'If a boy tells his mates that he's been with three different girls, his mates would all say: "Oh lucky you" or "Well done my son, you're a man"'. The pressure is on boys to boast about their sexual conquests. They have to act big in front of their friends. As one girl explained:

They might say, 'Oh I've had her'. Then it starts spreading round. She might be really quiet or something and they'll say, 'Oh she's not quiet when you get outside the school'. Someone else will take it in the wrong way and it'll carry on from there.

No wonder that girls always fear boys going behind their backs and saying, 'Oh you know, had it with her'. It is the girl's morality that is always under the microscope, whereas anything the boy does is all right. A number of girls described girls who had not slept around but had been out with a number of different boys in a short period 'because they were unlucky enough to be dropped by a number of boys'. This led people to start saying, 'Oh God, who is she with tonight?'

The crucial point about the label slag is that it is used by both girls and boys as a deterrent to non-conformity. No girl wants to be labelled bad and slag is something to frighten any girl with. The effect of the term is to force girls to submit voluntarily to a very unfair set of gender relations. A few girls did reject the implications of the label and the double standard implicit within it, but even they said they used the term to abuse other girls. What becomes important is not the identification of certain girls but how the term is used. A useful way to understand how terms like slag are used is provided in a study of the functioning of *categories of deviance*:

Their general function is to denounce and control, not to explain . . . They mark off the deviant, the pathological, the dangerous and the criminal from the normal and the good . . . [they] are not just labels . . . [but]

... They are loaded with implied interpretations of real phenomena, models of human nature and the weight of political self interest.

(Sumner 1983)

To call a girl a slag is to use a term that, as we have seen, appears at first sight to be a label describing an actual form of behaviour but into which no girl incontrovertibly fits. It is even difficult to identify what actual behaviour is specified. Take Helen's description of how appearance can define girls, not in terms of their attributes as human beings, but in terms of sexual reputation:

> I mean they might not mean any harm. I mean they might not be as bad as they look. But their appearance makes them stand out and that's what makes them look weird and you think, 'God I can imagine her, y'know?' ... She straight away gets a bad reputation even though the girl might be decent inside. She might be good. She might still be living at home. She might just want to look different but might still act normal.

You cannot imagine a boy's appearance being described in this way. How she dresses determines how a girl is viewed and she is viewed in terms of her assumed sexual behaviour. Whether she is 'good' or not is determined by how she is assumed to conduct her sexual life; that sexuality is relative to male sexual needs.

The term 'slag' can be seen as part of a discourse about behaviour as a departure, or potential departure from, in this case, male conceptions of female sexuality which run deep in the culture. They run so deep that the majority of men and women cannot formulate them except by reference to these terms of censure that signal a threatened violation. Girls, when faced with sexual abuse, react by denying the accusation rather than by objecting to the use of the category. It is important to prove that you are not a slag. So Wendy, when asked what she'd do if someone called her a slag, replies, 'I'd turn round and say "Why? tell me why?"' The term slag therefore applies less to any clearly defined notion of sleeping around than to any form of social behaviour by girls that would define them as autonomous from the attachment to and domination by boys. An important facet of slag is its uncontested status as a category.

A second important facet of the term is that, although it connotes promiscuity, its actual usage is such that *any unattached girl* is vulnerable to being categorized as a slag. In this way the term functions as a form of control by boys over girls, a form of control that steers girls into 'acceptable' forms of sexual and social behaviour. The term is incontestable. All the girls agreed that there was only one defence, one way for a girl to redeem herself from the reputation of 'slag': *to get a steady boyfriend.* 'Then that way you seem to be more respectable like you're married or something.'

Going steady establishes the location of a sexuality appropriate for 'nice girls', and that sexuality is distinguished from the essentially dirty/promiscuous sexuality of the slag by the presence of love. My research supported Wilson's finding that 'the fundamental rule governing sexual behaviour was the existence of affection in the form of romantic love before any sexual commitment'. For most of the girls, love existed before sex and it was never a consequence of sexual involvement. Deirdre Wilson (1978: 71), who studied a group of 13–16-year-old girls commented:

> given this threat of rejection [for sex without love] it was difficult to discover just how many girls actually believed in the primacy of love, and how many simply paid lip service to the ideal. Nevertheless the fact that the girls found it necessary to support this convention, whether they believed in it or not, was an important fact in itself.

Nice girls cannot have sexual desire outside love, for them sexuality is something that just happens if you are in love, or if you are unlucky, when you are drunk. As Tracy put it 'You might be at a party and someone just dragged you upstairs or something and then the next thing you know you don't know what's happening to you'. If this happens the general consensus of opinion is that it is the girl's fault. They had no difficulty in attributing the blame. 'It happens a lot. But then it's the girl's fault for getting silly drunk in the first place that she can't – she doesn't know what's going on or anything.'

Few girls were clear about what being in love meant, though invariably love was given as the only legitimate reason for sleeping with a boy. The importance of love seemed to be therefore in permitting sexual excitement while offering some protection from sluttishness. This failure to recognize sexual desire meant that girls often changed their minds about whom they loved:

> You think you're in love and then, when it finishes, you find someone else you like more, and then you think, 'The last time it couldn't have been love, so it must be this time.' But you're never sure, are you, 'cos each time it either gets better or it gets worse so you never know.

> You think you're in love loads of times and you go through life thinking, 'God, I'm in love' and you don't do anything. You want to be with this person all the time. Then you realize you weren't in love, you just thought you were . . . I thought I was in love and then I went away and when I came back I realized I wasn't. It wasn't love at all. So I finished it and I was much happier.

The girls here could just as easily be describing the way they felt attracted to a boy and then lost interest. Some girls said they had 'been in love loads of times' whereas others said they 'had never really experienced it'. This is how Debbie described love:

It takes a while to happen. I mean it sort of dawns on you that you finally love this person. Don't think it happens straight away. I mean you might say, 'Oh look at him, I love him', 'I think he's really nice', but you can't really say that until you know him really well.

Given the ambiguity about what love involved it could well be that love is used as a rationalization for sleeping with someone after the event rather than, as Deirdre Wilson (1978) suggests, as always existing before sex could occur. The confusion that girls experience over whether or not they are in love arises from the confusion of using the word 'love' to express what is really sexual desire. Love is supposed to last forever or at least for a long time, and is the main reason that girls give for getting married. The distortion of what is really sexual desire into love means that girls must find it difficult to separate their sexual feelings from decisions about marriage and long-term commitment. As Jacky said: 'Girls have got to keep quiet about sex and think it's something to be ashamed of'.

However, it is quite legitimate to talk of love. The legitimacy of love is precisely its role in steering female sexuality into the only safe place for its expression: marriage. The result is that a girl either suppresses her sexual desire or channels it into a steady relationship that is based on an unwritten contract of inequality – that she will be the one to make compromises over where she works, lives and spends her leisure. She will bear the main burden of domesticity and childcare without pay and adjust herself, and indeed contribute, to her husband's work, lifestyle and demands. The importance of the threat of being regarded as a slag in pushing girls to channel their sexuality into the 'legitimate' channels of love which result in marriage is illustrated by the realistic, as opposed to romantic, view of marriage that most of the girls had. Almost all the girls took it for granted that they would get married, yet they were remarkably clear about the grimmer aspects of woman's lot in marriage. As one girl put it:

The wife has to stay at home and do the shopping and things. She has got more responsibility in life and they haven't got much to look forward to . . . We've got to work at home and look after the children till they grow up, you've got to go out shopping, do the housework and try to have a career. The man comes in and says, 'Where's my dinner?' when we've been to work. They say, 'You don't work.' It's because boys are brought up expecting girls to do all the work. They expect their mums to do it and when they get married they expect their wives to do it. They're just lazy.

The realism about marriage was based on the observation of their parents: 'My dad won't do anything – he won't make a cup of tea. He says he does the work for the money and the rest is up to my mum. She does part-time work too.'

The most important reason that girls put forward for getting married was that they saw no alternative. Life as an independent, unattached woman is always open to risks:

> If you don't want to get married and want to live a free life and you go out with one bloke one week and another the next, everyone will call you a tart, like you've got to go out with a bloke for a really long time and then marry him.

Besides the constant fear of being regarded as a tart or slag, living alone is seen as too frightening. The need for protection emerged in a number of the interviews. Charlotte describes how her brother is treated differently from her:

> Boys are a totally different physique. I could go out and be raped whereas he couldn't. He'd have more chance of protecting himself. I think that comes up the whole time. It's not that a boy is more trusted. It's that he's freer.

The harsh reality existing in a male-dominated world was that women needed protection from sexual harassment. Girls could never go out on their own, or even with girlfriends, without fear: 'Say you have a boy protecting you. It's as if no one can hurt you or nothing. You're protected and everything. If someone does something to you, then there's him there too and it just makes you feel secure.'

The threat of male physical violence takes its place alongside the verbal insults associated with labelling a girl a slag to steer girls into the acceptability of marriage. It is not just the constraints on an independent sex life that lead girls to marriage but the need for warmth and intimacy and love. Lesbian relationships can of course offer these, but only if the girl manages to resist the pressure towards conformity and, of course, if she is attracted to other girls.

In the face of these strong pressures the girls inevitably subscribed to the idea that they wanted to marry. Nevertheless, their realism about marriage, based on their observation of their parents, led them to devise ways of rationalizing or cushioning its inevitable impact. Almost all the girls wanted to put marriage off for some time. By delaying marriage many girls thought that they would be able to have some fun; they often fantasized about travel and seeing the world. Marriage was something you ended up with after you had lived:

> I don't really want to get married 'cos I want to go round the world first like me dad did . . . they got married when they were 30, they just sort of had their life first and then they got married and had us but when you're an air hostess you don't start the job until you're 20 so I want to work until I'm 35.

Girls who did want a career often realized that relationships with boys might upset their intentions and therefore steered clear of them. As Annie said: 'If a boy does ask us out we say "no", don't want to know, because we want a career and go round the world and all that lot. So we just leave them alone.' Janey put it more strongly:

I don't really bother about boys now – just get on with my home-work. I was brought up not to like boys really 'cos I've heard so much about what they do, robberies, rapes and all that so I keep away from them.

When asked what she meant by being brought up not to like them she replied, 'Well my mum told me never to go with them because they're bad and they damage your health and things like that, don't know.'

Boyfriends and marriage could easily interfere with career intentions; the girls could see what had happened to their mums and how little autonomy they had. Another way of attempting to avoid the predicament of marriage was to attribute the unhappiness they saw in marriages around them to the wrong choice of partner. The subordinate position that many women found themselves in was often attributed to the lack of good sense in choosing the right husband rather than to the general structural constraints on women at home with young children.

Alice, looking at the 'mistake' her mother had made in choosing the wrong man, believed, 'but not all marriages are like that though are they? Like if your mum's goes bad, yours might go good, it's what husband you pick'. She is right in one respect. Some men allow women more autonomy than others. She does not however criticize the unfairness of the marriage deal itself, particularly if children are involved. Although having children was something that most girls wanted, again, the way in which this inevit-ably constrained freedom was recognized. Helen explained, 'I think that once you decide to have kids then you've got to accept the fact that you are gonna be tied down for a while. That's why it's important not to get married too early – until you're 28 or so.'

In short, the girls were not aware of positive attractions attaching to married life. Romanticism about choosing the 'right man' can be seen as a way of attributing personal responsibility for structural oppression, but the fact of structural oppression is realistically understood. Nevertheless, des-pite the unattractiveness of marriage the question is, as a girl from Diana Leonard's (1980) study in Cardiff put it, not of choosing to get married or not but whether you fail to get married. My argument has been that what forces this closure on all alternatives to married life is above all the power of the slag categorization for the unattached woman who is sexually act-ive. Once we understand the way in which female sexuality is constructed and constrained by the categorization of slag, how a woman's femininity and sexuality is only rendered 'safe' when confined to the bonds of marriage, we understand why until recently there is just no alternative, as the girls see it, to married life.

Race, class and subculture

As I have noted, most studies of male youth culture have been conducted from a subcultural standpoint in which youth culture is seen as resistance to, and temporary escape from, the pressures and demands of society. Yet the experiences of the girls portrayed here can hardly be seen as resistance or escape. On the contrary, the processes that have been illustrated are very far from resistance; they are the processes of constraint and the channelling of aspirations and behaviour along the well-established paths of sex and gender relations exemplified by the institution of marriage and the role of women in the domestic sphere. To see the rehearsal for entry into a major social institution such as marriage and the domestic sphere as a form of subculture or resistance is, in effect, to deny the reality of the domestic sphere as a social institution akin, say, to economic life and social class relations and to see it purely as a cultural phenomenon. In this way the questions of subculture and the debate over sex and class relations are crucially linked. If the main structural forces or forms of stratification in British society are seen as economic class structures then of course rehearsal for domestic life, when seen from the standpoint of those structures, will be seen as a form of cultural behaviour unrelated to class, or possibly as a form of resistance to the consequences of class-determined life chances – in the way in which, for example, Paul Willis (1977) describes the process whereby working-class boys reconcile themselves to working-class jobs. But if gender divisions are seen to be of equal significance to economic class in the constitution of social structure and social institutions then it is less easy to view girls' behaviour as 'subcultural'. It is important to analyse the constraints that the structuring of gender relations and the double standard of sexual morality places on girls.

The importance of reputation varies between different religious and ethnic groups. Amrit Wilson, who undertook the first British study of Asian girls in the late 1970s, described how in conversations she had with girls from many language groups and religions, in every part of Britain, 'reputation came up all the time' and was the 'bane of their lives from adolescence to the early years of marriage. It controls everything they do and adds a very tangible danger to any unconventional action' (Wilson 1978: 102). Girls as young as 12 are frightened to go out with boys lest it affect their reputation. Sofia, a Muslim girl of 19, described how if you go out with a man in Southall:

> He will go around and boast to his friends that he's been out with this
> girl and he's done this to her and that to her. Even if he hasn't, he'll

boast about it. Then they get the girl's name bad. That's why girls try and keep it quiet when they're going out with a bloke, because they don't want anyone to know. It's quite different for boys. They can get away with it. Their names can't ever get spoilt.

Reputation is a conservative force controlling everything in Asian communities, as male pride or *izzat* depends on it. A young woman's family can be disgraced by imputations on her reputation. Issues of identity, nationality, race, and religion (exacerbated by the rise of religious fundamentalism) intersect on Asian women's rights to self-determination. Some young women are very unhappy about this control and are resisting. As Roy (in Griffin 1995: 107) describes it, 'Asian girls constitute a battle-field that traditional male controlled community groups see as theirs to own'. In this way religious customs operate in such a way to control female sexuality, in so far as most relations lay down moral codes relating to virginity and sexual behaviour.

The processes by which girls are labelled slags becomes one component of the way in which racial stereotypes are constructed and perpetuated. The category of slag and slut is part of the raw material out of which racist views are elaborated. There are two reasons for this. First, racist and sexist stereotypes operate in ways which, although not identical, are in some respects similar. I have already argued that there is a vacuousness and ambiguity about the term slag which detaches it from any particular characteristics of a young woman's behaviour and thereby enables it to function as a general mechanism of control of her sexuality. Racial stereotypes operate, as Allport (1954: 23) explained, in a way which has some analogies:

> There is a common mental device that permits people to hold pre-judgements even in the face of much contradictory evidence. It is the device of admitting exceptions: 'There are nice Negroes but...' or 'some of my best friends are Jews, but...' This is a disarming device: by excluding a few favoured cases, the negative rubric is kept intact for all other cases. In short, contrary evidence is not admitted and allowed to modify the generalisations; rather it is perfunctorily acknowledged but excluded.

Sexual, like racial, categorization is a form of labelling which is difficult to pin down to any hard specific content which could be shown to be untrue and lead to a withdrawal of the label. For slag this is because of the ambiguous way in which it is used, and in the case of race, by refusing to allow any exceptions to modify the basic racist stereotypes (Allport calls this 're-fencing'). It is thus easy to see how slag can come to fulfil the requirements of racism. Racial stereotypes of blacks by whites and whites by blacks occurs among the girls at the same time as it is being used by both girls, and boys in a way which ends up constraining the freedom of girls, irrespective of racial group.

Morality and sexual behaviour: slags

My research into the language of sexual reputation amongst young women revealed three things. First, that names like slag function as terms of abuse to control single girls and steer them towards marriage as the only legitimate expression of sexuality. Second, what became clear was the interdependence of male 'non-gendered subjectivity' and female sexuality. This manifested itself in the way girls continually take on responsibility for male actions – especially violence or other behaviour that is irrational or sexually motivated. Girls also bear the moral responsibility for the consequences of sexual relations by taking steps to ensure contraception. Third, the repression of sexuality to the conventional pattern of marriage means that female sexuality has little autonomous expression but is constrained by social station and its duties. The woman becomes the housewife and her virtue comes to consist of the correct performance of the duties of the marital relationship, being a good wife, in which sexual expression is allowed only to the extent of meeting her husband's 'legitimate' sexual needs. When women are charged with petty criminal offences social workers and law enforcement agencies have been shown to give weight to sexual reputation and the performance of domestic duties in sentencing. There is also some evidence that girls are sent to institutions on grounds of sexual conduct rather than the nature of the offence. For men sexual reputation is, in the main, separated from the evaluation of moral behaviour and regarded as private and incidental.

If in the private sphere it is a woman's duty to keep quiet and be a good wife, in the public sphere her inability to achieve non-gendered subjectivity closely follows from her having to take on the responsibility for male sexuality. Because the male 'rational man' is only possible where his sexual and irrational behaviour can be attributed to 'woman trouble' or other feminine influence it is obviously impossible, under present circumstances, for men and women to co-exist as non-gendered subjects. Women's escape from sexual stereotyping in the public sphere would require men to take on responsibility for, and integrate their sexuality into their public behaviour.

For women, this situation limits the possible forms of behaviour in the public world. One can of course latch onto a man and go places but, conversely, a woman who does achieve in terms of skills and capacities other than sex stands in danger of either having her achievements attributed to her sex (that she slept her way to the top) or being regarded as sexless (one of the boys and therefore undesirable). To be an honorary man is to be so masculine and 'unattractive' that men and other women will come to dissociate her completely from any concept of sexuality. Thus a type of false non-gendered subjectivity is achieved but only as a residue; a woman is evaluated in terms of her achievements only because no men find her sexually interesting.

For men, on the other hand, virtue is achieved irrespective of sexuality; in public life sexual reputation is largely excluded from the moral evaluation of conduct. In private life too men's sexual conduct does not define moral standing. A man can still be a good father or a good husband and have illicit sexual relationships outside marriage.

Conclusion

Michel Foucault argues that identities have to be created by modern discursive practices and that power is produced in social relations. Rather than seeing power as possessions of a particular group, Foucault envisages a network of power relations 'as forming a dense web that passes through apparatuses and institutions' (1990: 96). In this chapter, I have shown how the policing of a woman's reputation takes place through language and is intrinsically connected to the development of identity. Foucault's ideas that prevailing forms of selfhood and subjectivity are maintained not through physical restraint but through the individual's self-surveillance and self-correction to norms is directly relevant to the way that women police their own and each other's behaviour. Such exercise of power therefore operates without any external surveillance or coercion.

Girls do of course resist, some more successfully than others. Foucault (1990: 96) envisages points of resistance:

> producing cleavages in a society that shift about, fracturing unities and effecting regroupings furrowing across individuals themselves, cutting them up and remoulding them, marking off irreducible regions in them in their bodies and minds.

Postscript 1996

> Stunned broad, dog, bag, and bitch are words that apply to girls as well as worse words. I don't hold these words against them. I don't think any of these words apply to me ... The trick with these silent words is to walk in the spaces between them, turn your head sideways, evade. Like walking through walls.
>
> (Atwood 1988: 244–5)

This research was undertaken over 10 years ago during which significant changes have taken place. In this postscript I shall briefly discuss some ways in which insults can be subverted and overview the changes in girls' approach to marriage. There is some evidence that young women are not only more aware of the atmosphere of verbal abuse and misogyny but are beginning to resist the insults. One strategy Margaret Atwood aptly depicts in the above quotation is walking in the spaces between the words, rather like walking the gauntlet. This can be seen as a precarious form of avoidance, but not so restricting as changing her behaviour to avoid abuse by not going out with boys, or not going out at all. Even avoidance carries the risk of being labelled too tight or a lesbian.

The most successful forms of resistance appear to involve verbally subverting or challenging the terms of the abuse or collectively resisting the insults. Occasionally girls did take action against the boys, as in the following account:

> The boys love coming into the girls' changing rooms. This boy, right, we made a decision next time he comes in, grab hold of him and start taking his clothes off and see how he feels. All the girls were watching him. He never came back.

One difficulty facing girls who resist is that there is no vocabulary of abuse to level at boys. The label 'stud' is a compliment and words such as 'poof' imply femininity. Criticizing the sexism of boys in no way enhances femininity. Quite the contrary. Girls who contest the unfair subordination of girls are likely to be regarded as show-offs, kill-joys or lesbians, which is why so few young women find it easy to declare themselves feminists.

Radical feminists in particular have argued that language is man made (Daly 1979; Spender 1980) and have attempted to develop a feminist language or way of subverting discourse. By adopting the word slag as subject rather than as object, it is possible to subvert the misogyny embedded in the term. Mae West and Madonna are stars who successfully subvert the term by applying it to themselves. Madonna is an example of a woman who enjoys her sexuality and avoids being portrayed as a sex object. 'I'm not ashamed,' she asserts. In an interview (*Madonna Live*, BBC 2, 1991) she told how her grandmother used to beg her not to go with men, to be a good girl. She plays on the madonna/whore dichotomy and declares that being sexual, being a 'whore' is fine. In videos she often plays two roles, one questioning the other as if debating the two views of female sexuality: the moral 'virgin' versus the voluptuous 'slag'. Singing voluptuously and dressed like a prostitute, she makes a mockery of her grandmother's and the church's view that women are either virgins or whores. She explained, 'If you can create yourself, you can recreate yourself.' Madonna's video company is named Slutco. She is a triumphant slut who challenges the derogatory meaning of the word and turns it into a symbol of female freedom. Nor is she unaware of the power involved in resisting male dominance: 'It's a great thing to be powerful. I've been striving for it all my life', she asserted.

Madonna sees change as important because it means you have grown. By wearing a suit and monocle, she ironically subverts the constraints of being constructed as male or female. She dresses like a prostitute. She is successful at gently exploding myths. Take her contribution to the condom campaign:

> You never really get to know a guy until
> You ask him to wear a RUBBER
> Hey you, don't be silly, put a rubber on your willy. (My Blond Ambition)

The use of the word willy cuts the embarrassment and male obsession down to size. There is a certain contradiction in the way Madonna presents herself both as a porn star and as a sexually liberated woman. Mae West too rose above the term and took on a dominant active role in her cinematic sexual relationships. Such subversion requires confidence, however, and for an ordinary girl to declare herself a slag carries considerable risks.

Donna Eder (1995), in a study of adolescents in the midwestern US, shows how talk (and teasing in particular) is used as a collective process as a way to transform gender relations and can be seen as a form of resistance to traditional female roles. Such mocking comments were directed at a boy as, 'Come over here, I'll ruin your family life'. She illustrates how girls mock many aspects of traditional female behaviour. Teasing often takes the form of goading girls about being sexy or can have a romantic aspect. Girls who are sexy are teased for having a 'dirty mind'. It seems to be OK to be sexual but not too sexual.

Another strategy girls adopt is to de-sex the interchange. On one occasion, described by Eder, the boys were doing pelvic thrusts to get the girls' attention. In their imitation of the boys, the girls described the behaviour as inept attempts at skiing. It seems the most effective way is to combine humour with an insult about ineptness or stupidity. Another strategy is for girls to mock boys' possessiveness. Eder quotes an example of this where two girls pretended to fight over a boy. Through satire, they transformed the concept of ownership to one in which boys are the property of girls instead of vice versa. By pretending to fight physically over him they mocked the stereotypical notion that girls are always competing for boys (see Eder 1995: 142).

On the other hand, Beverley Skeggs (1991) illustrates how sexualizing verbal interchange can also be effective. Referring to a study of young women and men in England, she describes how students felt able to make regular confrontational stands which sexualized classroom interaction in order to embarrass and humiliate male teachers by goading them about the assumed size of their penises. She quotes this example:

> *Mandy:* Bloody hell, what the heck could you do with that? Not much.
> *Therese:* Can't believe he's got kids with one that size. You'd think he'd never be able to get it up.

These comments challenge the prerogatives of masculine power even if only momentarily. Girls refuse to take masculinity seriously. They understand its vulnerabilities, size, performance and potency. These young women are able to use their knowledge of masculinity to subvert the regulatory mechanisms (Skeggs 1991: 134).

Some girls in my study were well aware of male power and the limitations of resistance. Lily, for example, described the way boys behaved as though they owned you by buying you drinks: 'Some boys think they're flash because they've got a bit of money and think they can buy you. I said to one boy, "Ditch your money" and he wouldn't let me so I thought, "He thinks he can just do what he wants".'

Other girls assimilate to the boys' behaviour by trying to be 'one of the lads', assimilating characteristics of 'maleness' such as bragging about sexual exploits. Tania told me:

She just turned round and said, 'Yeah, we went to his house and he put it in me and we had it off. My mate was sitting in the next room and she didn't even know. Then we thought his mum was back, but when we found out she wasn't, we went to the bathroom and we did it again.

Other girls boasted about being on the pill:

This group I know, certain groups of about seven girls are on the pill and they really love talking about it. Not sex but that they're on the pill. They say, 'I sort of went out with him and got off with him'. They just do it to impress.

Some boys resented tomboys for subverting 'natural' differences. Gender dichotomies require collective activity to maintain them and although individuals can deviate, their deviance will give rise to disapproval. An example of this was one boy's mixed feelings about Jasmin's tomboyish behaviour which he found threatening: 'The girls with the big mouths. They keep running me down. Jasmin. She copies all the words I use. In D & T [design and technology] she always talks to me. She's got the same type of interests. She likes the same type of music.' He is aware that Jasmin shares his interests and faces a contradiction in her refusal to adopt the submissive feminine role, and to criticize him. Such contradictions illustrate the complexity of identity formulation and how feminine and masculine identities are constantly evaluated.

Tomboys appear to be more confident than other girls. They may not see themselves as different from boys. Tania, a black girl, describes how she goes nicking with 20 or so boys aged between 15 and 25 years old. Chloe explained the meaning of butch: 'You're quite boyish, thinking about mostly boy things, you know, say you don't want a husband – think they're no good. You get a motorbike 'cos most girls have mopeds.'

Subverting racist language can also be seen as an effective form of resistance whereby the oppressed are enabled to break their silence and speak out. Three examples spring to mind. Grace Evans (1980), a black teacher in a London school, described how West Indian pupils used patois as a means of subverting the school curriculum in response to the racism of teachers who disparagingly referred to them as those 'loud black girls'. In another study group, Asian girls resisted teachers' stereotypes that Asian pupils had language difficulties by insisting on speaking Urdu in class (Brah and Minhas 1985). Finally, in Mirza's study of African Caribbean girls in the late 1980s, black girls rejected and challenged teachers' low expectations of them (Mirza 1992).

Girls adopt different strategies to deal with insults. Some of these are more successful than others and some (like feminism) carry the risk of ostracism. All girls spend an inordinate amount of energy finding a way to cope with or survive the objectification and subordination that entraps them. Yet increasingly girls are contesting the sexist discourses and questioning the sexism that a few years ago was so taken for granted.

As Howe (1994) explains, there are real penalties for breaches of the language of sexual reputation where the use of language becomes a pain in itself. Judy, for example, had stopped going to discos in London because all the girls were bitchy, shouting abuse at her making her life a misery. She described what upset her:

The main thing that comes to mind is 'Look at that slag' or something like that . . . I don't think most of them know the meaning of the word really 'cos calling someone a slag, you've got to really have proof, haven't you? I don't think it's very nice, but it does upset you. It starts me thinking that, 'Why are they saying it to me?' I don't go after boys all the time but I like to enjoy myself.

What is most significant about the stigma attached to sexual reputation is that young women police each other. Bitching typically involves calling other girls names and often casting doubt on their reputation. As one young woman said, 'What people say when they bitch. They say they think some girl's a slag or something like that. If rumours spread about you it can be unnerving.' Another young woman commented

If it undermines my own confidence to such an extent that I start feeling uncomfortable then yes, it bothers me. And if it isn't true, if it's false, it also annoys me if no one had a nice word to say about you, it's going to upset you. I must say I get quite paranoid.

Such policing has material effects in constricting young women's social life. The slag categorization and constraint on a young woman's sexual expression act as a very effective way of restricting both the expression of her sexuality and her freedom of action – her independence.

Change in the status of marriage

Resisting marriage by delaying or even rejecting a long-term commitment appears to be on the increase, which indicates that not all women are being policed into marriage (see Howe 1994: 183). More couples now cohabit rather than marry, at least prior to marriage. The number of women who have cohabited with their future husband before marriage has risen tenfold in a generation, from about 5 per cent in the mid-1960s to over 50 per cent in 1995. More children are born out of wedlock than ever. Births outside marriage rose from 54,000 in 1961 to 236,000 in 1991, and births within marriage fell from 890,000 in 1961 to 556,000 in 1991. Divorce in Britain has also increased sixfold over the past 30 years, a higher increase than in any other European country. Almost half of marriages now end in divorce, and 70 per cent of divorce petitions are taken out by women.

Other changes in young women's lives have occurred that have widened their choices. There has been a dramatic increase in university education and for the first time in 1993 more young women entered university than young men. Access to jobs, albeit low status and low paid, has opened up for women. During the period 1952–92 the proportion of women at work increased from 31 per cent to 45 per cent of the labour force. At the same time male unemployment, in particular of young men, has increased. While the trend to increased female employment runs in the opposite direction to increased male unemployment, they are, of course, both reflections of a single process of economic change. The old structure of the family established during the nineteenth century, in which the men worked for a family wage while women managed the family, is rapidly being undermined. Marriage is no longer a necessity for women and it appears that women are realistically weighing up the pros and cons of the marriage deal.

Research into the attitudes of young men and women to marriage and family life reflect this realism. Sue Sharpe, in her 1994 updated version of her book *Just Like a Girl*, first published in 1976, returned to the schools where she had interviewed 15-year-old girls then and compared them with girls today. The most remarkable change she found related to the girls' changed views of marriage, which had dramatically dropped in popularity. Over three-quarters of the girls she interviewed had said yes to marriage in 1972. By 1991 this had dropped to under half. Most girls did not want to get married, but saw it as something to be approached with extreme caution.

In unpublished research with Mike O'Donnell, she explored the attitudes, ideas and expectations of marriage and family life of 15–16-year-old boys. Boys' attitudes had changed far less. In contrast to the girls, three-quarters of the boys uncritically assumed that marriage would be part of their future life. Boys saw marriage as an important way of committing themselves to another person. As Jim said,

For myself I think marriage is pretty important and the father and mother have to be there for the child. I'd live with them and then I'd feel as you get older that marriage is the official statement of your love, like, so I'd get married eventually.

Note

1 A research fellow, Celia Cowie, was funded by the Inner London Education Authority, and the Nuffield Foundation contributed towards the project.

CHAPTER 2

Sex education in conflict

Recently sex education has become a burning political issue. Teachers, parents and social workers all agree that sex education is vital as a health promotion measure, but there is little agreement over what exactly it should contain. In this chapter, with reference to research I conducted in four comprehensive schools involving interviews and group discussions with over 100 15–16-year-old girls and boys, I propose a form of radical sex education which should be an integral part of the school curriculum. It should be far broader in focus than is the case in most schools at present. In particular, the different social experiences of young men and women and the double standard of sexuality should be addressed. There is a need for young men to develop the ability to communicate about their sexual feelings and relationships and for young women to discuss ways of subverting the sexism around them.

Concern with sex education is recognized under the 1993 Education Act which states that all state secondary schools must offer sex education, although parents have the right to withdraw children. On the other hand, the Conservative government sees sex education as a potentially dangerous instrument of the 'permissive' society, which could be used to undermine the already disintegrating family and promote immorality (see Kelly 1992). A clear split has recently developed between the 'health' concerns of the Ministry of Health and the 'moral' concerns of the Ministry of Education over the issue of sex education in schools (Thomson 1994). Education is seen by some as an answer to the problem and by others as the cause of increasing permissiveness.

This controversy has added fuel to the already delicate area of sex education, a topic which teachers find difficult to undertake. There is a fundamental tension and ambiguity about introducing questions of the body and sexuality, issues of responsibility and moral choice, quite apart from 'unmentionable' topics such as menstruation and childbirth, into the class-room. This is perhaps the main reason why the provision of sex education is patchy and sex education is a severely underresourced area of education (see Farrell 1978; Allen, I. 1987; Thomson and Scott 1991; Sex Education Forum 1992). There is also disagreement about what exactly should be covered and what knowledge sex education teachers need to broach the subject. Is biology or religion relevant or should knowledge of the sexual relations between young men and women be an essential prerequisite?

Background to the sex education debate

Britain has one of the highest rates of unplanned pregnancies in Europe and promotion of sex and HIV related education was one of the five prior-ities identified by the government in the white paper, *Health of the Nation* (HMSO 1992).Yet within Conservative party ranks there is a lack of clear thinking and coherent interdepartmental policy on sex education and sexual health.

This has led to some strangely contradictory political manoeuvres. In January 1994, the Health Education Council's promotion of safer sex and condoms was banned after Baroness Cumberlege, the junior Health Min-ister responsible, announced that only one of the planned advertisements was acceptable. Then on 18 April 1994, the Health Education Authority announced that it was to withdraw 10 of its sex and HIV related educa-tional publications after disputes with the government over the nature of its campaigning. Among those banned was Nick Fisher's (1995) booklet, *The Best Sex Guide* (*The Guardian*, 18 April 1994). His earlier booklet, *Your Pocket Book to Sex*, was referred to by the Health Minister, Mr Brian Mawhinney, as 'smutty'. David Blunkett, the Labour party's shadow Health Minister denounced what he called panic measures, which he argued would cause harm in a crucial area of health education.

To add to the confusion, on 26 April 1994 Baroness Cumberlege, re-versing her previous stance, provoked an uproar when she argued that as a last resort it was acceptable to provide children under 16 with 'the means to avoid pregnancy'. In a speech at the Royal College of Nursing, she argued that the decision to supply teenagers with condoms was a mat-ter of professional judgement (the *Sunday Times* report was headed 'Lady Cumberlege thinks it right to give condoms to girls like this but shouldn't she be teaching her "the art of saying No"!'). In contrast to recent minister-ial pronouncements condemning sex advice for its lack of moral content, she defended a family planning nurse who handed out free condoms in a

Birmingham youth club for girls aged 12–18 years. Dame Jill Knight, a Conservative member of parliament and a campaigner on moral issues, condemned the Birmingham initiative and argued 'sexual intercourse with a girl under 16 is illegal and to provide the means by which the law is broken is a loophole that must be closed'.

In May 1994, following a row over a sex education lesson in Leeds where a teacher answered questions from pupils about oral sex, John Patten, then Minister of Education, who had been incensed by the report, ordered teachers to deal with precocious questions outside class, provided they had consulted with parents. A week earlier he had apparently put forward the farcical idea that pupils should be streamed for sex education classes according to their degree of sexual awareness. On 5 May he published guidelines suggesting that teachers should not give advice to children under 16 without parental consent. The circular, to take effect from September, dropped references in an earlier draft to possible prosecutions of teachers for abetting unlawful sex, but stated, 'Teachers are not health professionals and the legal position of a teacher giving advice in such circumstances has not been tested in the courts'. It stressed that sex education should be presented in a moral context, promoting marriage and fidelity.

Changes in sexual practice

Both in the USA, continental Europe and Britain there has been a trend towards earlier and more frequent sexual intercourse among adolescents of both sexes. Farrell's (1978) work, which followed the so-called era of sexual liberation of the late 1960s and early 1970s, suggested that for adolescent girls at least, this trend was less far-reaching than imagined. The rise in teenage pregnancy and transmission of sexually transmitted diseases (STDs) was much lower than the media inspired moral panics might have led us to suppose, promiscuity was rare and teenagers were no more likely to have a casual sexual relationship than they would have been 30 years ago.

Nonetheless, some significant changes have taken place and the pace of change has been faster over the past decade. The availability of the birth control pill since the 1960s has made childbirth a real choice; the prejudice against unmarried mothers keeping their children is immeasurably less than 20 years ago, and unmarried girls are increasingly opting to keep their children. By the 1990s, therefore, in the United Kingdom, premarital sex is common (Ford and Morgan 1989). This was not only facilitated by the greater availability of abortion (following the Abortion Act of 1967) and of contraception, but also by advances in penicillin and antibiotic treatments for venereal disease.

The idea of a 'woman's right to choose' was applied by feminists not only to whether or not to give birth but to other realms of behaviour. The proportion of illegitimate births increased from 6 per cent in 1961 to 25 per cent in 1988 (*Social Trends* 1990: Ch. 2). The stigma attached to illegitimacy declined, following its dramatic rise since the 1960s, culminating in its abolition in the Legitimacy Act 1988. There is today far more tolerance of different types of sexual behaviour and it is argued that heterosexuality may well no longer necessarily be the norm in future years (Giddens 1992).

The changes of the 1980s and 1990s may not have made sexual relations easier to cope with for girls. There is less pressure to get married but more pressure to have sex. Girls are presented with more choices than ever before. Birth control and abortions are more available, but the level of teenage pregnancy and abortion has risen (Dollomore 1989) both in Britain and the United States. In Britain the rate of abortion has increased for under 20-year-olds (Francome 1986). In the United State the rate of teenage pregnancy is even higher. The rising teenage pregnancy rate led both the US and Britain to gradually recognize the importance of sex education (Hudson and Ineichen 1991).

A major change in the last five years is that AIDS is now seen as a threat not only to male homosexuals and drug abusers, but also to at least some sectors of the wider heterosexual population. Since reporting began in 1982 a total of 5684 AIDS cases (5295 males, 353 females) have been reported in the United Kingdom of whom 3527 (62 per cent) are known to have died (British Youth Council 1992). The majority of new adult cases continue to consist of homosexual men but recent figures confirm a steady spread of the disease among heterosexuals. One effect of the impact of AIDS has been to promote far greater discussion of sex than has ever occurred before. Condom was a forbidden word on the BBC in Britain until a few years ago.

Young people's sexual knowledge

Recent findings in Britain concerning young people's sexual knowledge, attitudes and practices are no grounds for complacency. MORI (1991) interviewed a sample of 4436 young people aged between 16 and 19 for the Health Education Authority, and the results are assessed in the authority's *Young Adults: Health and Lifestyle Report*. Most of those surveyed, approximately 88 per cent, had received some sex education at school, although this varied in different parts of the country. Most sex education concentrated on how bodies develop, pregnancy and childbirth. Even the 'plumbing and prevention' focus was lacking, quite apart from discussion of the dangers of such hazards as cervical cancer. Only two-thirds were taught about sexually transmitted diseases, only half about AIDS and a mere 14 per cent about lesbianism. An even larger gap concerned feeling and emotion, and only a third of young men and young women remembered being taught anything about them.

Another important finding concerning communication about sex education is that friends are a major source of misinformation. A study conducted in Australia indicated that sources of formal information were useless and 84 per cent of the sample said friends were an informal source of information (Szirom 1988). Thomson and Scott (1991) in Britain found that the acquisition of knowledge from peers, particularly in the school context, is often a case of 'Chinese whispers'. Messages are progressively distorted as they circulate from person to person, obscuring sexual meanings which were not explicit to begin with. The young women we spoke to reported learning by 'picking things up' and 'just catching on'. Often this took the form of hearing sexual innuendo in the form of jokes, which, like 'reputation' can also serve the function of social censure. In I. Allen's (1987) sample, 30 per cent of teenagers thought that others of their age knew more about sex than themselves.

Communicating about sex

Young people would like to have been taught about sexual relations and emotions, and more specifically about homosexuality and lesbianism. A report on unplanned pregnancy cited in Skelton and Hanson (1989) found lack of communication to be a major problem. Young people have difficulty in communicating verbally with each other. It was frequently assumed that people know a great deal about sexuality, sexual health, reproduction and contraception. This assumption was not borne out. They concluded that education about sexuality should include how to talk to each other.

I interviewed and held group discussions with 100 young women aged 15 to 16 in three London comprehensive schools and two years later, with a male colleague, Dave Phillips, expanded the project to young men (Lees 1993a). All the interviews were taperecorded and transcribed. The young men and women selected their own groups and the discussions and interviews took place in school time. They were of mixed ethnic groups, as is typical of London schools. There were, however, more Bangladeshi young men than African Caribbean ones, but more African Caribbean young women than Bangladeshi ones. Despite quite dramatic cultural and religious differences between them, the differences between young men compared to young women were stark.

The contrast between the boys' and girls' groups was startling. The young women interacted and talked about relationships and feelings, worries and concerns and knew all about each others' families. The young men all talked at the same time, interrupted each other, rarely listened to what others said and vied for attention and dominance. In one group I was astonished to find that the young men knew little about each others' families although they had known each other for several years.

The issue of whether sex education should be taught by men or women is often raised. Dave Phillips and I both held group discussions with groups of five to six boys and found that the groups behaved quite differently. His groups were noisier and livelier and at times he was drawn into joking with them. Controlling the groups was a bit like refereeing a football match. My groups, on the other hand, were quieter and more serious. Young men were on the one hand less at ease, yet they were in my view more thoughtful and less inclined to boast and brag. I seemed to calm their exuberance and they appeared to talk less jokingly, as though there was no need to impress me.

This suggests that with boys at least, a woman coordinator may have an advantage in attempting to develop boys' capacity for talking seriously and intimately about their relationships with girls. This is not to say that men should not play a role in sex education, nor that it may be easier for particular topics to be presented by a man rather than a woman to both young men and women. It also suggests that there may be advantages in holding same-sex as well as mixed groups.

Young men and women talk about sexuality in very different ways and both sexes find sex difficult to talk about. There is very little vocabulary available to us to talk about sexual intercourse and sexual anatomy which is not either derogatory or clinical. Carol Lee (1983) on setting up sex education classes, met with opposition from headteachers over using certain terms such as penis and vagina. Euphemisms for sex must be more common in Britain than anywhere in the world, where teachers are still censored for using words such as penetration and many girls have no idea where to find their clitoris or vagina.

The female body is still shrouded in secrecy and shame and regarded by male culture with contradictory attitudes of desire and disdain. Mothers are more reluctant to name the genital organs of their daughters than their sons and tend to do so at a much later age. Many mothers are embarrassed to name the girl's sexual organs except by referring to her 'bottom'. The only word the girl may come into contact with is cunt, which is depicted as dirty and shameful. There is not an acceptable word for female sexual parts, although 'fanny' is perhaps one possibility. Most social stereotypes define women's genitals as unpleasant, odorous and unattractive and these are internalized by the female child. Many of the obscenities directed at women are so taken for granted that girls and women stop noticing them.

The young women I interviewed all found it embarrassing to talk about their bodies or sexuality. Jane, aged 15, for example, explained that: 'If they're all girls and the boys aren't here, we can talk to the teacher about the facts of life and growing up and abortion and things like that.'

Girls find talking about sexuality and the body difficult precisely because their body is so much linked to their identity and is often the butt of boys' ridicule. Girls' bodies are subject to contradictory appraisal. Depictions of girls' bodies are the raw material of verbal sexual abuse. At one moment her appearance is presented as a girl's passport to success both in private and public life, and at the next moment she may be called a dog, unattractive, or beyond the pale. One of the strongest bases of self-esteem rests on pride in your body image. The widespread dissatisfaction that girls express about their physical attractiveness was startling. Not one girl expressed pride and confidence in good looks. Anxiety focuses on their bodies.

Young women are more likely than men to report that they have difficulty in adjusting to their changed body images between the ages of 12 and 16. Research indicates that women are more likely to experience depersonalization because their self-concepts are much more volatile at that age. A young woman is constantly warned that her body may let her down by emitting unpleasant odours or leaking. Menstruation is a constant concern. The sense of shame attached to menstruation is reflected in advertisements which all emphasize cleanliness and discretion.

Wood (1984: 64) in a study of how boys talk about sex, describes how 'the reproductive and excremental aspects of the female body was constantly referred to by the boys in that fixated, disgusted tone, edged with nervousness and surrounded by giggling'. He concludes that women are presumed to exist primarily in and through their bodies as opposed to their whole selves. These bodes are there to provide pleasure for men but at the same time these bodies are alien and therefore weird, dirty and even sinister. He points out that there is no equivalent way girls discuss boys' bodies. Paul Willis (1977) also portrayed many of their views as blatantly sexist. Boys in both studies talk endlessly about bodies in relation to sex. Sophie Laws (1991), who undertook an in-depth study of men's attitudes to menstruation, argues that these taboos are inseparable from how men see women generally. Viewing menstruation so negatively makes it difficult for women to talk about it or to feel positive about themselves.

The significance of reputation

Girls and boys talk about sexuality in quite different ways, which is leading relations between them on a collision course. Girls talk about sexual experiences in terms of feelings and relationships whereas boys distance themselves from intimacy and talk about sex in what Giddens (1992) refers to as 'episodic' terms – how far they got, how many conquests they made, who they managed to 'have'. Boasting about alleged sexual conquests functions to enhance boys' status with their peer group. As one of the girls commented, 'Boys are boys and if they don't get what they want, they're going to lie about it anyway, 'cos they're show-offs.' This is how Lesley, a black girl, referred to a boy, mouthing,

Oh I've slept with someone. I done this. I done that and it's not true. Fair enough if it's true. But to lie about it, that's the worst. If they don't get what they want they lie about it anyway. That – to me – that's stupid.

Boys need help in talking about intimate relationships to counter the pressure towards the macho culture where sensitivity and feelings are taboo. Angela Phillips talks about the process of attaining manhood as a process of desensitization, in which the openness of the young child shrinks further and further into the shell of the man (Phillips 1993). Deborah Tannen (1992), Professor of Linguistics at Georgetown University, Washington DC, illustrates how women and men use language in very different ways, women primarily to make connections and reinforce intimacy, men to preserve their independence and negotiate status. This makes it difficult for girls and boys to communicate with each other.

Girls face an irreconcilable contradiction in regard to sex. They are under pressure to be seen as competent and confident sexually but not as slags and it is a fine line to tread. Sex is a difficult area for everyone; for young women it's even harder to know what they want. The boys in my research did not on the whole envisage marrying virgins. When asked in a group discussion whether they would mind having a girlfriend who was sexually experienced, they replied:

B1: Well, it's OK, she's been touched by someone else.
B3: What, not like a packet of frozen peas?
B2: So you can touch them before anyone else?
B3: So you can put a mark on the chart on the wall?
B2: Like truck drivers?
Q: Would you like your future wife to have sexual experience?
B3: You can't find a woman who hasn't had sexual experience. Not round here you can't, not in London.

I asked girls what they got out of their sexual relationships. Few spoke about sexual experience as pleasurable. They were aware that they had a great deal more freedom than their mothers but they experienced sex as an anti-climax and, as we shall see in the next chapters, often felt pressured into it. Take Miranda's account of her friend Sarah's experience of losing her virginity on a one night stand:

It happens a lot. I've got a friend called Sarah who went to the Lyceum for the Greatest Disco in Town and I know she was a virgin. She went there and a kid decided that he really wanted to sleep with her and he said: 'Well I'm not going to go out with you if you don't.' So she did. I could never do that. Never ever. I'd just turn round and say, 'Forget it if you're like that'. Just walk off. But she didn't. She lost him the following day anyway.

When asked how she felt afterwards, Miranda replied: 'I think she feels it was a waste. She didn't enjoy it and she was pressured into it and now it's gone. If I was in her situation and that happened to me I think I'd just be so down.'

More optimistically, there is some evidence that young women are becoming more confident. This is reflected in young women's magazines which have radically changed in the last two decades with the decline of photo love stories around which many of the girls' magazines were marketed, where female passivity and traditional sex role stereotyping took on a heightened form. In her analysis of *Jackie* and *Just Seventeen* McRobbie (1991) indicates how these love narratives lost popularity in the 1980s as a result of readers informing the editors that they thought they were insulting and silly. Stories have since become far more realistic.

Lesbian girls have been ignored in most of the British surveys of young people and since Clause 28 of the Local Government Amendment Act 1988 (which prevented local authorities from promoting homosexuality through funding and licencing of local groups or through the purchase, production and promotion of educational and other materials), it has become very difficult for homosexuality to be raised as an issue in schools. Yet the problems gay and lesbian young men and women face need to be addressed. A Canadian report (Lesbian & Gay Youth 1988) found that young lesbians and homosexuals were faced by pressure and hostility which lead to problem behaviour such as drug and alcohol abuse, delinquency, heterosexual promiscuity and pregnancy (as a last attempt to prove their heterosexuality). One-third of the young people interviewed reported dating members of the opposite sex in order to conceal their sexual orientation. Not only pupils, but lesbian teachers face harassment both on account of their lesbianism and their gender, which makes it very difficult for them to provide role models for girls (see Squirrell 1989). They stress the importance of preparing teachers to confront the name calling and harassment in schools. Young men in my research differed in their views of gays:

> *B3:* I don't feel hatred against gays. I just feel a bit uneasy.
> *S:* What would happen if a boy admitted to being gay?
> *B2:* If he was West Indian he'd probably get beaten by his West Indian friends and kicked out of his clan. In a group of normal London kids they'd take the mickey out of him and want nothing to do with him no more, an outcast. Then the rest another group might say it was all right but deep down inside they'd want nothing to do with him.

The introduction of information on AIDS in sex education provides an opportunity for teachers to raise the whole issue of homophobia. Lesbians in my research were frequently associated with women's lib and many girls expressed marked prejudice against them. Jacky, for example said:

Have you seen them? Two girls walking along, one of them's got cuff links on and everything, just like a man. I think that's terrible – I think it's disgusting. Poofs I can tolerate, but lesbians I can't. I suppose because it's my own sex.

Fear of seduction by lesbian girls was a constant theme – astonishing in the light of the real harassment that girls experience in their day to day life from boys. Girls made such comments as: 'Maybe we feel threatened by them – so we think to ourselves "Oh my God, maybe if they tried to drag me into that thing."' Another girl said that in the event of a close friend coming out as a lesbian: 'I wouldn't talk to her as much as I used to, not because I didn't like her as much but because I'd be threatened by her.'

Information about AIDS has clearly improved during the past few years but it is likely that the confusion expressed by these boys is still common:

Brian: A girl and a boy go out to get a baby. A boy and a boy go out to get AIDS.
Jimmy: AIDS is punishment for someone who goes fucking around.
Mike: You can get AIDS from anyone.
Jimmy: You can't catch it from women.
Mike: Yes, you can. People think AIDS is only for queers. You can get it from a blood transfusion, from women, from sperm.
                    (Group discussion, 16-year-old boys)

After conducting a survey of 4500 women, Shere Hite (1988) reported that most women were distressed and despairing about the continued resistance of the men in their lives to treat them as equals. She describes how women are subtly undermined in the home by men using disparaging stereotypes and being condescending. In the survey 70 per cent of women who had been married for more than five years said they were having extramarital affairs, although almost all believed in monogamy and believed their husbands to be faithful. Some 91 per cent of those who had divorced said that they, not their husbands, had made the decision to divorce, not because of adultery or an unsatisfying sex life, but because of a sense of emotional isolation in the marriage.

There is, however, evidence that attitudes are changing. As we have seen in Chapter 1, girls are less romantic and more realistic about what lies in store for them, mocking and being critical of boys who boast about their sexual prowess. They are more aware of the double standard and are contesting a passive view of femininity.

A new more confident femininity appears to be particularly true of black girls who through economic necessity have often had to take on the breadwinner role. Mirza (1992) found that the forms of femininity among African Caribbean girls differed fundamentally from their white peers. In the black definition, few distinctions were made between male and female attributes with regard to work and the labour market. She argues that this results in greater equality between black couples, where though they may not necessarily stay together for life, nonetheless both parties are seen as autonomous individuals in their own right.

On the other hand, the constitution of masculinity has changed little. Sexuality for girls is a matter of falling in love and individual passion. For boys it is more a group phenomenon between themselves. There is pressure to score – a sporting word. To be a man you've got to be hard. Boys talk about what they do. To talk about feelings or relationships is soft. They may know girls as friends until adolescence. Then suddenly they start talking about them in terms of their body parts – tits and bums – and seeing them as people they have to be different from and control. They cut off from feeling. A conversation between two boys quoted by James Walker (1988) in his ethnographic study of an inner city Australian school epitomizes this approach:

A: Fucking mole.
B: That's what I'm going to do. I swear it. I promise and I'm going to do that.
[smacks hands together hard indicating a slap]
A: See. I don't like hitting girls. He likes hitting girls. Like if they do something bad to them, he'll hit them you know.

A few boys I spoke to are aware of issues of equality but the majority, while not necessarily overtly sexist, do little to oppose the sexism around. Calling girls slags is a way of objectifying them, not recognizing them as people of equal worth. It is also an effective way of controlling female sexuality. The disgust of the female body, unless as an object of their desire, epitomized by their views of menstruation, is another form of distancing themselves from everything female. They cannot see the benefits of feminism as their identities have been constituted in opposition to femininity. Sexism should not, therefore, just be seen as chauvinism. It is deeply ingrained in identity formation, continually endorsed and celebrated by the dominant culture. The mass media, the daily press, pornographic magazines and videos all reinforce the objectifying of women's bodies, and celebrate a form of macho, aggressive masculinity. Violence against women is condoned and the fear of violence constricts the lives of women of all social and ethnic groups.

How possible is it to change sexual practices?

The AIDS campaign has been aimed at altering the attitudes and sexual practices of young people to the use of condoms and other methods of birth control. These studies generally find that knowledge alone of the risks of HIV infection is not a sufficient determinant of safe sex practice. Information-giving is simply insufficient to bring about clear cut and lasting behaviour change. People actively 'make sense' of new ideas they encounter by assessing them in the light of pre-existing beliefs, interpreting them and fitting them in with their present knowledge. It is therefore essential to study the meanings attached to sexual relationships and how these change over time.

The reluctance of young people to alter their sexual behaviour has been well documented. According to a study involving interviews with young women, their identification as slags or drags is still prevalent, and current health education programmes, based on increasing knowledge of condoms for protection against AIDS, overlook the meaning that the use of contraceptive technique has for young women and men and the ways in which their understandings differ (Holland *et al.* 1990).

The low use of contraception by girls was partly explained by girls' hesitancy about approaching doctors and birth control clinics but what could be more significant is the operation of the double standard. For young women to carry condoms around implies premeditated sex, which conflicts with popular ideas of romantic spontaneity and implicitly labels them as slags. The operation of the double standard condemns a girl as irresponsible if she does not use contraception and condemns her as not respectable if she does. If she uses contraception on a casual date this contravenes the dominant code of romance which opens her up to savage criticism. To use contraception involves premeditating sex which is only legitimate with someone you are going steady with. For a girl to have sex without contraception can only be explained by something which 'happens' without previous intent, unless of course the girl is a slag.

There is some evidence from Australian sources (Moore and Rosenthal 1991: 20) that girls are expected by boys to take responsibility for contraception. However, some of the British boys I interviewed thought that contraception was a joint responsibility. Tony, an Italian boy, had listened to his father's advice. When I asked him who should take responsibility for contraception he replied:

> Both of you discuss it beforehand. One, cause I don't want a kid. 'Cause my dad told me there wasn't any contraception around in his day and he doesn't know how many kids he has around Italy. And I got a message from that.

Jenny described when she went to a birth control clinic with her mum who needed contraception, the lady at the clinic asked her if she wanted to go on the pill too. She refused but the lady said she might need to. Jenny replied:

I've got will power, I didn't know what to say to her, I wouldn't go on it. I don't think it's right really because I know if you go on the pill you're going to lose will power in the end and just let yourself go.

Intriguingly, the phrase 'letting yourself go' has connections with both sexual excitement and becoming sluttish. Love seems to play an important ideological role in permitting the former while offering some protection from the latter.

In addition to these considerations, condom use, unlike the pill, involves the boys' active collaboration and also requires a degree of confidence to handle. It involves talking about the sexual encounter rather than 'letting it happen', which is not only far more embarrassing to negotiate but also involves carrying condoms around with all the risks of exposure. Even if the girl wants to use contraception that decision has to be negotiated and they have to be able to communicate with each other about it. Research undertaken by Moore and Rosenthal (1993) indicates that girls are very diffident about raising issues relating to contraception, which leaves them vulnerable to being overruled by a boy when he is resistant to using it.

A programme of sex education which would empower young women to take control of their own bodies to resist abuse and exploitation would be needed to begin to overcome these obstacles. Yet there is little sign that such action will be taken. For a woman to carry condoms can be seen as challenging the patriarchal definition of her as innately responsive to male initiative, as reactive rather than proactive. Such a challenge demands more than assertiveness training for women. It means shifting the meaning of sexuality and sexual identity. The importance of a young woman's self-confidence is crucial to her ability to insist on the use of condoms.

Generally surveys have found that young people are complacent about their risk of infection from HIV. Ford (1992) in his study found only 30 per cent had used a condom in their most recent sexual intercourse. Only one-fifth of the casual recreational group who condoned sex outside a casual relationship used condoms. Abrams (1991) found that young people overestimate other people's involvement in casual sex. He concluded that most young people are adopting safe practices but, among the minority who are not, the key seems to be that they are unaware that they are in a minority. Those most at risk were also those who saw themselves as least able to control the infection. Moore and Rosenthal (1993), in their study of Australian youth, also found that the failure to take on board the importance of safe sex was due to the linking of HIV/AIDS with risk groups rather than risk behaviours. A common theme in their responses to the threat of AIDS is the not-me phenomenon. Young people who saw themselves to be least at risk had a strong stereotype of an AIDS victim and imagined that since they were different (although this difference might be superficial or irrelevant), they therefore were not at risk.

The content of sex education

Critiques of the traditional nuclear family and the existing state of gender relations have hardly infiltrated the popular marriage literature or sex education in schools. In the US sex education is also deficient. Szirom (1988), who carried out the most comprehensive study of sex education provision undertaken in Australia, found that 60 per cent of young women chose their mother as their preferred person to learn about sex from compared with 15 per cent of young men. Fathers were not a major source of information for either females or males. Some parents still do not provide even basic information, such as telling their daughters about periods.

Schools reinforce the suppression of female desire through the lack of discourse about female desire in sex education discussions. Girls are not seen as the initiators of sexuality but are constantly presented as potential victims. Michelle Fine (1988) in her research on sex education found that girls were taught to defend themselves against disease, pregnancy and 'being used'. Female desire was tied to negative emotions and seen as having moral and reproductive consequences. Male desire, on the other hand, was typically represented as a normal biological process, consisting of such phenomena as wet dreams and ejaculation. When a girl asked about orgasms in one discussion, the topic shifted to better awareness of sexual disease. Fine calls for the need for open discussion where girls could examine what feels good and bad as well as examining their own needs and limits. They could then become subjects of their own desires rather than simply objects of male desire.

Consequences for the education of girls

What implications does this analysis have for the way that social relations and sex education are handled in school? Sex education in the traditional sense usually focuses on different methods of contraception and descriptions of the biological make-up and the mechanics of the sex act. A broader approach is needed where sex education is taught within this context of how sexual relations are structured by the norms and constraints outlined in this chapter.

Sexual harassment and violence are also areas that urgently need to be addressed. Feminist approaches have been developed in the United States which challenge men's violence and the traditional therapeutic interpretations that see the problem of male violence as a family problem. EMERGE, which was set up in 1977 in Boston, involves a coordinated community approach involving services for women, men's programmes and the coordination of criminal justice and social service agencies (Sousa 1991). Pro-feminist programmes directly challenge men's violence. A fundamental principle is to make men responsible for their violence. The appropriate use of confrontation is crucial. Confrontation involves attempts to persuade men to acknowledge their violent behaviour and to accept responsibility for actions and for the need to change (see Dobash and Dobash 1992: 244). These are the kinds of programmes which need to be introduced into schools in Britain.

Conclusion

Over the past decade therefore changes have taken place in gender relations which are unlikely to be reversed, however much Conservative party ministers wish. Premarital sex is now the norm rather than the exception, marriage is no longer conceived as necessarily lasting for life, for better or worse, and involving the subordination of the wife, who is expected to provide domestic services, fidelity and obedience to her husband who in return provides economically for her. Rather relationships are negotiated on a more equal basis and conceived as lasting as long as both parties find it satisfactory. Already these changes are reflected in the rising divorce statistics. In the short term, however, there is a danger that young men, deprived of their breadwinner role, may find it too hard to move to a more democratic relationship with women and may be more likely to resort to violence in an attempt to put the clock back and reassert their authority. Sex education should be an educational priority.

CHAPTER 3

Judicial rape: researching rape trials

Have you ever asked a woman who has been raped whether she enjoyed it? Have you ever asked her whether she asked for it by wearing a short skirt, going out late at night or inviting someone in for a coffee? Have you ever asked her to describe loudly and clearly in a roomful of people what exactly happened in the assault, where and how she was touched, what she felt at each point and why she did not fight back more strenuously? Probably not, but this is what we inflict on the minority of women who are brave or foolhardy enough to allow their cases of rape or sexual assault to be taken to court.

These are the types of questions which defence counsel, in wigs and gowns, and drawing salaries well over six figures, are encouraged to put on the grounds that this is the only way men can be protected from false allegations. Rape is not the expression of love or passion. It is the expression of sexuality used as a form of power and desire to humiliate. Another form of domination is practised by the courts where men, highly paid and unscrupulous, defend this right that men hold to power over women. The judicial 'rape', where a woman's reputation is put on trial by the court is, according to many victims, as humiliating as the actual rape. In some respects it is worse, more deliberate and systematic, more subtle and more dishonest, masquerading in the name of justice.

This chapter documents the difficulty of obtaining convictions for rape in the British adversarial system of justice. The research is based on a study conducted in 1988–89 of jury trials undertaken at the Old Bailey, the Central Criminal Court in London. After a preliminary hearing in magistrates courts, cases are sent up to the higher court which usually takes over a year. This means that women have to give evidence a year after the rape and relive the ordeal again. Each rape case lasts about four or five days, the complainant's evidence usually lasting a whole day. I only accidentally started to attend rape trials. At the time I was undertaking research into the defence of provocation in murder trials, and one day when waiting for a relevant trial for my research to be heard, I wandered into a rape trial. In my innocence at this first trial, I imagined there was no way, in the light of the evidence presented, that the defendant would be acquitted. He was however discharged.

Access to the well of the court took two years to negotiate. It is only in the press seats that it is possible to hear adequately to record the proceedings. The court system in Britain is unbelievably old-fashioned. Records are kept in a vault in the cellars. Courts number one and two are vast nineteenth-century galleries, with high chapel-like ceilings, the judge up high – a terrifying setting in which women who have been sexually assaulted have to give evidence. The other courts are smaller but the atmosphere is still very formal, exacerbated by the fact that the presiding judge wears a wig and is adorned in red and ermine apparel.

I managed to obtain a small research grant to investigate further trials. I sat in on 10 trials and a further four retrials, with a research assistant, and both of us made transcripts of the trials. (A court stenographer takes down the evidence but this is only transcribed if the case goes to appeal and it costs about £2000 to obtain an official transcript). By the time seven out of 10 defendants had been found not guilty of rape, and another case abandoned, I came to see these trials as a cruel hoax, equivalent to a second rape by the judiciary and legal profession which functions to condone violence against women, ideologically reinforcing the relations of domination and subordination. In three trials the defendant was found guilty of a lesser charge than rape, either buggery or indecent assault, for which he was given a short sentence or in one case set free.

I also conducted an analysis of 52 case records of cases heard between June and September 1988, which revealed a similar picture to my small sample. Ten of these defendants pleaded guilty. Of the remaining 42 who pleaded not guilty, only nine were convicted of rape, a mere 23 per cent. This figure is a higher acquittal rate than for any other crime and is similar to Wright's (1984) findings that only 17 per cent of those arrested of 204 cases he followed up were found guilty of rape.

Once a woman has reported the alleged rape, she is drawn into a process from which it is very difficult for her to withdraw without facing contempt proceedings and possible imprisonment.[1] It examines why so few alleged rapists are convicted. Instead they are set free, to rape again. Women are subjected to a trial in an adversarial court system where two versions of events are pitted against each other and the woman's account is discounted or disbelieved, her credibility and reputation undermined. The intimidation faced by women from their attackers is frequently discounted or ignored. Jurors are rarely aware of how few cases even reach court or how unfair the procedures are.

The only previous study in England and Wales of rape trials was conducted by Zsuzsanna Adler (1987) who followed up 82 trials at the Old Bailey in 1978 to 1979 for her PhD thesis. At that time, both the conviction rate and length of sentence were very low, the average sentence for convicted rapists being only two years. She found that recent amendments to the Sexual Offences (Amendment) Act 1976, intended to avoid cross-examination of the victim about her previous sexual history, had been largely ineffective as this was still allowed at the judge's discretion, which was given in 60 per cent of the trials she attended.

Factors affecting the outcome of trials

The judge and jury

There are a number of ways in which the odds are balanced against the complainant. Let us first consider the jury. There is evidence that jurors find many of the court procedures bewildering. Recognition of this problem has recently led to the piloting of a video to try to prepare juries for their task in 12 courts. This was commissioned by the Lord Chancellor's department to explain the role of the barrister, solicitor and usher and the order of speeches and evidence, to facilitate recognition of the trial participants, and explain how to get the judge's attention, how to take notes and how to claim expenses. Jurors frequently complain that they could have done a better job had they understood the trial process better.[2] It would help if jurors were given a great deal more information about what happens from the time a woman reports sexual assault to the police until the high court hearing. Many jurors have little idea of the pressure many women are under to drop cases or how long it has taken for a case to reach the Crown Court. Over and above this, some judges fail to clarify the court procedures. There are various strategies that judges adopt, intentionally or unintentionally, which distort the complainant's situation and lead juries to gain a false impression of how cases come to court, and various court procedures imbalance the trial in the defendant's favour.

Judges sometimes mislead juries into believing that it is up to the woman complainant whether or not the case comes to court and do not inform them of how few cases reach court at all. It is well documented by victimization studies (see Jones *et al.* 1986) and figures from London Rape Crisis Centre (1989) that rape is one of the most underreported serious crimes. Many women never tell anyone until years later. Of reported rapes only one in 10 of the women who go to rape crisis centres go on to lodge a complaint with the police. The police still do not record every case as a crime. Between 30 per cent to 40 per cent of cases are 'no-crimed'. Few women, therefore, even report sexual assaults to the police. In a recent survey conducted at Cambridge University, it was found that one in five of 1500 students surveyed had been victims of rape or attempted rape and one in nine had been raped. Only one in 50 had told the police (*Public Eye* 1992).

Judges however often openly state that it is all too easy for women to bring cases to court, implying that it is their decision to do so. For example, I heard a judge say: 'It is easy for women to make false allegations of rape but difficult for a man to refute them'. In reality it is a great deal easier for men to get away with sexual assault. It may be easy to make false allegations, but it is very difficult to take a case of sexual assault to court and it is not the woman's decision to do so. It is not even the decision of the police alone. Only 40 per cent of the cases proceed to court at all and only one in four of the defendants who plead not guilty are convicted. In the United States, conviction rates are also low. According to the Federal Bureau of Investigation (FBI) statistics, of every 100 reported rapes, only 16 per cent of the accused persons are actually convicted of rape (Steketee and Austen 1989).

With procedures so weighted in favour of the defendant, only a small proportion of cases ever go to court, and furthermore, contrary to what judges argue, it is not at all easy to make allegations. The woman will have spent hours, even days, under police questioning, she will have had a thorough medical examination, she is likely to have had pregnancy and venereal disease testing, she may have spent hours at the police station involved in an identification parade, she will have gone to the magistrates court (lower or preliminary court), she may well have been subjected to threats from the alleged defendant or his friends.

Court procedures

Various court procedures weight the trial in favour of the defendant, making it very difficult for jurors to convict, even when the evidence is convincing. This is mainly a result of all the extraneous factors that can be introduced and often involve attacks on the woman's reputation, as not merely her sexual history but all kinds of irrelevant factors relating to her past are discussed. She is subjected to a ruthless character assassination, a humiliating trial, a form of judicial rape. Some lawyers have recognized the fraudulence of these procedures and are refusing to defend rapists who insist the woman consented. The grounds for their refusal is twofold. First, they object to the way in which rape cases are frequently defended and believe the processes in such cases are unnecessarily harrowing for women.

Second, many of their clients are victims of male violence which, they say, presents a conflict of professional interests as the whole conduct of the defence may be based on a series of stereotypes.[3] The prosecution barristers, as we shall see, are inept at countering myths and prejudices about women, indeed they often share them. Often jurors, when faced with all sorts of information about the woman's character which they assume must be relevant to the case since it has been presented, can only deal with the conflict between the doubts they have been presented with by the defence and the need to find the defendant guilty beyond any reasonable doubt by failing to reach a decision. This results in a retrial where the complainant often cannot face attending and going through all the painful details again. If a decision cannot be reached on the second retrial the defendant goes free.

In the cases I attended jurors were not encouraged to come to a verdict, nor was it explained to them what the outcome would be if the jury twice fails to come to a decision. The jury do not, of course, know whether or not they are participating in a retrial. Instead, in one case I attended after the jurors had spent three or four hours deliberating and had failed to reach a consensus, they were brought back to court, where the judge told them that having failed to reach an unanimous verdict, they could settle for a majority verdict which he would give them half an hour to try and reach. When they returned having failed to do so, he dismissed them instead of insisting that they should spend more time deliberating. He told them not to worry as there could always be a retrial. They were not encouraged to take time to come to a decision, as would be the case in a murder trial, where juries are often put up overnight if they cannot easily reach a verdict. This case was not unusual and few of the cases I attended ever went on after 4.30 p.m. Failure to reach a verdict was the outcome in four of the 10 trials I attended. Of the retrials, one woman could not face another humiliation and did not turn up. In another the jury again failed to reach a decision and in the two remaining retrials, the defendant was found guilty.

The complainant is only a witness for the prosecution so has no separate representation in court, whereas the defendant can consult with his defence lawyer before the case comes to trial. The complainant, as the main prosecution witness, is not allowed even to speak to the prosecution counsel, indeed she may not even know which of the barristers he is. The ban on the prosecution counsel consulting with the witness is to prevent the briefing of witnesses, but in a rape trial where often the victim rather than the defendant's reputation is under attack, she needs some representation. In the United States, as described by Judith Rowland (1986) a state attorney in San Diego, the prosecution and complainant prepare the case together over several months before the trial. In Denmark and Norway, the complainant is entitled to legal representation from the moment that she reports a sexual assault. Under this provision the police are obliged to inform the victim of her rights and to provide a list of suitable advocates in the absence of her having her own lawyer. These lawyers are provided by the state and have had training specifically related to sexual assault cases, which is not currently provided upon completion of either the Law Society's Finals or the Bar Finals in Britain. My own preference would be for the San Diego system where separate legal representation is not provided, but the prosecution and complainant are able, in sexual assault cases, to prepare the case together. The complainants should, however, be eligible for expert advice and counselling from the time that they report a case to the police. At present in some areas victims are offered victim support, a voluntary service which, with limited resources, provides some emotional support and help in preparing complainants for a court hearing. This is often inadequate and more resources need to be available to provide a specialist service. Often complainants are not kept informed by the police of what has happened to their case, and are not even told whether or not the case reaches court.

The failure to provide a barrister for the complainant results in a highly disinterested representation on the woman's behalf. Forensic evidence is repeatedly ignored by the jury, as defence lawyers expertly create red herring tales, which can make it difficult for a jury to bring in a guilty verdict. Calling her as a prosecution witness leads to a certain confusion about the order in which evidence is heard. Normally in trials the prosecution presents their case, and witnesses are questioned by the defence, who then presents their case.

The confusion arises when the defence starts to introduce contradictory allegations after the witnesses have given evidence and are therefore not available to answer them. In other words we have a 'contest' system of trials where each of the witnesses appear for one side or the other and each advocate must have a turn at questioning them. Evidence from a witness can be contradicted some hours later when the witness is no longer available to be cross-examined. This is a major problem with the adversarial system of justice and puts considerable strain on the jury to remember exactly what was said.

This can raise particular problems in rape trials where it gives an advantage to the defence who can contradict what witnesses argued without their retort. For example, in one case of a man who was charged in two separate trials of raping three women, an outlandish story was presented by the defence about the marks around the neck of one of the women having been caused by the boyfriend of another girl living in the house. He had been called as a witness but had not been asked about this allegation. The prosecution is on the defensive without knowing exactly what the defence is going to argue. Other relevant questions are not asked and the character of the defendant is rarely challenged in the same way as the complainant's. The defendant has the advantage of having met with their counsel beforehand whereas the prosecution cannot speak with their chief witness. The complainant is not allowed to see her statement.

The Crown Prosecution Service (CPS), led by the Director of Public Prosecutions, was set up as an independent body in 1985 to separate the prosecution from the investigatory police role. There are 31 Chief Crown Prosecutors under whom are Crown Prosecutors who are barristers or solicitors. Starved of funds from the start, and in London starting at a mere 50 per cent of its proposed strength of lawyers, it has led to bureaucratic delays and has been much criticized for the poor calibre of staff that it has managed to recruit, mainly due to inferior rates of pay compared to independent barristers. The resignation of the Head of Public Prosecutions, Sir Allen Green, in 1993 for alleged kerb crawling cannot have helped its image. The task of the CPS is to continue criminal proceedings only when there is a realistic prospect of conviction or when it is in the public interest to prosecute. These criteria are set out in more detail in the Code for Crown Prosecutors, which is included in the service's annual report, a public document. Victims should have the opportunity to work more closely with the Crown Prosecution Service barrister. In Canada, as soon as a sexual assault is reported the complainant has the right to free legal advice and is put in contact with a lawyer who can represent her in court. Certainly in rape trials the prosecution rarely presents a convincing case for the complainant.

Little recognition of the trauma women experience in reliving the attack is made, and women still appear in court without support or preparation for what is a horrendous ordeal. Imagine what it is like to give evidence against a man who has raped you. The case does not come up until over a year later. You have already given evidence at the magistrates court. You are now obliged to relive the whole life-threatening experience, face to face with the man who assaulted you, the mere sight of whom brings back the horror of the attack. You avoid looking at him. You face ranks of barristers in wigs, the judge up high, police everywhere, all in the awe inspiring surroundings of the Central Criminal Court. You have no legal representative of your own, and you are not allowed to meet the prosecuting counsel, so you are probably not sure which one he or she is.

As we shall see in the next chapter, you must describe in intimate detail every part of your body that was assaulted in words which would embarrass women under any circumstances, let alone in such a public setting in a loud voice. To describe such details carries the implication that the woman is sexually promiscuous. It is for this reason perhaps that so many women find being cross-examined such a nightmare. You are liable to be mercilessly cross-examined about every aspect of the assault, how long every move lasted (which breast did he hold, for how long and how did it make you feel, where did he fondle next), about your lifestyle, relationships and (at the judge's discretion) your past sexual experience. As if this ordeal was not enough it is continuously implied that you have lied, invented everything and even enjoyed it. You have gone to court in the expectation that the accused will be convicted. But you begin to feel that it is you, not he, who is on trial. A range of tactics are used to discredit your character and every word. You are subjected to aggressive verbal attack while the defendant does not even have an obligation to take the stand. Finally, as he is three times more likely to be set free than convicted, you are likely to emerge from the ordeal with your own credibility and reputation undermined by the jury's dismissal of your evidence. You also may fear that he will come after you again to punish you for taking the case to court. Jurors can have no idea of the impact of a 'not guilty' verdict on a complainant who has been raped. Women who have been raped all agree that it is an experience from which you never recover. Then to not be believed, to be humiliated in court and to be the object of scorn and ridicule, is quite devastating.

How to define rape

The definition of rape, which focuses on penetration, diverts attention away from the coercive and life-threatening experience of rape as described by complainants. There are two different conceptions of rape, the male judicial view and the woman's view based on her experience of the rape. According to the judicial view, rape is defined as penetration of the vagina by the penis without the consent of the woman, when the man knows she does not consent, or does not care whether she consents or not (Section 1 Sexual Offences Act 1956).

Women describe rape as a life-threatening event, as sexual coercion aimed to humiliate rather than give pleasure, in which their main concern is to survive. To explain why juries do not believe such accounts needs some explanation as it is difficult to believe that any of the cases I heard could have been fabricated. Take for example this statement by a woman who was allegedly raped on waste ground at 2 a.m.:

> He was holding my shoulder, and he grabbed me tighter and pulled me down. He had me by the neck. I asked what he was trying to do. He said, 'I'll never hurt you'. I said, 'Are you going to kill me?' He said it would not be worth it. I was too scared to run or move.

Or these statements by women who alleged they had been raped in their own homes:

> I kept saying, 'Don't hurt me. Please don't hurt me.' He picked me up with a hand round my mouth and one hand round my throat with my feet off the floor and carried me into the bedroom. I put a slap here and there and I scratched him. I panicked. I was scared. I'm asthmatic. I couldn't breathe. He was carrying me by the throat so I couldn't scream. He threw me on the bed. I said, 'I have a period at

the moment.' He said 'Don't give me that bullshit.' He ripped my skirt and my blouse. There weren't any injuries because I did not let myself get injured. I didn't want a bottle over my head.

He said he had chosen me as a victim because he could control me with violence. At knife point he ordered me to masturbate him. He was unable to penetrate. He forced me to have oral sex and when he could [when he had an erection] he raped me.

In defining rape in terms of penetration by the penis rather than all forms of sexual degradation, from threats and bullying, to forcible oral sex or penetration by other objects, attention is diverted from the broader context of the woman's actual experience. All the attention is on whether he penetrated or not rather than what led up to the sexual assault and how sex was negotiated, if at all, or forced. Excessive detail of where exactly the penis went and how long it penetrated, whether or not ejaculation occurred and so on takes the focus off the woman's strategies for survival, where her terror at the man's threats and demands for sex is disregarded.

The focus should be on what evidence can be produced that she consented, what led him to believe she was willing, rather than on whether she actually fought, where many women see their best chance of survival as submitting to the attack or are simply frozen with fear. Men can get away with arguing that the woman enjoyed penetration, even when she vehemently denies it and describes the experience as terrifying. Even when defendants walk off, leaving a woman on waste ground or in a lift shaft in the middle of the night, or the woman runs half clothed into the street, such events are not regarded as relevant to her account because the whole focus is on penetration. This, for example, is how a defence counsel (DC) cross-examined a woman complainant (C):

DC: Do you recognize that garment?
C: Yes.
DC: Your knickers. Are they clean?
C: I don't know.
[The usher ostentatiously puts on rubber gloves and picks up the exhibit.]
DC: I think they are the ones you took off.
Judge: [to C] Would you like some plastic gloves? Or I don't suppose you mind handling your own knickers?

The defendant's pants are not the subject of debate and his knickers are never handed round. Judge Perleman, in an interview on the *Panorama* programme *The Rape of Justice* (1993), remarked that many rape complainants found the handing round of their panties the most appalling part of the trial, even worse than describing the actual assault.

The myth of equal justice for all is no more blatantly exposed than in a rape trial. The whole procedure loads the dice against her. Not only her testimony, but her very life up to her complaint of rape and her motives in making that complaint are brought into question, and often aggressively or mockingly so. The judge pulls this bias against the complainant together in his directions to the jury; people lie more about their sexual behaviour, he warns, than about any other area of human conduct. Here, for example is how one judge put that proposition to the jury in two cases I attended:

> There is in all cases of sexual allegations a special warning. Experience has shown that people who say they have been the victims of sexual attacks do not always tell the truth. Such allegations may be very easy to make and very difficult to refute. It is dangerous to convict on the evidence of the complainant alone.

> What is the most difficult and the most intimate part of our lives? It is our sexual life. It is not only the most difficult but the most unstable part of our lives. It has become a rule of law that some supporting evidence is needed that is wholly independent.
>
> (my transcript, summer 1988)

Rape is the only crime where this warning is given. The judge combines it with the usual direction that it is not up to the defendant to prove his innocence, but for the prosecution to prove his guilt beyond any reasonable doubt. As one judge put it: 'He does not have to prove anything. The proof has to be so strong that you are sure that the defendant is guilty. Then it is your duty to convict. But the defendant gets the benefit of the doubt.'

Put in conjunction, these two directions make it very difficult for a jury to convict. Only in sexual cases does the defendant get this double indemnity. The Common Sergeant of London set out the thinking which lies behind this judicial caution in September 1989: 'In complaints of a sexual matter, made by men and women, it has been found that whether out of spite, excitement, jealousy, sexual gratification or malice, false allegations are made and once made are extremely difficult to disprove.'

Jennifer Temkin (1987) points out that if a woman reports a burglary, or makes an insurance claim, her word is not automatically doubted, though of course investigation would take place to substantiate her report. But her integrity would not be questioned, her statement would not be picked to pieces, and her whole life would not come under investigation. Myths about women making false allegations override common sense explanations of why they should run naked into the street, cry compulsively, spend the night in police stations for fear of retribution for taking the case to court, change their name or even move house. Only if a woman contrived to be physically assaulted such is the burden of proof, could she be sure of being believed. The judge fails to warn the jury with equal solemnity that experience has shown that accused men lie to escape conviction. Indeed, many men convicted of rape continue to deny that the woman did not consent (Wyre and Swift 1990). Nor does the judge draw the jury's attention to the fact that most women who have been raped cannot face the ordeal they will have to go through if they complain to the police (many, indeed, cannot face telling anyone) and that they are often threatened with retaliation if they do go to the police. One woman, when asked why she had not gone at once to the police, replied, 'Because he told me that if I told anyone or went to the police, he'd come back for me and the children.'

The corroboration warning

One main barrier to gaining convictions in rape cases is the belief that rape can never be corroborated. Since the act takes place in private and rests on the presence or absence of the woman's consent, it is argued that independent corroboration is impossible. This is not always true as trials often rest not simply on the question of consent but on two divergent accounts of what happened. Evidence to back the man or woman's story is given but is often not treated as corroborative. For example, in one case a defendant said he had never been on the wasteland where the complainant claimed rape had taken place. A can of beer with his fingerprints on it was found close to where the grass had been flattened as though two people had lain there. Yet the prosecution did not emphasize this as corroborative evidence. In several cases evidence was given by witnesses that the complainant had been in a state of shock when she had rung desperately half-clad in the middle of the night at a neighbour's door. This was however not regarded as corroboration, nor did the defence find it even necessary to explain why else she should have been in this state. The argument is put forward that she could be faking it. It is not considered necessary to explain why as the myth lives that women are known make false allegations.

The woman will usually show signs of distress or other psychological reaction, but this is at once viewed as suspect. In one case, several police officers, including a police surgeon, gave evidence that the woman was shaking with fear and distress, tears were streaming down her face, she wanted to wash herself frequently and was afraid afterwards to go out alone. They all agreed she was in acute distress and showing every sign that she was suffering from what has been identified as the rape trauma syndrome. Yet the prosecution counsel failed even to mention her distress in his summing up. In this case I abandoned my role as participant observer and followed him out of the court and asked him why he had not mentioned her distress. He responded that it was absurd to regard the woman's state as corroborative and dismissed the judge's view as irrelevant. This exemplifies the lack of sympathy between the prosecution counsel and the complainant and the way it can prejudice her case.

Rarely does the prosecution counsel challenge the defendant in the same way as the complainant is challenged about whether or not his behaviour was aggressive and violent and whether it is credible that he believed she consented. The prosecution often fails to ask such questions as: How does he view women? Why has the woman gone through all the agony of reporting the rape to the police and living with the anxiety for at least a year after the alleged offence if her agony is all faked? All sorts of questionable criteria are used to determine whether or not the victim consented, most of which refer to her assumed sexual character. Factors determining social respectability include virginity, marital status, class, race, employment, housing, past sexual experience. Most of the women in the trials I sat through were unattached. Only one was married; over half were living alone in bedsits and the rest with children. They were mostly working class, often working in low paid jobs.

Chambers and Millar (1986: 89–91), who interviewed 20 women whose cases reached the Scottish courts, found that women said they felt 'let down' and poorly represented by what they believed to be their side. The majority of women were very critical of the questions which they were asked by the defence, and expressed great annoyance with questioning which insinuated that they had led the guy on or that they were a willing partner or that she was a 'liar'. They also criticized the defence questioning for being difficult to understand.

Criteria for credibility

The question of whether a woman has had sexual experience outside marriage is frequently raised as a criterion of her credibility. The Sexual Offences (Amendment) Act (1976) precluded such questioning about the sexual past of the victims, except at the discretion of the judge. In two cases in my research, the judge used his discretion to allow the defence to focus on the woman's past sexual history. Over and above this, one judge himself questioned the woman about her sexual experience in the absence of any application from the defence; and defence counsel on one occasion conducted what clearly amounted to improper cross-examination without intervention from the trial judge. A woman who has been a drug addict in the past, or who smokes cannabis, is particularly at risk of having her credibility undermined. One woman, who had broken with heroin two years previously, was continually asked if she had been taking drugs, and the defence suggested that she was stoned and had been drinking when the defendant arrived at her flat. This was in spite of police evidence that she was sober. Another woman was asked about having had an abortion and having sex with her boyfriend, neither of which was the least bit relevant to the alleged rape.

> Q: With regard to your stomach hurting, you said this was because you had had a termination and you weren't supposed to have sex? When had you previously had sex?
> C: I think it was Saturday.
> Q: So you were able to have sex?
> C: Having sex with your boyfriend is different to someone raping you.

Being homeless and on social security came up in one case and was used to imply that the complainant had 'asked for it'.

> DC: You didn't have anywhere to live, did you?
> C:　I've got friends, that's where I went.
> DC: I suggest you asked him if you could stay at his flat.
> C:　No I didn't. He suggested it.

Lack of marital status was emphasized in another case:

> DC: Being a single mother must be hard?
> C:　Not really.
> DC: Were you keen to have a relationship?
> C:　Not really.
> DC: Were you keen to have a man around?
> C:　Not really.

Lack of contact with her children's father was used as evidence for her 'being embittered towards men'.

> DC: As far as your two children are concerned, you don't have contact with either of the fathers?
> C:　No.
> DC: You don't know where they live?
> C:　I do know. They have got nothing to do with this case.
> DC: They don't support you in any way?
> C:　No.

The importance of reputation based on allegations rather than evidence was underlined in a case where the defendant pleaded guilty. Judge Richardson, in his summing up, commented:

> She is not a promiscuous person. She is a sober, sensitive and religious young lady who will bear the mental scars for a very long time to come. Did she 'provoke' the incident by the clothes she wore, the amount she had drunk, by dancing provocatively, going to the defendant's flat, being out late at night, asking the defendant back, taking drugs or soliciting?

Any indication of autonomous behaviour or taking an active rather than a passive role was argued by the defence as implying consent. For example, since the defendant alleged that she had insisted on coming back to her flat (in the afternoon) the defence counsel argued:

> She is not a young innocent girl straight off the boat from Ireland. She has worked around public houses. The sort of young woman who is well able to look after herself. She is not delicate and retiring in her appearance. Not a small girl. Why did she invite him back to her flat?

In another case the defence counsel asked:

DC: In your account, he asked you to go back to your place for a drink. Why did you ask him to come?
C: To accompany me.
DC: When you left the pub, was it not that you said 'Let's go get some more drink and come to my place?'
C: No.
DC: He asked to go back several times. What did you expect?
C: I didn't expect it to happen.

The myth of false allegations

The focus of rape trials is therefore to ascertain whether or not the woman is making a false allegation. In the conduct of trials she appears to be more on trial than the accused. She is under greater attack for allegedly making false allegations than he is for lying. Reasons put forward for false allegations are often specious. It is argued that complainants allege rape through fear of admitting to their boyfriends that they had been unfaithful and enjoyed making love with someone else, or that they are acting in revenge for being jilted or that they are unable to differentiate between fact and fantasy.

In one case, the defence alleged that a complainant had made false allegations due to fear of the defendant's girlfriend. Since she had told the girlfriend about the rape, this seemed completely far-fetched. The defence counsel in his summing up said: 'Did she lead him on, prostitute herself, or consent and then changed her mind at the last minute when the man was unable to control himself?' This is based on the commonly accepted idea that male sexuality once aroused is uncontrollable. If the defendant's wife is pregnant at the time, the man's presumed sexual frustration is presented as an excuse for the offence.

In the following case, the absence of injuries was taken as evidence of consent:

Police Constable: [questioning the defendant] She says she screamed.
Defendant: She was squeaking, not screaming.

PC: What did you think that meant?

D: I thought she was enjoying it.

PC: [questioning the complainant] You're bigger than him. How could he make you do anything?

C: You probably haven't ever been scared in your life . . . He said he'd punch me in the face if I didn't do what he wanted . . .

The phrase 'false allegations' needs unpacking. The malicious woman who concocts a false story to revenge her past lover would not get very far in the legal system where a past sexual relationship usually precludes cases even getting to court. It is possible that on rare occasions women who have perhaps been raped or abused in the past may allege that it has happened again, but it is unlikely that a sensitive investigator would not be able to uncover this. Temkin (1987) points out that there is no evidence that fabricating allegations happened more often in rape cases than in other types of crime.

In Lorna Smith's (1989: 12) study the police decided they had evidence of this in only 17 of the cases reported in the two London boroughs over the three year period of the research. More commonly, false allegations refer to the woman's word pitted against the man's protestation that she consented. In most trials the fact of sexual intercourse is not disputed; the issue is about the meaning of consent. Men's exaggerated fear of false allegations says perhaps more about some men's fantasies about women. It reflects a society where the forcing of sex by men on women is far more common than generally imagined and where women who are forced into sex often do not name this as rape. In all but one trial exaggerated or unfounded allegations of drink or drug use were made against the women. In three trials it was argued that this 'loosening of inhibition' led women to have sex with strangers in car parks, waste ground or lift shafts. The far greater inebriation and in some cases violence of the defendant is hardly questioned by the prosecution.

Powers of the defence

The defence can even employ solicitors to question relatives and neighbours of the woman for information to use against her in court. In one case defence solicitors had actually called on the woman's mother, who had not known about her daughter's rape, as well as spying for several days outside her own house. The defence counsel had the gall to use the fact that the complainant had shouted at them to 'fuck off' as evidence of her lack of respectability, but even the jury could not stomach that. The complainant, a single mother, had not wanted her mother to know about the rape, but the defendant's solicitors had written to her mother. She began to cry when questioned about this:

DC: You stopped your mother talking to solicitors representing the defendant?

C: I didn't stop her. She didn't know anything.

DC: You stopped your next-door neighbour from speaking to solicitors?

C: No . . . Mrs P can't speak English.

DC: You shouted abuse at the solicitors?

C: That's right . . . They weren't embarrassed.

DC: Half the street could hear you.

C: No . . . I didn't shout as loud as I could.

DC: What did you shout?

C: I told them to fuck off and leave me alone, she doesn't know anything about the case.

DC: You shouted, 'Fuck off you cunt'.

C: Yes . . . What interview is that? A woman who can't speak English.

DC: Isn't your neighbour allowed to decide who she speaks to?

C: She can't speak English. She doesn't understand. She was frightened.

DC: She was just below you. She could hear everything.

C: At 4 o'clock in the morning she would be asleep.

DC: So the solicitors retired.

C: They just stood there.

DC: You went upstairs to your window and you shouted at them again.

C: Yes . . . He wouldn't go. He just wanted to come round and tell anyone.

At this point the jury passed a note to the judge. It read, 'What is the role of the interviewers and who are they?' The complainant explained that her neighbours had told her they were the defendant's solicitors. The prosecution never criticized this harassment, yet the defence used the woman's outrage as evidence against her.

I have argued that two opposing views are presented in rape trials and it is usually the woman's view that is discarded. The unreliability of the woman's word compared to the supposed rationality of men is a bias that judges express quite blatantly.

The acceptance that there is something dangerous and uncontrollable about male sexuality has led women to be held responsible for male violence. It is assumed that it is they who should take evasive action if they are to avoid blame. A police video on ways women can avoid or defuse a dangerous situation urges women to take self-defence lessons from professionals (*The Guardian*, 15 September 1989). They fail to suggest that more women should join the police force to encourage more reporting of violence and changes in legal procedures. At present men can get away with violence, and the law supports this entitlement.

So what is the effect of this failure to hold men responsible for their sexual behaviour? Does rape serve to control women both actually and potentially by means of the fear it inspires and is it an important agent of the perpetuation of male domination over women? Is it 'nothing more or less than a conscious process of intimidation by which all men keep women in a state of fear?' (Brownmiller 1976) Certainly rape and fear of rape act as a strong form of social control over female sexuality and independence.

Court of Appeal decisions

There is some evidence that convictions can be quashed on appeal on very questionable grounds. In 1986 a group of paratroopers was convicted of indecent assault. On appeal their sentences were drastically reduced on the grounds that the victim was 'dissolute and depraved' and the paratroopers were described by the judge as 'fine men and good soldiers who had thrown away their careers for activity, albeit disgusting, that lasted for only minutes' (Temkin 1987). In another appeal case a man who was convicted of raping a 16-year-old girl on 10 July 1989 and sentenced to seven years' imprisonment won his appeal which was heard in February 1991. Three Appeal Court judges ruled that the original judge had misdirected the jury by laying too much stress on the girl's distressed state after the alleged assault (*The Guardian*, 15 September 1989).

In another rape case that I attended, the judge in the first trial used his discretion to allow the defendant to call a character witness, and the defence was allowed to question the young woman's 'reputation'. The jury at this trial was unable to reach a verdict. This led to a retrial before a woman judge who disallowed the calling of character witnesses by the defence. The defendant was convicted and sentenced to five years. He appealed. At the appeal the three Court of Appeal judges ruled that the judge in the second trial was wrong to disallow character witnesses for the defendant, and consequently quashed the conviction.

Little is known about decision making in regard to appeals in sexual assault cases, but most of the convicted men in my sample planned to appeal. Preliminary evidence indicates that appeal courts are reducing sentences and overturning convictions of men convicted of rape by juries; this is a disturbing finding and requires further investigation (see Temkin 1993).

Conclusion

Rape trials appear to have the function of controlling women rather than protecting them. Barristers, in order to argue their case, play on the prejudices of jurors. A rape trial can be seen as a barometer of ideologies of sexual difference, of male dominance and woman's inferiority. The ideology condones and legitimates a degree of male violence. The conduct of rape trials has the manifest function of limiting the degree of violence against the few women who bring cases to court but its latent function is to reinforce male dominance, to undermine women's experience, and hold their autonomy in check.

The present system is a mockery of justice. The following reforms are long overdue: the legal definition of rape needs to be widened; the prosecution counsel should be allowed to prepare the case with the complainant as is the case in some American states; and the Sexual Offences (Amendment) Act 1976, which had failed to implement in full the recommendations of the Heilbron Committee (1975), designed to restrict the use of sexual history evidence about the complainant, should be tightened up. Where such evidence is permitted, equivalent information about the defendant, including previous convictions, should automatically be allowed. A radical overhaul of the way in which prosecution barristers handle rape case is needed, including training in the *modus operandi* of rapists and the effects of rape; an opportunity to meet with the complainant before the trial; greater use of expert evidence regarding typical reactions to rape; and the provision of screens in all courts so the complainant would not have to face their assailant. The lengthy delays in trials coming to court should be cut. There should also be some monitoring of trials and the analysis of acquittal and sentencing rates in different parts of Britain.

Notes

1 In 1989, for example, Michelle Renshaw, called as witness in a rape case, was sent to prison for three days by Judge Pickles for refusing to give evidence because she was scared of retribution from her attacker. See woman appeals against Pickles' sentence. *Observer*, 12 March 1989; Pickles, read Shame. *Daily Mirror*, 14 March 1989.
2 Video to train jurors and 'demystify' court system. *The Guardian*, 3 May 1992.
3 Andrew Hall's firm of solicitors and Hodge, Jones and Allen refuse to defend alleged rapists.

CHAPTER 4

The representation of the body in rape trials

→ used as torture to police presence

Within patriarchal society women who are victimized by male violence have had to pay a price for breaking the silence and naming the problem. They have had to be seen as fallen women, who have failed in their 'feminine' role to sensitize and civilize the beast in man.

(hooks 1989: 89)

In this chapter I explore how the rape trial can be seen as a public spectacle which functions as a warning to all women against speaking out about male violence. Just as we saw in Chapter 1 how such terms as slag operate as a form of social censure on all women, so too can rape trials be seen as a way of warning women to keep silent by punishing complainants, an experience which has been described by survivors as a 'second rape' (Lees 1996). I show how the portrayal of women in rape trials reflects myths rooted in medical, religious and philosophical discourses about the nature of women's bodies and of female sexuality. The depiction of the woman's body in rape trials is used to cast aspersions on her credibility and reflects mechanisms of power and control operating within legal and medical discourses.

The politics of the body has relevance to this issue as it illustrates how power operates not as a negative prohibition, but at the level of the production of bodies and their materiality, their forces, their energies, sensations and pleasures (see Bordo 1993). The first court hearing of an English woman police officer's rape allegation against a colleague, Michael Seear in February 1995, illustrates the way the rape victim, her body and her sexuality are reproduced in the trial and operate as a form of power which serves to discredit her testimony. The woman police officer explained the way the distortion operated in her case and was reproduced in the press:

For the first day I was the poor weeping WPC, then I became this drunken temptress, covered in love bites, causing trouble . . . Everything was put under a microscope. I have no sordid past, nothing lurid to hide, thank God, because I felt as though my character, my whole soul, was being judged, and found wanting . . . Anyone who knows me could tell you the picture the papers painted wasn't me.

(*Observer*, 26 February 1995)

The research on which this article is based was conducted for a Channel 4 *Dispatches* documentary, *Getting Away with Rape* (1994) which involved the monitoring of all contested rape trials over a four month period at the London Central Criminal Court, the Old Bailey in the summer and autumn of 1993. Researchers sat in on trials and took transcripts of 30 trials and some official transcripts were also obtained. The research indicated that many rapists go free, endangering other women and giving men a licence to rape again. This picture is confirmed by the official Home Office statistics which indicate that only a small proportion of reported rapes result in a conviction. Although the number of reported rapes has more than doubled between 1985 and 1993 the conviction rate for cases reported to the police according to Home Office figures has decreased from 24 per cent in 1985 to only 8.6 per cent in 1994 (Home Office Statistics 1994). I show how the use of evidence regarding the complainant's bodily processes and the reliance on medical opinion are tools used by the defence to cast doubt on the woman's evidence and is an important factor in undermining her credibility. As we have seen in the last chapter, court procedures imbalance the trial in favour of the defendant, making it very difficult for jurors to convict. Juries are directed that in rape trials, it is a question of judging one person's word against another. Yet they are instructed to judge the credibility of the defendant and complainant according to totally different criteria. In the defendant's case what is considered relevant is his reputation based on his lack of previous convictions and his occupation. In the woman's case it is her character and past sexual history.

Foucault outlines in *Discipline and Punish* how in the seventeenth century the feudal notion of punishment embraced the deployment of the public, spectacular power of the monarch over the body of the rebellious subject. The authorities punished deviant behaviour by direct punishment with such methods as branding, whipping, or even execution. This was displaced in the modern era by a discourse of the soul which sought the reclamation of the offender through the exercise of a regime of disciplinary power such that punishment was no longer a public ceremony of degradation, but 'a whole series of subtle procedures' embodied in legal and penal institutions which made 'each subject find himself caught in a punishable punishing universality' (1991: 178). Therefore modern institutions attempt to punish and prevent criminal behaviour by studying 'the criminal personality' and reform the mind rather than torturing the body. According to this perspective, the criminal trial becomes less a spectacle of degradation and more part of a diagnostic process in which the law 'operates more and more as a norm, and that the judicial institution is increasingly incorporated into a continuum of apparatuses (medical, administrative and so on) whose functions are for the most part regulatory' (Foucault 1990: 144).

According to Foucault power is exercised through discourses which define and therefore regulate and control the objects of their expertise. In the nineteenth century, with regard to women, this control has increasingly focused on sexuality. Stress was placed on purity as a measure of woman's worth and the idea that respectable women would be safe only at home. Davidoff and Hall (1987) show how the middle class developed an identity not only through capitalist economics but also through this development of 'separate spheres'. As Anna Clark (1987) points out such restrictive moral standards of separate spheres stemmed from the middle-class efforts to control the activities of working-class women in public space, in particular their sexual activities. This is reflected in the way reformers, for example, portrayed factory work as fraught with perils of seduction and violation and where the bourgeois discourse of seduction regarded both a seduced woman and a rape victim as fundamentally fallen. Moreover, victims of rape were often treated harshly. Clark (1987: 65) showed how women could even be arrested for indecent exposure while being assaulted and some men who molested women on the street accused them of theft in order to avoid punishment. An increased legal surveillance over the sexual behaviour of working-class women therefore coincided with an intensification of the notion of women's sexuality as property. What Clark (1987: 10) refers to as 'the invention of rape as a warning' must be seen in the context of the greater sexual and economic independence of working women who were drawn into the mills and factories.

More and more, therefore, women hesitated to report sexual assaults, fearing rape would be seen as a taint on their reputations (Clark 1987: 63). In a similar way, rape trials today can be seen both as operating as a warning, and a way of restricting the activities of women through inciting fear of the public sphere, but also through punishing a victim for breaking the silence enforced by the emphasis on female respectability and chastity. To return to Foucault's notion of the changing nature of punishment, I suggest in this chapter that the rape trial retains something of the older notion of spectacle that Foucault saw as being displaced by disciplinary power and scientific reason, but a spectacle of degradation visited upon the victim rather than the offender.

The rape complainant, who is usually unmarried, a single mother, separated or divorced can be seen as occupying space in particular need of regulation and control. Marriage can be seen as a control over autonomous female sexuality. Until 1991 marital rape was not against the law and in my monitoring of cases in 1993 only one case involved a cohabiting couple, who were in fact separated at the time of the rape. It is unlikely that many marital rape cases reach court but at present no statistics are available to identify them. Nor do cases of married women raped by other men often reach court. There is some evidence (from discussions with rape crisis workers) that such women often do not tell their husbands in fear of their anger, let alone take out court proceedings.

Various manifestations of misogyny have centred on the female body, all of which can be seen as forms of control over women's autonomy – from foot binding, genital mutilation and corsetry, to the more modern less overtly misogynist practices of plastic surgery, constrictive fashions (wearing of high heels and tight skirts) and dieting. In consumption-driven capitalistic societies, anxieties about controlling desires become displaced onto anxieties about the body which are frequently focused around eating disorders and sexuality (Vines 1993: 11). Rape trials where the woman's body, its secretions and its desires are the subject of close examination, function as a form of control over female sexuality. By focusing on the woman's body, rather than on her testimony, the impression is given that she is ruled by her body and therefore her 'consent' or 'rationality', the core issue of dispute in rape trials, is implicitly questioned. Women are blamed for not taking sufficient precautions to protect themselves from male violence or for actively provoking violence by wearing short skirts or low tops, fashions which are actively promoted by the fashion industry, and if not adopted by young women, ironically render them unattractive, 'dogs', or lesbians.

The legal control of women's reproduction has been widely studied (see Stanworth 1987; Phillips and Rakusen 1989). Reproduction raises legal issues of inheritance and legitimacy (see Smart 1989: 92). The law both draws heavily on medical knowledge of the body to establish legal questions and to control bodily functions. The laws on divorce and on the control of prostitution exemplify how the legal controls operated in a discriminatory way in the nineteenth century. The Divorce Act of 1857 stated that a husband could divorce his wife for a single act of adultery whereas a woman has to prove adultery plus bigamy, cruelty, desertion, incest, rape or unnatural offences to obtain a decree. The Royal Commission on the Contagious Diseases Acts argued that there is 'no comparison to be made between prostitutes and the men who consort with them'. In the one case, the offence is committed as a matter of gain, in the other it is an irregular indulgence of a natural impulse. Walkowitz (1980), in her study of Victorian prostitution, illustrated how working-class women's bodies came to be seen as the sites of dangerous sexuality and as carriers of disease in need of Draconian methods of regulation. The Contagious Diseases Acts of the 1890s gave police powers to restrain girls and women considered to be prostitutes and to force them to undergo compulsory medical examinations, while leaving their clients free to reinfect them immediately afterwards.

The law's involvement in the regulation of desire is less well appreciated. Male and female desire has to this day been conceptualized very differently. Male desire is regarded as more normal, more aggressive and more straightforward than female desire. As Havelock Ellis, founder member of the British Society for the Study of Sex Psychology, argued in the nineteenth century, the male sexual impulse is 'predominantly open and aggressive' and its needs are inscribed 'in the written and unwritten codes of social law' (Hall 1991: 22). Female desire was conceptualized in contradictory ways. It was openly described as more dangerous and in greater need of legal control, yet respectable women in the nineteenth century were also seen as lacking desire. Respectability and lack of desire were closely connected to class where working-class women were seen as lascivious and promiscuous.

The insatiable female is overtly expressed in the eighteenth-century term 'nymphomania' which Groneman (1994: 337), an American anthropologist, describes as a symptom, a cause and a disease in its own right. Women whose symptoms consisted of committing adultery, flirting, being divorced, or feeling more passionate than their husbands were described as suffering from this disease. Groneman argues that female sexual desire was seen to be particularly dangerous and irrational; women were seen as more easily overwhelmed by the power of their sexual passion because they were closer to nature and thus more volatile and irrational than men. By the late nineteenth century all sexualized women such as nymphomaniacs, lesbians and prostitutes were grouped together and described in very similar terms. Groneman argues that the meaning of nymphomania changed in the twentieth century and was seen as a disordered psyche, but the assumption that women of a particular class have an overwhelming need for sex is evident in rape trials. Working-class unmarried women are depicted in trials as particularly unrespectable and prone to promiscuity. Middle-class women, in particular professional women, appear to be treated as more discerning. The complainant in the Diggle case, heard in January 1993, a respectable middle-class solicitor whose case resulted in one of the few convictions, was treated with respect in her cross-examination in spite of having had a great deal to drink on the night in question.

The meaning of consent

The portrayal of the female body in rape trials reflects contradictory views about the nature of desire. The woman's body is seen as dangerous, seductive and unpredictable. Defence counsels and judges insinuate that women are neither honest nor aware of their desires, implying that they are ruled by their bodily urges, and therefore are not fully aware of what they want. Judge Dean, 67 years old, in his summing up of a case which he said lacked independent corroboration in April 1990, told the Central Criminal Court at the Old Bailey, which subsequently cleared a London property consultant of rape: 'As gentlemen of the jury will understand, when a woman says "No" she doesn't always mean "No"'. When criticized later he replied: 'In saying that, I was simply repeating something I have heard over the last 40 years. If that remark, as it seems to have done, has upset certain people, I regret it. I did not wish or intend to upset anybody' (*The Guardian*, 12 April 1990). He is voicing a common view which is used to support the argument that women do not share male rationality, in other words their evidence is no evidence at all. If women do not know whether or not they want sex, then rape cannot happen as their will is always confused. It is argued then that women regret their lust and are thus prone to make false allegations, to pretend that they did not consent at the time. This makes them irrational and untrustworthy. If women do not know their own minds the whole concept of consent becomes irrelevant and the very definition of rape as sexual intercourse without consent is undermined. To return to Judge Dean, he added that he might repeat the remark if he was trying a case where there was no support of any allegation of rape. Audrey Wise, Labour MP, said the judge's comment was appalling: 'It is an invitation to rape and it makes men feel it is okay. I do not think this man should be a judge.'

'They say no but mean yes' refers both to the woman's hesitation at appearing to be sexually desiring to protect her reputation, and to the myth that women do not really know what they desire, as they are irrational beings. There are various ideas confused here. Clearly, in the nineteenth century, many women feigned resistance when they really desired sex, but women's pleasure in sexuality is so taken for granted today that there is no reason why such feigning should still take place. There is a world of difference between feigning and refusing. The argument that 'women mean yes when they say no' has dangerous implications. If the female body has an existence of its own, totally out of control of its occupant, evidence of lack of consent is rendered irrelevant. Implicit in these ideas is that not only does a woman not know her own desires, but that she is responsible for the 'uncontrollability' of male desire once it is aroused. The defence counsel then puts arguments forward such as, 'Did she lead him on, prostitute herself, or consent and then change her mind at the last minute when the man was unable to control himself?' The idea that male sexuality once aroused is uncontrollable firmly shifts the blame onto the woman. Despite her own irrationality and lack of control, she is expected to exercise control on behalf of both of them.

Evidence in British trials is presented to imply that the woman enjoyed the experience against her better nature or in order to support the man's argument that she consented. In other words 'she said no but meant yes': Witness this exchange which comes from one of the trials Zsuzsanna Adler (1987: 10) covered in her research:

Prosecution counsel (PC): And you say she consented?
Defendant (D):   I didn't say she consented.

PC: Did she agree?
D: She didn't agree.
PC: Having said no at first she just gave in?
D: She enjoyed it.
The judge intervened: 'The enjoyment wiped out her initial resistance
– is that what you are saying?'
D: Yes.

This discussion is important as it depicts one of the major underpinnings
of rape trials. The conception of what comprises sex is based on an archetypal male model where a male predator overcomes the resistance of a
passive female whose resistance is against her better interests. Penetration of the penis is what is presumed to give pleasure to women regardless
of any foreplay or other sexual activity and assumed evidence of 'enjoyment'
represents consent. The assumption here is that a woman could want sex
without even knowing herself. It reduces the whole issue of consent to
absurdity, in which the woman is denied any subjectivity or knowledge
of her own desire. This becomes clear in the cross-examination of the
defendant:

PC: You gave her a kiss but there was no response.
D: No.
PC: That is because you frightened her into submitting.
D: No . . . Women, they're really complicated you know. I've come
    across women who play hard to get, but when I make a move
    they respond . . . I'm saying she wanted it. Her body wanted it
    but her mind was somewhere else.

Here we see a different version of Judge Dean's 'no means yes' argument, implying the woman has no subjectivity of her own. The implication
is not only that the man knows what she really wants better than she herself does, but that she is also ruled by her body. Similarly lubrication of
the woman's vagina is presented by some defendants as evidence that the
woman wanted sex. I was horrified to find that a police officer I interviewed believed that forensic tests could ascertain from the vaginal fluids
whether or not the complainant consented. If some police believe this,
jurors could well be confused, and such an argument might plant a seed of
doubt in their minds. Such discourses reflect the hysterization of women's
bodies which Foucault (1990: 104) argues was one of the mechanisms of
knowledge and power centring on sex.
    Sex and violence are seen to be interrelated. Violence during a sexual
encounter is neutralized or seen as part of sex. It is a legitimate part of the
'courting' process. Even where the complainant gives evidence of violent
assault or threat, this does not necessarily preclude her consent. The defence
will argue that only extensive injury or evidence of her active resistance

provides adequate proof of her non-consent. The woman is a sexual being, her rationality is therefore always debatable and her claim of rape always suspect. Men know best what her body really wants, and she is not more than her body. This is what renders women fickle and untrustworthy.

The trial focuses on what men define as sexuality, not on women's experience of sex or rape. Men are presented as having a biological need for sex. Sexual appetite, it is argued, is synonymous with hunger. If therefore the man is deprived of sex, a sexual assault is understandable, even pardonable. The man's alleged sexual frustration is then presented as an excuse for the offence and legitimates a low sentence. An example of this is where Sir Harold Cassell, aged 72 (Kennedy 1992: 111) freed a child molester, saying his pregnant wife's lack of sexual appetite had caused three sexual assaults on his 12-year-old stepdaughter. He argued 'pregnancy led to a lack of sexual appetite in the lady and considerable problems for a healthy young husband'. He went on to accuse the woman of 'encouraging' the assaults. The mother described how her daughter's life had been ruined and went on to say, 'As far as the sexual side, my husband did not go without the whole time through my pregnancy, so I do not know where the judge got his information from'.

The vindictive woman intent on revenge also hovers over rape trials as exemplified by one defence counsel who argued

> This is a case of a woman scorned. Hell hath no fury like a woman scorned. An emotional case, a case of love-hate, passion and ultimate destruction. The heights she went to destroy this man, the utmost to pull the wool over your eyes – rape is an emotive word. Don't be fooled by her tears.
>
> (own transcript of trial, October 1993)

Rape trials as pornography

In rape trials as in pornography, the female body is publicly portrayed and debated. It is her body, not his, that is put on trial. Her body's secretions and underclothing are scrutinized, her photographed injuries distributed as exhibits, her body's level of sexual arousal debated without regard to her testimony. She is objectified in similar fashion to her objectification in rape itself. This is the meaning of the term 'judicial rape'. The analogy with porn is relevant here:

> Porn puts into circulation images of sexuality that have definite meanings connected with them; sexual pleasure for men is initiation and dominance, and for women submission to men's depersonalised needs. The problem is that these meanings feed general definitions of sexual identity and sexual activity.
>
> (Coward 1984: 176)

Catherine MacKinnon (1987) drew attention to the rape trial as a pornographic spectacle; by being forced to speak about sex, the woman herself becomes a pornographic vignette. The complainant must describe in intimate detail every part of her body that was assaulted in words which would embarrass women to refer to at all, let alone in such a public setting out loud. Questioning women about male penetration can be seen as giving pleasure synonymous to a pornographic vignette.

Judges frequently direct complainants to 'speak up' in the lofty setting of most Victorian court chambers. For a woman unused to speaking in public it can be shattering. The paradox is that the very use of such language, referring to private sexual parts of the anatomy, is sufficient to render a woman unrespectable. Many women never say such words even in the privacy of their homes, let alone to strangers in open court. Giving evidence about rape can be seen as a process of 'shaming' the complainant by forcing her to describe in open court the details of the assault. According to Anna Clark (1987: 29), in the eighteenth century to even admit to being raped was so shaming that women tended to use euphemisms to describe what happened to them, with such terms as 'ill used'. Clark describes (1987: 54) how male judges and lawyers were obsessed with the explicit details of rape and would question her as to 'how her assailant could stop her mouth, hold down her hands, pull up her petticoats and pull down her breeches all at the same time'. Clark recounts how women often faced laughter from the gallery and transcripts of rape trials were sold as titillating literature. The curiosity about the details of the rape is also derived from patriarchal concern with chastity. Even today, what matters is whether penetration of the penis has taken place, which carries the implication that the victim's value as sexual property is damaged. The effect of such a stigma is the suppression of women's speech about sex.

Only in pornography would the kind of details of sexual activity – where the man put his hands, who removed her knickers, her tampon if she had a period, and other pieces of clothing – be described in public. It is for this reason perhaps that so many women find being cross-examined such a nightmare. As Carol Smart (1990: 205) comments: 'She is required to speak sex, and figuratively to re-enact sex: her body and its responses become the stuff of evidence. The act of describing in exact detail what the man did and how she responded is enough subtly to render her "unrespectable".'

Another issue of great concern is evidence that prosecution statements of victims of rape, child abuse and indecent assault are being circulated as pornography in prison, a practice which has apparently existed for years. Such statements may also be circulated when convicted rapists are released. A probation officer in Wales reported that she knew of two convicted rapists who had prosecution statements in their possession including the victims' names and addresses and details of rape in total opposition to the law on victim anonymity (see Radford 1989, 1991; *The Guardian*, 26 October 1989).

Rape trials as defiling the victim

Various themes relating to the female body emerge with regularity in rape trials. The frequent portrayal of the female body as bloody or slightly disgusting is combined with its portrayal as dangerous, enticing and brimming with uncontrolled sexuality, incitement to male lust, implicitly a danger to the moral order. Comments made by defence counsels in cross-examination are often fused with desire and repugnance, disgust and fascination. Alison Young's analysis of the representation of women's bodies in Greenham Common women's anti-nuclear protest is relevant here. She argued that women were subjected to defilement through the language and images of revulsion and disgust which equated them with excrement, dirt, blood and disease. The Greenham Common women have been policed in the general literal sense through the increased deployment of personnel at the base and in a less usual sense through the repeated accounts in the press of 'their dirtiness, their insanitary habits, their morally defective values' (Young 1990: 62). She points out that both their bodies and their moral selves were attacked. The Greenham women were transgressing lines of gender, territoriality, sexuality and familiarity and had to be policed in the same way that the suffragettes were policed through force feeding.

The emphasis on menstruation and handing round used panties in rape trials can be understood as a similar process of defilement. Menstruation, even today, is regarded with ambivalence. In some communities women have been confined to menstrual huts and menstruating women have been seen as contaminated and banned from the worship of God. They are defiled. Disordered menstruation, gynaecologists argued in the nineteenth century, could lead to injury to the nervous system and thus to mental illness (Groneman 1994: 337). The menstrual taboo is also evident in rape trials. The defence counsel's disgust is often blatantly expressed. In one trial heard in August 1993 the judge intervened in the defence counsel's (DC) cross-examination of the complainant (C):

DC: Let me put it to you that in fact you were just coming off, finishing your period at the time of having sexual intercourse with Mr Jones. Do you agree with that?

C: I was on for another couple of days.

DC: Another what?

C: Two days. I was on for another two days after that.

DC: This is the early hours of Wednesday, so do you mean until the Friday, or when?

C: I can't remember. What has my period got to do with that?

DC: Just answer the questions please.

C: I don't know.

DC: You see, let me tell you what I'm driving at. I am putting it to you that you were a willing partner in having sex with Jones.

C: No, I wasn't. It's not right. I wouldn't go near him with a barge pole.

DC: These questions may not be very tasteful, but I have got to put them to you. In order for him to insert his penis, he has to cope then with the debris of your period and the tampon, is that right?

Judge: Well, she can't answer what he would or wouldn't find easy.

DC: The point is – I am sorry to have to put it to you – that the channel was obstructed.

Judge: I think you're making a comment.

DC: Am I? All right.

                    (transcript of trial at Old Bailey, summer 1993)

There are links between the medical preoccupation with women's menstruation and contemporary social and cultural concerns. Shuttleworth (1990) draws an analogy between the obstruction and accumulated waste that dominated Victorian theories of female menstruation with the *laissez-faire* economics elaborated by economists. Like the body, the economy could only thrive with the free flow and circulation of commodities, unimpeded by blockage or government interference. Female thought and passion, like government interference, were seen as throwing the whole organism into a state of disarray.

Forcing complainants to discuss menstruation is another means of shaming them and rendering them unrespectable. No respectable woman would speak about menstruation in public but in rape trials it is not uncommon for intricate questions to be asked during the cross-examination. In one trial the defence counsel asked: 'He [the defendant] was able to insert his penis easily because you were turned on in the normal fashion – nothing to do with periods or anything else; that is right, isn't it?' If it can be established that the complainant was menstruating, this also carries the implicit assumption that she was a bit off key, perhaps totally irrational, and perhaps prone to make false allegations. The frequent reference to menstruation in rape trials also alludes to women as seducers whose powers are overwhelming when menstruating.

Another common way of discrediting victims was where there was evidence of alcohol or drug use. The use of alcohol and drugs has quite different meanings for men and women. For men heavy drinking serves to enhance their male status, it signifies 'real manhood'. For women, on the other hand, alcohol carries the taint of immorality and promiscuity. Elizabeth Ettorre (1992: 38), a British sociologist who studied attitudes to women and alcohol, suggests that 'a woman who drinks does not need to be a prostitute to have a promiscuous image. She is promiscuous by the very fact that she is a drinker'.

Drinking and drug use were used to discredit complainants in two ways, first by suggesting that consumption would lower the woman's inhibitions and thus she would have been likely to consent to something which she would regret later, and second, to suggest that a woman under the influence of alcohol would be more likely to act irrationally or vindictively and make a false complaint. Drink and drugs are seen as particularly dangerous in unleashing a woman's sexuality, which once unleashed is irresistible to men. A man is not held responsible for his sexual desires; all the onus is on the woman to control his sexuality. According to Stanley Brandes's (1981) study of sexual relations in an Andalusian town, women are portrayed as dangerous and potent while men are seen as suffering the consequences of female whims and passions. Women are viewed as seductresses and whores possessed of insatiable lustful appetites. When women wielded their power, men cannot resist temptation and are forced to relinquish control over their passions.

Notions of 'purity' and 'pollution' are intrinsic to sexuality and drug abuse. Mary Douglas (1966: 113), a British anthropologist, defines pollution as 'a type of danger which is unlikely to occur except where the lines of structure, cosmic or social, are clearly defined'. With women the social boundaries are more clearly defined in the sense that there are clear lines between what is and is not legitimate or respectable behaviour for women compared to men. The controls over their social behaviour are more stringent. Transgressing such boundaries (poisoning themselves, being out of control and so on) turns female heroin users into polluted women. As Ettorre (1992: 76, 151) argues:

> In private they are regarded as potentially sexless, bad mothers, uncaring for their children, or irresponsible wives, not considering the needs of their husbands. In public they are viewed as unforgivably out of control in their domestic and/or work situations, fallen angels, evil sluts or loose women who cannot be trusted . . .

> As a polluted woman with a spoiled identity the woman heroin user is low on the hierarchy of women generally and women substance users in particular. Being viewed as 'deviant' and a 'whore' she is engaged in using a drug which is seen as low (bad, evil) on the hierarchy of drugs. The lower the drug the closer the connection to the whore image.

Medical discourse to discredit the victim

Although doctors are seen as expert witnesses, they are called to give evidence either for the prosecution or for the defence; it is therefore no surprise that doctors give conflicting evidence, evidence that is sometimes based more on opinion than fact. In rape trials a common source of disagreement relates to the effects of alcohol on the complainant. This can however be very confusing for jurors, particularly those who may have faith in doctors' judgements. For example, in the Donnellan case, where a student at Kings College was acquitted of what was alluded to as 'date rape' in October 1993, Dr Robin Moffat, a senior forensic expert, gave evidence to the effect that although the complainant's alcohol level would not have been enough to have induced coma, drink was an aphrodisiac and the complainant would have been 'very very drunk and very very sexy' (*Daily Mail*, 19 October 1993). It is rare that a doctor gives a genuinely balanced judgement as in the following case, where, when asked what the effect of drinking the equivalent of four to five pints would be and the likelihood of it 'reducing inhibition', the woman doctor of 36 years' experience replied, 'In some people it can. It depends on the person. Some people can become quite stubborn or stroppy'. Indeed in many drink induces deep sleep.

Medicine and psychiatry are power-knowledges and are therefore called on to contribute to discrediting the complainant. As Foucault (1990: 45) pointed out 'medical and psychiatric investigations often had the apparent objective of saying no to all wayward or unproductive sexualities'. In this way medical and psychiatric knowledge and practice are part of the means by which gender divisions in society are maintained (Doyal 1983: 379). How the reports are obtained is important since the prosecution (representing the complainant) can only call for two psychiatric or medical reports but the defence, on the other hand, can shop around for doctors who are prepared to write medical reports which are sympathetic to the defendant's case – and presumably receive a hefty fee for doing so. It appears that forensic and medical evidence is a crucial area of dispute between the prosecution and defence lawyers where conflicting medical opinion is often used to plant seeds of doubt in the jurors' minds about whether or not the woman consented. Such evidence is based far more on bias and prejudice, and no reference is ever made to research findings on, for example, the reactions of rape victims or the tactics commonly used by rapists.

Medicine is deeply involved in the reproduction of a specific view of the intrinsic character of women and of sexuality. For this reason even when the complainant has extensive injuries she will not necessarily be believed on the grounds either that 'she liked a bit of rough' or that the injuries could be self-inflicted. In one of the few cases (heard in August 1993 at the Old Bailey) involving a couple who had been previously married, but had separated as a result of the husband's violence, a wife who had been hounded by her husband and had two injunctions out against him, failed to convince the jury that she had been raped in spite of her appalling injuries. Her nose had been broken and, according to medical evidence, she had strangulation marks around her throat. She had reported the rape and assault immediately and been examined by a doctor within hours. In court she was faced with a barrage of such questions as, 'Did you rub his penis through his jeans?' and statements such as, 'You helped him put his penis into your vagina and had consensual sexual intercourse'; 'You weren't frightened'; 'He never put his arm round your throat'. Her denials went unheeded even when she insisted it was the first day of her period and she would never have had sex during this time. The defence counsel argued that the defendant did not know she had a period, to which she replied, 'He took the tampon out so he should have known'. The defendant was acquitted of rape but was found guilty of gross bodily harm and given a short sentence of the length he had already spent in custody. He was immediately released and waved his thanks to the jury.

The rape trial subtly silences and discredits the complainant's voice, using medical and legal discourses to distort her testimony. Absence of injuries is taken as evidence of consent rather than a paralysing fear that she might be killed, which leads to a decision that the best chance of survival is to submit. In one case the complainant was asked why she did not dig her fingernails into her assailant's penis, or 'put a construction in front of the door' when her assailant went to the toilet. Both of these actions are ludicrous for a woman who is in fear of her life to contemplate. Women certainly have reason to believe the threats. The defendant knows their name and sometimes where they live or work. The gravity of the threats is grounded in real experience. In two cases I encountered, the rapists had returned to rape the woman again. In court however these threats are trivialized. Complainants are cross-examined in detail about whether they enjoyed the sexual attack, whether they were drunk at the time and consented to sex but regretted it later and made false allegations, whether they were having another relationship on the side and had to cover up their infidelity to a boyfriend with a false story and so on. One of the difficulties is that women subjected to threats often do not suffer visible injuries or the injuries consist of slight bruising. Many defendants argue that because the woman did not resist, they did not know that she did not consent. Some rapists, according to Wyre and Swift (1990: 6) who set up a treatment programme for convicted rapists at the Gracewell clinic in Birmingham, argue that they kid themselves that it was not rape and say, 'Why didn't she stop me? . . . she must have known I didn't want to do it', as if it was her responsibility to save him from himself. Among rapists Scully (1990) interviewed, 69 per cent agreed with the idea that most men accused of rape were really innocent and 65 per cent believed women cause their own rapes by the way they act or clothes they wear.

Doctors play a crucial 'expert' role in analysing women's responses and sometimes give conflicting and distorting accounts of the 'typical' bodily signs and symptoms of rape. A common argument is that if really raped, the complainant should have had vaginal injuries. This does not fit with the evidence from the medical examination of rape victims; vaginal injuries are rare for the simple reason that most women are too terrified to resist. Yet again and again, doctors called by the defence argue that women who have been raped should have vaginal injuries. The prosecution is inept at countering such claims and fail to draw on the common response of both men and women to attack when threatened with violence or with their lives. Men who are raped or assaulted behave in exactly the same way.

In one case, several police officers, including a police surgeon, gave evidence that the woman was shaking with fear and distress, tears were streaming down her face, she wanted to wash herself frequently and was afraid afterwards to go out alone. They all agreed she was in acute distress. Yet the prosecution counsel failed even to mention this in his summing up. The judge did make reference to it and implied that the prosecution counsel should have mentioned it. In this case, I abandoned my role as participant observer and followed the barrister out of the court to ask him why. He said it was absurd to regard the woman's distress as corroborative and dismissed the judge's view as irrelevant. This instance exemplifies the lack of sympathy between the prosecution counsel and the complainant and the way it can prejudice her case. Forensic evidence is relevant only in establishing that intercourse took place, not whether it took place with or without consent. There is often disagreement over what constitutes corroboration. In England and Wales the woman's distress is not regarded as corroborative, but in Scotland it is (see Brown *et al.* 1993).

Judge Smedley on 1 September 1993 in a case heard at the Old Bailey comments on why evidence of the complainant's distress should not be regarded as relevant at all: 'A word of warning. If the account the complainant is giving was completely fabricated you may think she is clever, then clever enough to act out distress.' Women's distress is excluded mainly on the grounds that she is the source of the distress and corroboration has to be evidence from a different source. Yet as we have seen, judges do not agree as to its relevance which is one reason why training judges is so necessary.

One of the main findings of research into the reactions to rape (Holmstrom and Burgess 1978; Roberts 1989; Foley 1994) is that although there are common patterns, there is no typical reaction. Some women express anxiety immediately, for others the reaction may be delayed. Likewise, men do not all react to traumas in a similar fashion, but this is not held against them in the same way. However, a common tactic used by the defence to support the idea that the woman is making a false allegation is to suggest that her reactions are not typical of a rape victim. In several trials I monitored, evidence that the complainant had not broken down was used to imply that she had not been raped. In one case where the complainant was being cross-examined, the defence counsel argued that according to the doctor the complainant was 'not at all distressed'. Witness this cross-examination:

> *DC:* What signs, in the light of his Honour's questions were you show-
> ing of distress to this doctor?
> *C:* Well I did cry and . . .
> *DC:* Anything else? I mean, is this doctor right or wrong or just
> mistaken?
> *C:* Well maybe. I wasn't showing signs of distress at some times,
> but I was feeling it.
> *DC:* I see. So this doctor, it was a woman doctor, failed to see that
> underneath it you were, in fact, distressed and, as you said, you
> were not at all distressed, making the point you cried for about
> 20 seconds but then smiled and carried on talking. What is the
> picture that we should have?
> *C:* I was distressed, but she was doing her best to try and, you know,
> be nice and cheer me up.

The complainant little realizes that the doctor's evidence is used by the
defence counsel to imply that since she was not distressed during the examination, she could not have been raped. What is apparent here is the way
the complainant's description of her state of mind is disregarded and the
doctor's view prevails.

On a number of occasions the defence counsel appeared to have gleaned
information about the complainant's past sexual history from forensic
medical reports of the examination at the time of the rape. Such reports
can sometimes reveal sexual history evidence in the form of uncensored
medical reports – which reveal a mass of background detail often inappropriate for the ears of the court. In one of the trials a 19-year-old girl was
cross-examined by the defence counsel about an abortion she had had
three years previously. He presumably had gained this information from
the medical examination carried out on her at the time of the rape. He
asked, 'When did you have an abortion?' to which she replied, 'When I was
16. That's got nothing to do with it, has it?' This indicates that doctors
are either unaware that such comments will be passed to the defence or are
not aware that such information can be used as ammunition in trials.

Conclusion

Insufficient attention has been paid to the function of the trial process in
policing women's sexuality. Several studies have examined how power and
discipline produces 'docile bodies', in particular, Foucault pointed to the
emergence of a new disciplinary power in the modern era directed against
the body. Forms of violence against women, from rape and domestic violence to sexual harassment and sexual abuse are perhaps the most oppressive byproducts of what Foucault calls 'technologies of sex'. The disciplinary

techniques, such as power reflected in the use of abuse, both verbal (such as slag and slut) and physical, have a direct effect on regulating how women and girls behave, how she feels about her body, her desires and her self-confidence and how constricted her life can become. Through court procedures, women who do not behave in a stereotypical 'feminine' way, or women who speak out about male violence, render themselves open to such disciplinary techniques which are laid bare in the court drama.

According to Adrian Howe, an Australian criminologist, the reason why women so rarely commit criminal offences may well be due to the greater powers of surveillance and discipline they are subjected to both in childhood, adolescence and adulthood. She calls on the reconceptualizing of penality to include a wider range of sanctions and controls and 'refuse the discursive boundaries which separate policing from punishment' (1994: 201). The women who are brave enough to speak out about such disciplinary powers should not be named victims or even survivors but rather rebels who are unprepared to remain silent. By reporting assaults to the police, they become targets of disciplinary punishment themselves for such transgression. This is one of the pernicious aspects of Katie Roiphe's (1993) book *The Morning After* as she joins in the ostracizing of the victims of rape by arguing that they have a 'victim mentality'.

Foucault (1980: 96–7) called for an examination of how power and discipline produces docile bodies 'at the extreme point of their exercise, and to explore punishment and the power to punish at the local level', especially how they are embodied in 'local, regional, material institutions'. The cross-examination of rape complainants is an example of just such a practice. The latent purpose of trials can be seen to strengthen the control and disciplinary practices over young women who are considered to be 'leading men on', acting independently by being single parents or complaining of enforced sex, part of the normal oppressive system of subordinated sexual relations. The trial subtly turns what is purported to be a judicial examination into a condemnation of the complainant, her punishment. Press reports often then add to this character assassination, as shown in the *Guardian* report (26 October 1993) of the Kydd case where 'Man was acquitted of raping "slut of the year"' was the headline.

The task of the jury in rape trials is to weigh up one person's word against another's in order to decide whether the prosecution has proved that the defendant is guilty 'beyond any reasonable doubt'. By constantly questioning women about their most intimate bodily processes regarding, for example, lubrication and menstruation, their 'moral character' is undermined. The association with women and the body is aimed at dissociating women from the faculty of reason. The implication that women's bodies are out of control, particularly when under the influence of drugs or alcohol, leads to the assumption that a woman's rationality is in doubt, and her word cannot be relied on. The man's body is rarely a matter of debate even when under the influence of far greater quantities of drugs. His rationality and credibility are taken for granted.

Rape trials can be seen as a spectacle of torture, a feudal remnant, by which rather than protecting women, the trial can be seen as a public mechanism for the control of female sexuality. The defilement of the complainant through language puts her publicly on trial. The purpose of the cross-examination of the complainant appears to be to uncover the real culprit of the trial, the whore, the insatiable female harridan, vengeful and often in disguise; behind the young beautiful girl lurks the archetypal Eve who ensnares male rationality and drags men down. Such myths protect men from allegations and thereby from responsibility for their own violence. It is a consolidation of heterosexual privilege; the privilege of men to decide when a woman says 'yes'; the right of men to have sex when, how and when they want; the right of men to control female sexuality and prevent female autonomy.

CHAPTER 5

Male rape

In this chapter the meaning of male sexual assaults on men is explored in relation to consultancy and research undertaken for a Channel 4 *Dispatches* programme on *Male Rape* (1995). The research is small-scale but is one of the first attempts to investigate the hidden problem of sexual assaults on men by men. The idea that rape can be seen as a way of enforcing hegemonic heterosexual masculinity is developed.

Male rape or non-consensual buggery of men by men is one of the most underreported serious crimes in Britain. Only a minority of such assaults are reported to the police. For this reason we know very little about what victims suffer or about the men who carry out the attacks.

Mezey and King (1992) undertook a small study involving interviewing eight men and analysing 22 questionnaires, and concluded that male sexual assault was a frightening and dehumanizing event, leaving men feeling debased and contaminated, their sense of autonomy and personal invulnerability shattered. They also found that, like women, most men reacted with helplessness and passive submission, engendered by an overwhelming sense of fear and disbelief. Most attackers were known to the victim. The consequences for the victim's view of himself as a man is drawn out. King suggests they strike at heart of 'hegemonic' or the dominant form of masculinity in western societies where men are supposed to be in control, invulnerable and heterosexual. He argues that although there were many similarities between the reactions of male victims and those reported for women, 'the stigma for men may be even greater however, in a society which expects its male members to be self-sufficient physically and psychologically' (1992: 10).

In this research, two surveys were undertaken. The first survey, which shall be referred to as the victim survey, located victims through three telephone lines which were set up by the *Dispatches* team for men to ring over a two month period in response to advertisements placed in the local and national press. Respondents were asked to fill in questionnaires, anonymously if they wished. Questionnaires were also distributed to victim support groups and various agencies throughout the country. These were completed by victims themselves or counsellors on their behalf. Most of the questionnaires described unreported non-consensual anal penetration. Eighty-five valid questionnaires were received. In addition 20 questionnaires were returned which related to serious sexual assaults – fellatio or anal penetration by objects which did not fall within the present legal definition of rape, but which victims regarded as rape. Some of these men agreed to be interviewed.

The second survey, referred to as the police survey, was an investigation into police recording of male rape. Questionnaires were distributed to 43 police districts. Only a minority of police forces took part in the survey. Some were unwilling or unable to cooperate. Others said that no rapes of males over 16 have been reported to them in the previous two years. Eighty-one questionnaires were received from 15 forces in total where they were completed by investigating officers. Of these, 60 questionnaires relating to rape (i.e. using the widened legal definition of rape which now includes anal intercourse of men without consent) were returned and another 21 which related to reported sexual assaults. Transcripts of two trials of male rape were also obtained – the first which I shall refer to as the Richardson case (not his real name), heard in April 1995, of a young man raped when on remand in prison by a fellow prisoner twice his age, and the second case involving a man who had sued the armed forces for his harassment, alleging male rape.

The programme was shown on 17 May 1995 and a helpline was available for viewers to ring until midnight. The helpline organizers were astounded by the response to the programme. Phonelines were jammed all evening and (because such a large response was not anticipated) insufficient counsellors had to deal with all the calls. British Telecom figures showed that there were 4169 ineffective calls, that is, by people who could not get through that night and only 210 calls could be dealt with. These callers reinforced the main findings of the victim survey carried out for the television programme. Many had never before told anyone about the assault, and expressed relief that they were able to talk about the attack for the first time. 'I thought I was the only man this had happened to' was a common response. Victims spoke of the appalling effect the rape had had on their lives. Some described their lives as 'ruined', some had suicidal feelings and many were still unable to cope with the mental trauma. One of the men in this research was devastated and wanted to kill himself.

Male rape and the law

The number of reported cases of coercive buggery rose from 516 in 1982 to 1255 in 1992. Indecent assault on a males rose from 2082 to 3119 cases (*The Times*, 12 July 1994). According to Gillespie (1996: 152) Home Office figures for 1984–89 indicate that offences of buggery increased by 90 per cent and indecent assault of boys by 24 per cent.[1] The number of men proceeded against for indecent assault of men over 16 years at Magistrates Court in 1994 (before the definition of rape was widened to include rape of men) was 532. Of these, 419 were found guilty, an incredibly high rate of conviction. Only 21 of these were dealt with by Crown Courts (Home Office Statistics Division, 2 July 1996). This indicates that comparatively low sentences would have been awarded, and that the offences would not have been taken very seriously.

It is only recently that non-consensual buggery (anal penetration) has become incorporated into the rape legislation, a development which has raised some controversy among feminists (see Naffine 1994). The Criminal Justice and Public Order Act 1994 (which came into force in January 1995) widened the definition of rape to include non-consensual penetration of the anus (buggery) as well as of the vagina. It carries a maximum sentence of life imprisonment. Previously such attacks on men had been categorized under indecent assault which carried a maximum sentence of 10 years imprisonment (Section 12, Sexual Offences Act 1956) and buggery of women had been a criminal offence in itself, whether consensual or not. This meant that consensual anal sex between heterosexuals was legalized for the first time.

These changes are in line with other countries. Male rape was recognized in Sweden in 1984, and has been recognized more recently in Germany, Canada, Holland and most US states (where rape is defined more broadly as non-consensual penetration of vagina or anus by a penis, hand or other object). The change in the law followed on from various campaigns by male rape survivors' groups.

Rendering rape a non-gendered crime raises problems for the feminist explanation of rape as a form of coercion used to keep women subordinate. According to Florence Rush (1990: 170), 'Gender neutrality is rooted in the idea that both genders, male and female, are equally oppressed and that any attempt to hold men and male institutions accountable for transgressions against women is no longer fashionable or acceptable.' Other feminists have expressed concern that men raping men will be seen to be a more serious problem than rape of women. However to embrace non-consensual buggery of men under the same legislation is not, in my view, to deny the relation between rape whether of men or women and male domination, and in particular, domination of the particular hegemonic form of macho masculinity characteristic of western cultures.

The gender neutrality of the new rape law also raises the question of whether other forms of sexual coercion such as oral sex or penetration with an object should be included in the definition of rape. The definition of buggery has not always been confined to anal penetration as is the case today. In 1817 a man was sentenced to death under the buggery laws for oral sex with a boy. Jeffrey Weeks (1977/1983: 14) in tracing the development of harsh legal laws against homosexuality at the close of the nineteenth century points out that 'sodomy was a portmanteau term for any forms of sex that did not have conception as their aim, from homosexual acts to birth control'. In 1885 the Criminal Law Amendment Act made all male homosexual acts short of buggery whether committed in public or private illegal. Some countries, such as Canada and some states in Australia have replaced the crime of rape with degrees of sexual assault (see Temkin 1987: 101–5).

The police survey: reporting rape

It is frequently argued that male rape is even less likely to be reported than female rape. Such assertions are impossible to prove and are not helpful. It can be said that like female rape, the numbers of reported attacks on men may well have increased over the past decade and overall, a higher number numerically are reaching court. The police have adopted a far more sympathetic approach to the treatment of rape victims, both male and female, in recent years, and certainly appear to be making an effort to provide a more user friendly service. In the early 1990s the London Metropolitan police (the Met) introduced special training and extended services provided for female victims to male victims. In some areas a chaperone system has been set up, similar to that provided for women victims. This involves specially trained officers taking the statement from the victim and remaining attached to the case until the investigation has been completed. This means taking the officer off other duties.

Over half the callers to the TV researchers over the months of the research had not reported the assault to the police. Of those that did report to the police, two-thirds did so on the same day or the day after the incidents. However one in 10 took several days to report and a significant proportion (18 per cent) took several weeks, months or years before confiding in police officers.

Many women experience rape as shameful. For victims of male assaults, the problem is slightly different and often involves a crisis of sexual identity. As Adler (1992: 128) points out,

> when the victim is male, any claim that he consented projects onto him a homosexual identity . . . Where the victim is heterosexual, the

very fear of being thought a homosexual may well stop him from reporting. In fact, the reasons for not reporting for male victims are much the same as they are for female victims, and include shock, embarrassment, fear, self-blame and a high degree of stigma.

They may question their masculinity and doubt their manhood. According to McMullen (1990), who set up Survivors, a helpline for men, it is not unusual for heterosexual victims to actively seek homosexual contacts after having been raped. They may question their masculinity and doubt their manhood.

As is the case with women rape victims, some men did not think they would be believed. Additionally, they feared the police would assume that they themselves were gay. Victims were particularly anxious if they had not resisted, which they feared would lead people to assume they had colluded. Social assumptions that 'real' men would fight to the death if put in that situation lead men to feel guilt and self-revulsion if they have complied with the demands of their attacker. Sometimes the assailant played on such fears, as this account reflects:

> I threatened to go to the police. He told me he was a solicitor and the police would believe his story rather than mine, also that they would think I was a rent boy. I was terrified not just for me but for my family who would be named in the papers. I didn't struggle. I just let him do it to me. I feel so ashamed now. I could have cried or begged him to stop but I didn't, I just let him fuck me until he was finished. I didn't say anything when he asked me if I was enjoying myself. He wasn't really asking, more telling me I was enjoying it and he wasn't aggressive. I *hate him so much.*

The likelihood of gaining convictions in the event of a case reaching court is slim in spite of the change in the legislation. Just how slim was graphically shown in the case of a young man, on remand in prison who reported being raped by his cell mate, a man just coming to the end of a 15 year sentence. *Dispatches* attended the trial and obtained a full trial transcript. He described how terrified he was: 'I was too frightened to do anything. I just lay there like a plank of wood. I just froze.'

Around 15 per cent who did report rape to the police had unsatisfactory experiences, that is, they felt the police had not taken their complaint seriously or had made it difficult for the complainant to continue with the case. The response from the police was not always appropriate. A common complaint was that police officers reacted with embarrassment. This discomfort on the part of the interviewer inhibited victims from giving a full account of the incident. Most victims were interviewed by Criminal Investigation Department (CID) officers with no experience of dealing with victims of rape. Some victims reported sniggering behind their backs, while some police officers admitted that male rape is still a subject of black humour in their police stations.

Victim feedback suggested that gay men are treated less sensitively and sympathetically by the police than heterosexual men. Some police officers seem to believe that rape is less traumatic for gay men. Analysis of both police and victim questionnaires shows that police officers are more likely to regard the testimony of homosexual victims as 'unreliable' – either to assume that the sex was consensual or that the complaint was malicious. Feedback from gay victims suggests that this scepticism is unfounded.

Ten of the rapes were by pairs or gangs, which is roughly the same proportion (17 per cent as compared to 15 per cent of the female sample) as were found in the survey we undertook on female rape for a previous *Dispatches* programme (*Getting Away with Rape* 1994). Eight of these were by two men and two involved three men. Seven out of the ten pair/gang rapes were by complete strangers. Most assailants were in their twenties. All the victims were white but assailants were more likely to be black than in single rapes. Three of the seven rapes by strangers (43 per cent) involved at least one black assailant. This is perhaps significant as the percentage of black Asian and Mediterranean suspects overall who featured in single assaults in the police survey was only 14 per cent.

The vast majority (about three quarters) of suspects had previous criminal records and half the suspects had been given a prison sentence for past criminal activities. The most commonly committed types of crime by those suspects who had a prior criminal record were dishonesty, and burglary. The majority had no previous record for sex offences. In almost two thirds of cases, the suspects prior criminal activity was serious enough to warrant a prison sentence. This finding suggests that sexual offending against males forms part of a general pattern of criminal behaviour and that most perpetrators will already be known to the police.

The majority of the rapes reported to the police involved indecent sexual acts other than anal penetration. Almost half of the men had forced fellatio on the victim. In three cases the assailant forced the victim to reciprocate by penetrating them. Several gay victims commented that a common misconception is that all gay men practice anal sex. This is by no means the case. Police officers interviewing gay victims should be aware that anal sex has a particular significance in the gay community. It is seldom carried out in casual relationships but almost always between partners in long-term relationships of love and trust. This is partly because anal sex can be extremely painful if the person penetrated is not relaxed and also, because of the fear of HIV, the person penetrating must be trusted to wear a condom. Indeed it is because anal penetration is most commonly an act of intimacy and love between gay men, that rape is just as great a violation for gay men as for heterosexual men. One man who said his sexual orientation was gay said, 'this was the first time I had been penetrated.'

Unless victims are confident that their complaints will be treated seriously and sensitively by the police, they are unlikely to find the courage to report. The police are concerned to improve their treatment of male rape and their involvement in the police survey is indicative of their concern.

Victim survey: reasons of non-reporting

By the nature of the act of buggery men appeared to be rendered effeminate, or to be 'not real men'. One man revealed that he had never told anyone because his friends would think he was a tart. Victims described how the assailants had made comments such as 'my arse was like a cunt.' Another threw money at him and said 'that was all that was, worthless.' Male rape victims are often stigmatized as female or homosexual, whatever their sexual orientation. This was a major reason why men did not report the offences to the police. When asked why he didn't tell the police, one man replied 'Only women are raped.' It appears that forcing sex on a man who for some reason is seen to be inferior, is a way of the assailants enhancing their masculinity.

Research on the coercive buggery of men indicates that, like the rape of women, sexual violence is more about power and domination than eroticism, as commonly understood. It is the use of sexuality to dominate, humiliate and degrade. Additionally, a common myth is that, because of the nature of the act, male rape is perpetrated by *homosexuals*. This is a myth that needs to be dispelled. It is far more related paradoxically to the enhancement of heterosexuality. Research both in the USA and Britain indicates that male rape is often carried out by men who see themselves in terms of their sexual orientation as predominantly *heterosexual* (Seabrook 1990). McMullen (1990), an English researcher, argued that male rape is generally carried out by straight men who rape men *they regard as homosexuals*. The sexual identity of the rapist is then wrongly thought to be homosexual and homosexuals are blamed for the rape. McMullen argues it is very rare for homosexuals to rape. Although our survey found that gay men did rape other gay men, overall assailants were more likely to be heterosexual than homosexual.

Rapes can be differentiated in terms of relationship between the assailant and victim. Twenty-one (31 per cent) of the reported rapes involving single assailants were sudden attacks involving assailants who were complete strangers. Forty-eight (44 per cent) were reported rapes involving assailants whom the victim had known for longer than 24 hours and 28 (25 per cent) were where they had met within 24 hours (the higher number of assailants is accounted for by the number of assaults in which the assailants operated in gangs). In terms of victims' views of the sexual orientation of their attacker, a third had no idea but 41 (51 per cent) considered their sexual orientation to be heterosexual, usually when they were previously known to the victim.

Some assaults appeared to be motivated by revenge, either concerning a past lover (in one case a man raped his wife's lover in revenge for his adultery) or for some grievance. Some assaults appeared to be homophobic, where victim was known or assumed to be gay. For example, a black gay student who was raped said: 'I felt it was a homophobic attack. He had something against gay people. I think he called me a queer. I am still scared of intimacy, even with my boyfriend although I have never told him about the assault.'

Several rapes took place in all-male institutions such as male prisons or boarding schools. Examples of such rapes from our questionnaires included two rapes taking place in prison and a gang rape by a rugby team. These may represent only the tip of the iceberg. The extent of rape in US prisons is horrific. The US Stop Prisoner Rape, a national non-profit organization dedicated to combating rape of prisoners and providing assistance, estimates the number of rapes in US prisons is in excess of 60,000 taking place every day. They estimate the level of rapes in the course of one year as 130,000 adult males in prisons, 30,000 in jails and 40,000 boys held in juvenile and adult facilities. It is quite possible that the rising level of young prisoner suicides in Britain is associated with this phenomenon here.

Reactions to assaults: similarities and differences to female rape

Being raped totally destroyed my life. I went into a marriage that broke up within months. After that I had a nervous breakdown which caused me to have daily psychiatric treatment for two years. I am still unable to socialize properly or work.

There were many similarities between the victims' accounts of the effects of male rape with studies that have been undertaken of the aftermath of female rape. Rape, whether of men or women, is often an appalling experience which takes a very long time to come to terms with. In the case of women victims, many felt rape stained their reputation as good women. Similarly male victims considered their reputation as 'real men' to have been undermined. Feelings of worthlessness and feeling dirty paralleled women's reactions to rape. One man described how he couldn't get clean:

I don't feel clean any more. The feelings I had for people have completely changed. I'm very bitter and angry. My dignity, my self-worth, it's gone. It's everything. He's just messed up my life completely. I'd like to tell him what pain he put me through psychologically and physically.

As is the case with women victims, sexual relationships were often affected. One man who did not tell anyone about the gang attack until seven years after, described how it had put him off sex and people found him boring. He described how

> I went through a breakdown of some kind. It was the worst period of my life. I phoned the Samaritans. The stupid bastards told me that it wasn't the kind of thing they dealt with and that there were special numbers for that but they didn't tell me what they were. I was unemployed for a year. I stopped drinking, suffered a stomach complaint, probably an irritable bowel and lost four stone through the summer.

Buggery was rarely the only humiliating sexual act that took place during the rape. An additional factor was that being forced into various sexual activities which aroused physical reactions often lead the victim to experience a *crisis of sexual identity* whether they identified themselves as homosexual or heterosexual. This was one of the main differences between the effect of rape on men and on women. Women who are raped often experience serious disturbances in their future sexual behaviour, but do not have a crisis of sexual identity in the same way, although their sexual relationships are usually affected and many who have partners break up.

Analysis of police questionnaires too showed that the majority of assailants make some attempt to 'arouse' male victims through fellatio or masturbation. This can be just as distressing for the victim as the act of buggery. In addition, many victims achieve an erection or ejaculate themselves, which greatly adds to their feelings of shame and humiliation. In-depth interviews with a subsection of the male victims (20 men) revealed that most got an erection – frequently because the assailants aroused them, either through masturbation or oral sex.

Kinsey (1948), the American psychologist who carried out the first survey of the incidence of homosexual behaviour in the United States, found that penile erections need have nothing to do with pleasure. In his investigation into adolescent boys who had been sexually assaulted by men, he discovered that violence and non-erotic stimuli and horseplay can lead to erection and even to ejaculation. He published a list of emotional states in which boys experience sexual excitation including erection and ejaculation. The list includes among others, being scared, fearing punishment, anger, and being yelled at. Kinsey (1948: 164–5) concludes 'the record suggests that the physiological mechanism of any emotional response (anger, fright, pain etc.) may be the mechanism of sexual response. These reactions need have nothing to do with sexual desire or pleasure.' The act of anal penetration stimulates the prostate gland and an erection in such cases is automatic. Apparently stimulation of the prostate gland can cause an automatic erection in impotent and disabled men. Reports from victims make it clear that erections during sexual assault are never experienced as pleasurable by victims. On the contrary, all the victims the authors spoke to felt horrified, shocked and ashamed by their physiological reaction to the assault. Additionally, assailants often demand that victims perform sexual acts on them – most commonly fellatio. Confusion and anxiety about their sexual orientation is often very distressing for victims.

A parallel can be drawn to the experience of some women who lubricate when raped or may even have an orgasm. Some doctors are not immune to drawing false conclusions about rape from the physiological state of the vagina. A woman I interviewed about her medical examination described how she felt when the doctor who examined her commented on the state of her vagina:

> At one point the doctor examining me said, 'Well your vagina feels moist, seems like a normal vagina,' and I thought, 'What is he telling me that for, is he saying I enjoyed it or there is no trauma there so it did not happen? I did not really know what his comment was for.

Evidence of physiological response is used by defence counsels to imply desire even when there is no evidence of lubrication. In one trial of a man who had raped a woman, for example, the defence counsel said, 'He touched your vagina and it was lubricated.' The significance of the suggestion of lubrication is to imply that the woman is enjoying the experience. The confusion arises over the meaning of biological or physiological changes. Sexual arousal may cause the vagina to lubricate but this does not mean that a moist vagina necessarily implies sexual arousal. There is great variability among women as to the changing state of the vagina at different points of the menstrual cycle and lubrication does not necessarily have anything to do with sexual arousal. Fear could affect lubrication as could alcohol. Yet the idea the defence counsel is advancing is that a woman could want sex without even knowing it herself. Such a view reduces the whole issue of consent to absurdity, in which the woman is denied any subjectivity or knowledge of her own desire. As one defendant argued, 'Her body wanted it but her mind was somewhere else'!

A physiological reaction to sexual assault therefore means nothing about consent. With male rape where victims are often forced to have erections, this can then be used as evidence of consent. In the case of the remand prisoner, Richardson, heard in April 1995 the victim was cross-examined about his erection and the following cross-examination ensued:

Defence counsel: Nothing in your behaviour would have indicated that you were not consenting – yes?

Richardson: Just lying there is giving consent, is it? Getting a hard-on is giving consent? Does it actually say: Yes,

> bum me – please do it now? . . . I feel if a person is to
> give consent, they give consent through their mouth.
>> (official court transcript)

A major concern for men who saw themselves as heterosexual was to question why it had happened to them and some felt vulnerable to further attack. Victims often assumed that male rape is a gay crime and therefore blamed themselves for 'giving off gay signals'. One man wrote, 'Why me? I can't tell anyone. No one would believe me. I feel hurt, smelly, degraded, isolated, disbelief, awful . . . no feeling like it.' Another wrote: 'I felt trapped, powerless, that the next assault was inevitable. I felt confused because of my physical reaction to the assault.'

It is of course true that some men are 'targeted' as they leave gay clubs or in gay cruising areas, for example, but most attacks are on heterosexual men. This appears to be a similar process to the way women blame themselves or are blamed for being raped, on account of, for example, the way they dress or for being out late at night. Additionally victims fear that they will be seen by the police and others as homosexual.

Another similarity with female rape is that assailants often forced victims to say they were enjoying the assault. This can be seen as a way of rendering the rape legitimate. One victim said, 'He kept asking me if I liked it. What he actually said was, "You like it, don't you?"' A waiter raped by his boss, the head waiter, described how 'I had to tell him I was enjoying it. I had to pretend because I was very afraid of him. He said, "You love this, don't you?"'

Mezey and King (1989: 205) argued that men who are raped were more likely than female victims to regard rape as life-threatening and that in some respects their trauma is greater since their masculinity is undermined. While it is true, as Adler (1992: 117) points out, that in some respects, male victims may face even more formidable obstacles in reporting and substantiating rape than female victims there is little justification for believing that men suffer more than women from rape. Gillespie (1996: 149) puts forward two arguments to challenge the backlash which she sees as aiming to marginalize feminist services. First, she points out that 'for a woman to be raped by men is deemed "normal" while for men it is abnormal, an experience which feminizes men and one which is viewed as somewhat more shocking and horrifying'. Second, she underlines that a rape victim is not merely a victim, whether male or female, but a victim of the gendered power relations between men and women (Gillespie 1996: 161).

Pair and gang rape

Where male rape is carried out in pairs, the assailants' camaraderie is enhanced. An 18-year-old described how he had accepted a lift with two smartly dressed young men who had laughed and joked with each other during the assault. One man described how he was raped by rugby team mates in the shower. He thought they were joking when they said 'Don't bend over to pick up the soap,' but it was not banter. When he turned round, two men 'descended on him just like animals'. He described it as a pack mentality and had been appalled that men he had regarded as friends could have done this to him. It had profoundly shaken his confidence in men.

The following report from a man who had been raped 20 years before shows how homophobia often arises from fear about one's own sexual orientation:

> I felt I had done something to cause it. I felt if I went to the police or told someone they would think I was gay and concern that I'd be ruined. Later I was fearful that I was gay. Felt asexual for over a year. Later beat up gays for several years.

In both the victim and the police survey perpetrators were more likely to be heterosexual than homosexual. This finding needs to be widely publicized since the most prevalent myth about male rape is that it is a 'gay crime'. In the police survey, over half the known suspects (i.e. named or identified by victims) who were interviewed had sexual relationships with women. Furthermore, over a quarter of known suspects were either married or cohabiting with females at the time of the offence. Analysis of both surveys indicates that victims are also more likely to be heterosexual than homosexual. This finding is predictable in view of the predominance of heterosexual men in the population.

Resistance

It appears that men are no more likely than women to resist assaults. Rapists usually take care to isolate the victim to make it hard to fight back. Where men did resist, as with female rape, resistance was met with higher levels of violence. The most common reaction among victims was to be frozen. A 20-year-old who said he was raped by a vicar, aged 52, and had never told anybody said:

> I couldn't think coherently. Because of the violence I was just too scared, and I just gave up trying to struggle. Get it over with and he'd go. That's all that was going through my mind. It doesn't matter where I was at what time of the day or night. It's still my body. I still have the right to say 'no' to anybody. He took the right away from me and raped me.

It is not uncommon for men not to resist. The police survey found that extreme violence is not usually necessary to carry out rapes on men.

Weapons were used in less than a quarter of cases, and weapons combined with physical violence (like punching and kicking) used in less than half the cases. The threat of violence was usually sufficient to carry out the act.

There were no major differences in the degree of violence used in stranger and acquaintance rapes. Stranger rapists were more likely to use weapons (e.g. knives were used in 28 per cent of cases compared to 17 per cent in acquaintance rapes), but the acquaintances were more likely to use threats to kill. Actual injuries sustained were greater in acquaintance rapes.

The court response

In law rape, whether of men or women, is seen as primarily about sexuality rather than dominance. Evidence of coercion and dominance is often ignored or explained as 'what the victim wanted'. Evidence that erections can be caused by fear and bullying is denied. Evidence of the state of the victim is seen as irrelevant. Instead the protagonists within the legal system generally do not believe that men get raped, but see it, as with female rape, as a sexual encounter where the victim must have consented.

It is important to consider why such evidence is denied. One possibility is that the barristers and judges cannot face the idea that sexuality can be about power and dominance, especially when it is carried out by seemingly 'respectable' men. It is more acceptable to write it off as homosexual and therefore not a reflection of hegemonic heterosexuality. Enforcing and maintaining the dominant (or hegemonic) form of masculinity is not only achieved through violence towards women but violence towards subordinated and marginalized other groups.

Connell (1987) was one of the first contemporary sociologists to analyse the relation between power and masculinity. He challenged the taken for granted conception of masculinity as a unitary construct and pointed out the diversity of *masculinities*. Of particular significance to the understanding of male rape, he pointed to the importance of recognizing and analysing the relations between these different kinds of masculinity, relations of *alliance, dominance and subordination*. These relationships are constructed through various practices or systems of representations within certain social contexts such as the school, the workplace and sport. Such practices exclude and include, and involve power relations between different groups of men. Connell refers to the dominant form as *hegemonic*, by which he suggests they exercise power through moral authority underpinned by the threat of violence (see Kenway 1995) and the other forms as marginalized or subordinated. Men raping men and men raping women can both be seen as forms of promoting the dominant hegemonic heterosexuality. Likewise, Walker (1988) who undertook a study of the relations between boys in school in Australia, shows how hegemonic forms of masculinity among boys leads to derogating everything feminine or related to femininity in order to purge masculine identity from any such association. This wards off threats to gender identity and 'reduce[s] the level of disgust and revulsion caused by "poofs" and any undermining of male authority by females who were less submissive than it was thought they should be' (Walker 1988: 90).

In the US, as reported by Connell (1995: 218–19), the early 1990s saw a new wave of homophobic campaigns depicting gay men as 'an army of lawbreakers, violating God's commands, threatening first the family and then the larger social order'. The homophobia evident in Walker's (1988) ethnographic study of Australian school culture is evident in educational studies carried out in Great Britain. Mac an Ghaill (1994) undertook a three year ethnographic study between 1990–92 into the social construction and regulation of masculinities in modern society. He viewed school as a complex gendered heterosexual institution where dominant forms of masculinity are confirmed by institutional, material, social and discursive practices. He saw this as based on a particular construction of the family and nation that lies at the heart of the New Right.

Beynon's (1989) ethnographic study of a tough English secondary school is one of the few studies of real life violence in the making. He sees violence at the heart of contemporary masculinity which must be understood in the context of social structures, relationships and interactions. Encoded messages regarding masculinity and by implication femininity were embedded in all kinds of social practices. Violence took different forms in the day to day life of the school he studied and was not merely condoned but sanctioned by the ethos of the school. Some teachers physically assaulted boys, who were hit, pushed and shaken. He found that in the lower school a hard core of male teachers regarded coercive measures as synonymous with good teaching and a virtue to be upheld. Teachers generally prepared to write off most pupil violence as normal, healthy boyish exuberance and horseplay. Much of the violence was homophobic and there were widespread attacks on boys regarded as queers or poofs. The same 'effeminated' boys were often rejected by many teachers.

Understanding homophobia

Homophobia appeared to be the motive in a number of attacks in the *Dispatches* research and appeared to be motivated by fear of one's own homoerotic feelings. Raping gays or men who are perceived as 'weaker' can paradoxically be seen as a way of defending oneself against homosexual feelings. When carried out with a friend or gang, rape can be seen as both a way of enhancing relationships with them (victims often report that the assailants laughed and joked with each other) and, by humiliating the victim, showing oneself to be a 'real man'. Humiliation was reported by many assailants, some of whom had been left lying naked and wounded in the street or urinated on. The homoerotic nature of gang rape has been pointed out in relation to gang rape in the US. In her study of fraternity gang rape on university campuses, Reeves Sanday (1990: 14), an American anthropologist, describes how 'pulling train', an activity where a group of men line up like train cars to take turns having sex with the same woman (who is usually unconscious), is defined as normal and natural by some middle-class men and women. She explains this as a form of male bonding which enhances male identity and dominance. She argues that in such gang rapes, the sexual act is not concerned with sexual gratification, but with the deployment of the penis as a concrete symbol of masculine social power and dominance. Seduction means plying women with alcohol or giving them drugs in order to 'break down resistance'. A drunken woman is not defined as being in need of protection but as 'asking for it'. The fraternity brothers watch each other perform sexual acts and then brag about 'getting laid'. Female participants are degraded to the status of what the boys call 'red meat' or 'fish'. The woman whose body facilitates all of this activity is sloughed off at the end like a used condom. It is assumed that male sexuality is more natural and more explosive than female sexuality and men are expected to find an outlet with male friends or with prostitutes. Men who do not join in or object to such behaviour run the risk of being labelled wimps, or worse still in their eyes as 'gays' or 'faggots'. It is this last group that are open to being raped themselves.

Sanday explains this behaviour by arguing that participation in such behaviour is a way of legitimating homosexual feelings otherwise outlawed by heterosexuality. Likewise, Enloe (1988) argues that in all-male institutions such as the army, gang rape can be seen as a form of control over homosexual feelings, which may be important for the cohesion of all-male groups but dangerous in terms of heterosexual identity. For men in the army to have close relationships with women weakens their loyalty and ties to the other men. Yet to develop too strong relationships with other men endangers their sexual identity. By participating in gang rape they enhance their solidarity with each other, but still confirm their heterosexual identity.

The men vent their interest in one another through the body of a woman, but this can also be on the body of a man who is not a 'real' man. The fact that the victim is often unconscious highlights her status as a surrogate victim in a drama where the main agents are the males interacting with each other:

The victim embodies the sexual urges of the brothers; she is defined as 'wanting it' – even though she may be unconscious during the event – so that the men can satisfy their urges for one another at her expense. By defining the victim as 'wanting it' the men convince themselves of their heterosexual prowess and delude themselves as to the real object of their lust. If they were to admit the real object, they would give up their position in the male status hierarchy as superior, heterosexual males. The expulsion and degradation of the victim both brings a momentary end to urges that would divide the men and presents a social statement of phallic heterosexuality.

(Sanday 1990: 13)

Homosexuality and male rape

The control of consensual sexual relations and homosexual desire between men has always been a particular concern of all-male communities, groups or institutions such as the armed forces. The law against homosexuality (buggery) was introduced to control such behaviour in the navy in the nineteenth century. In 1816, for example, four members of the crew of the Royal Africaine were hanged for buggery after a major naval scandal (see Weeks 1977/1983: 13). The death penalty for buggery was re-enacted in 1826 by Sir Robert Peel at the same time it was removed for over a hundred other crimes. It was abandoned in 1836 and finally abolished in 1861. According to Weeks (1977/1983: 13) the armed services believed themselves to have special problems of order and discipline since 'sexual contact between men and especially across ranks, threatened to tear asunder the carefully maintained hierarchy'. There is a delicate balance between enhancing male camaraderie at the same time as controlling sexual relations between them which could so easily disrupt the patterns of authority and class. The expression of sexuality as a form of power and humiliation on the other hand, as in male rape, could be used as part of military strategy both as a means of enhancing masculinity within battalions and as a strategy of war. According to some authorities (see Seabrook 1990), non-consensual buggery is a common practice of invading armies where the defeated are raped in order to break their spirit. It is estimated that 10 per cent of the rapes in Bosnia were of defeated men (Stiglmayer 1993).

There are all kinds of all-male activities – from the initiation ceremonies of the Masons to football 'hooliganism' and drinking binges – which can be seen to enhance male solidarity. Connell (1995: 31) describes how in some societies various kinds of homosexual behaviour have been regarded as central to the survival of the society. He describes the initiation rituals of the 'guardians of the flutes' in the highlands of Papua New Guinea which involve the sustained sexual relations between boy initiates and young adult men in which the penis is sucked and semen is swallowed. The semen is regarded as the essence of masculinity that must be transmitted between generations of men to ensure the survival of society.

Understanding masculinity

The construction of masculinity is central to an understanding of male rape. How males see themselves as male, and how that perception is enabled in the family, schools and other institutions, is central to any understanding of rape, both of women and other men. Studies indicate that adolescent boys are preoccupied with forming a masculine identity. Masculinity is not, as is often believed, genetically programmed, but is socially constructed and is only meaningful in relation to constructions of femininity. Achieving manhood involves a permanent process of struggle and confirmation. Arnot (1984) sees this as a dual process of men distancing women and femininity from themselves and maintaining the hierarchy and social superiority of masculinity by devaluing the female world. Connell (1995: 80–1) illustrates that masculinity is *not* a unitary construction, and points to different forms of masculinity which co-exist, some more dominant than others in particular societies at different historical periods. He makes the important point that hegemonic masculinity, that form which is ascendant in western capitalist societies, is defined not only in relation to the subordination of women but also in relation to other subordinated 'marginalized' masculinities. Marginalized masculinities (identified in school as groups of the 'swots', the 'cool' lads and the 'wimps') are less aggressive, and often are targets of the dominant group. A confusing irony is that although the overall effect of male violence is the subordination of women, a large proportion of victims are other men.

There may be a particular need at present to enhance 'manhood' with the rising male unemployment and women increasingly entering the work force, albeit in low-paid low-status jobs. All-male groups may increase in periods of changing sex roles. For example, the development of all-male societies in the nineteenth century such as fraternities, male clubs and lodges, could be seen as 'a defence against threatened manhood at a time when manhood was under assault due to industrial capitalism, the rise of female values and the cultural critique of masculinity' (Nardi 1992: 41). One of the main characteristics of such groups was to valorize 'all that was not female' which served to enhance male power.

Male upon male bullying in schools is all too often positively sanctioned and treated by both parents and teachers as normal behaviour (McMullen 1990: 27). An important means of achieving this is by putting down other boys in various ways. The most common of these appears to be by insulting those boys who are less 'macho'. Donna Eder (1995), an Australian sociologist, in a fascinating study of the social relations of adolescent boys and girls in school found that great importance was placed on men being aggressive and tough and that the boys conveyed the importance of toughness through ritual insults. Many of the names the boys used to insult each other implied some form of weakness such as 'wimp' or 'squirt'. Other names such as 'pussy', 'girl', 'fag' and 'queer' associated lack of toughness with femininity or homosexuality. She quotes a number of studies which indicate that boys police masculinity in each other's peer groups. Boys enhanced their masculinity by throwing homosexual insults at boys who failed to engage in stereotypical masculine behaviour. One of the boys I interviewed in my research who preferred the company of girls whom he regarded as friends, was stereotyped as a gay despite his clear heterosexual orientation.

Additionally, Eder found that in all kinds of ways school authorities legitimate aggressive domination, particularly in relation to sports. Avoidance of tough behaviour can lead to challenges to a boy's masculinity. Some of the toughest behaviour was seen in the boys from lower working-class backgrounds. They are known to feminize certain other boys in order to enhance their own self-image as 'real men'. This involves distancing oneself from all that is considered female and the disparagement of everything associated with weakness or femininity, which includes gays and women. Sexual domination can thus be used as a way of gaining power.

We found in our analysis of the questionnaires that exactly the same kinds of insults were directed at the victims of male assaults. It is the victims who are stigmatized as gay, soft, cripples, or 'not real men' or who by the nature of the act are rendered effeminate. One of the most damaging insults to be thrown at a man is to call him a woman, a bitch, or a cunt. The act of coercive buggery can be seen as a means of taking away manhood, of emasculating other men and thereby enhancing one's own power. Studies by Mezey and King (1992) and McMullen (1990) indicate that the assailant's sense of masculinity is heightened.

Conclusion

In this chapter, drawing on one of the first studies of male rape, the finding that male rape is predominantly carried out by men whose sexual orientation is heterosexual is explored and related to the control of homosexuality and the enhancement of hegemonic heterosexuality. As is the case with female rape, men rape men for a variety of reasons and rapes are likely to vary depending on the relationship between the assailant and victim. It appears however that a significant proportion of male rapes are to some degree homophobic. Raping gays or men who are perceived as weaker can paradoxically be seen as a way of defending men against homosexual feelings and enhancing masculinity. The relation of male and female rape is explored in relation to the enhancement of hegemonic masculinity, the form of masculinity which is ascendant in western capitalist societies, and is defined in relation to the subordination of women and to other subordinated marginalized masculinities (see Connell 1995).

Note

1 Eighty-five per cent of male victims of indecent assault were under 15 years old. Thus there is evidence of widespread sexual abuse of male children by men.

CHAPTER 6

Marital rape appeals

In August 1994, three days after Daniel Collins was cleared at the Old Bailey of raping his estranged wife, he beat her to death with a wrench in front of their children. On 9 February 1995 his plea of not guilty to murder was accepted by the Crown Prosecution Service after two psychiatrists concluded his responsibility for the crime was diminished (*Daily Telegraph*, 9 February 1995). Where plea bargaining is successful, the defendant does not have to stand trial. The most common ground for commuting murder to manslaughter is diminished responsibility, for which, according to Section 2 of the Homicide Act (1957), the defendant must be shown to have suffered from an abnormality of mind arising from an injury, a sickness or a developmental problem which substantially impaired her or his responsibility at the time of the killing. Such a diagnosis must be supported by two psychiatrists. For a murder conviction the mandatory sentence is life imprisonment.

In the Collins case, Judge Gerald Butler heard that the defendant had brooded over his five months in custody awaiting trial for rape. Three days after his acquittal, he lay in wait for his wife (from whom he was separated) outside the family home and beat her to death with a wrench. After he was arrested Collins told the police: 'She put me inside for months. I was up at the Old Bailey. The judge kicked it out. She said I raped her, my own wife. I was inside for nothing. I regret what I did but I'm not sorry for her because I am still very angry.' The prison psychiatrist, on the other hand, whose report was presented by the defence counsel found that there was 'no pre-existing evidence of intent'.

Mr Bevan, prosecuting counsel, said the Crown had decided the couple's two children, aged 10 and 17, who witnessed the attack would not be asked to make statements because they had been traumatized enough. Mary Collins had suffered a history of violence from her ex-husband and had spent time in a refuge. According to a neighbour who witnessed the horrendous attack, Mary had been terrified that he would come and kill her. On her return from the court, where the rape charge was dismissed, she had spoken of not being around to see her children grow up and said that she knew she did not have much longer to live (see Channel 4 1995).

The judge, in sentencing Collins to seven years' imprisonment, commented, 'It was a horrendous killing and although your responsibility was substantially impaired, I have to conclude you must bear a very considerable degree of responsibility.'[1] Mary's family collected 1500 signatures in a week requesting that the Attorney General should refer the case to the Court of Appeal which has the power to increase the length of sentences. However permission to appeal was refused.[2]

The case indicates that the lives of married women who are raped by their husbands, particularly after separation, can be in severe danger, but threats and intimidation are still not often recognized as such by the judiciary.[3] Yet marital rape and murder are associated. Both typically occur where the wife has finally decided to end or has ended the relationship – either at the point of separation or some days, weeks, months, or even years afterwards. Both appear to be forms of extreme coercion fuelled by revenge directed at the woman daring to leave or planning to leave, and are often preceded by extreme possessiveness.

Contrary to judges' opinion, rape by a past or present lover or husband is often more serious than rape by strangers or acquaintances. Wife and lover killings account for 45 to 50 per cent of the homicides on female victims (see Radford 1993) and such murders are taken less seriously than murder by strangers.[4] Nor are the dangers women face often recognized by the police. In May 1991, for example, Jayanti Patel killed his second wife, Vanda, at Stoke Newington police station in London. The Domestic Violence Unit had arranged the meeting to explore possibilities of conciliation, but no one had searched the defendant to make sure he was not armed, although he had been previously convicted of violent assaults and of stabbing his first wife, quite apart from the previous violence Vanda had suffered (Radford 1993: 179).

Marital rape during and after the break up of a marriage

Research has shown that violence experienced by women is most likely to occur in intimate relationships with men. As Dobash and Dobash (1992: 269) point out the onset of systematic and severe violence against women is almost exclusively associated with entering a permanent relationship with a man . . . Only in a prison or similar total institution would an individual be likely to encounter such persistent abuse, violence and terror.

Researchers have found that some men force women to engage in sexual acts against their will as part of a process of humiliation and domination. In such circumstances British and American research reveals that women usually remain physically passive in order to avoid more serious or prolonged attacks.

Marital rape is a form of coercion by which husbands maintain dominance over their wives. Most cases that reach court involve women who are desperately trying to escape from their husband's violence. Many are separated and yet, as in the Collins case outlined above, their husbands continue to persecute them. Finkelhor and Yllo (1982) interviewed American women who had experienced rape by a husband or lover and found that wife rape is most likely to occur during or after the break up of a relationship. Diana Russell (1982/1990), who carried out a comprehensive study of wife rape in the US, found that most of the cases that reached court involved separated couples. In only one-fifth (21 per cent) of the cases in which wife rape occurred was the couple still married.

It is also at the point of separation or divorce that women are most vulnerable to being killed by their husbands or cohabitees. Ann Jones, who undertook a major American study of women who killed their partners, found that at least half of all women who leave abusers are followed and harassed or assaulted again, many of them fatally. She found that the reasons for men killing women appear to be very different from the reasons women kill men. Both cases are associated with a history of violence from the husband. In explaining why women are killed she concludes that 'it is because women leave or try to, that they are killed' (1991: 367). Women most often kill, on the other hand, when violent men simply will not quit. As one woman testified at her murder trial 'It seemed like the more I tried to get away, the harder he beat me'. According to several studies, survivors' experiences show that up to a third of women who leave violent men suffer abuse after separation. Some of them are killed (see Radford 1993: 178).

In another study Angela Browne found that 90 per cent of the women subjected to violence in the family thought the abuser could or would kill them and many were convinced that they could not escape this danger by leaving. She found that some violent men searched desperately for their partners once the woman left, often spending days and nights 'stalking her'. Even if she had moved away, they frequently attempted to follow her, travelling anywhere they thought she might be. They considered that 'she is theirs. She cannot leave and refuse to talk to them. They may nearly kill their mates, but they do not want to lose them' (Browne 1987: 115). Some of the women had been separated or divorced for up to two years and yet were still experiencing life-threatening harassment and abuse. Many women stay in violent marriages because they believe their partner would retaliate against an attempt to leave him with further violence (see Browne 1987: 113).

All the cases of murder, attempted murder and manslaughter in the Crown Courts in England and Wales were monitored over a three month period in the summer of 1995 in research undertaken for the Channel 4 documentary, *Till Death Do Us Part*. Detailed information was collected on 113 cases. This information included the previous relationship between the killer and victim, the circumstances and details of the killing (including the weapon used, if any), whether a plea of guilty to manslaughter was accepted by the Crown Prosecution Service, defences run at sentencing hearings and trials, verdict options put to the jury at trial, outcomes and sentences. In over 12 cases, verbatim transcripts of murder trials were taken. The three main findings were that domestic cases were more likely than non-domestic cases to end up with manslaughter rather than murder convictions. Pleas of manslaughter were accepted in around a third of cases by the Crown Prosecution Service so that there was no trial. The defence of 'diminished responsibility' often formed the basis for the acceptance of manslaughter pleas by the CPS, while the defence of 'provocation' rarely did so. The severity of mental illness in cases where 'diminished responsibility' was the main defence to murder was significantly lower in domestic manslaughter cases than in non-domestic, for example, typically depression, compared with schizophrenia in non-domestic cases. Sentences for manslaughter (60 per cent of domestic cases), whether or not the case went to trial, were substantially lower (four years or less) than in non-domestic cases (only 12 per cent of such cases were given under four years). Overall 62 per cent of non-domestic cases were given life imprisonment and 40 per cent of domestic cases.

Reported wife rape and wife murder are likely to occur when the marriage is breaking down or after separation and divorce. We also know that injuries are just as serious in cases where women are attacked by their husbands, cohabitees or ex-husbands/cohabitees as where they are attacked by strangers. This association needs to be recognized and marital rape taken more seriously. We know that very few rapes are reported and that the rapes *least likely* to be reported are marital rapes. There are two main reasons why women do not report such attacks: they do not think they will be believed or receive support from the police and they fear retaliation from their husbands or lovers, their assailants.

The incidence of marital rape

It is difficult to assess the incidence of marital rape as many women who are coerced into sex do not define this as rape. The question of how exactly rape or lack of consent should be defined has preoccupied lawyers as well as researchers. Section 1 of the Sexual Offences Act (1956) defines rape as penetration of the vagina or the anus by the penis without the woman's consent.[5] Emission of semen is not required. Attempted rape occurs where an assault stops before actual penetration has occurred. Three issues have to be proved for rape itself: first, that sexual intercourse took place; second, that it was without the woman's consent; and third, that the defendant knew that she did not consent or was reckless as to whether or not she consented. If a man believes that a woman consented to sex he cannot be guilty of rape even if his belief was unreasonable. This shall be referred to as the 'mistaken belief' defence. In deciding whether or not a man believed that a woman was consenting to sex, the jury is instructed to have regard to the presence or absence of reasonable grounds for such a belief in conjunction with any other relevant matters.[6]

This definition has been criticized on several grounds. It focuses on penetration of the vagina, which diverts attention away from the coercive and life-threatening experience of rape as described by complainants. Most women who are raped fear for their lives. Yet in law it is whether penetration of the vagina or anus has occurred that is all-important and other forms of sexual coercion such as forced oral sex, which many women report as more humiliating, are not classified as rape. The defence can make out for example that injuries have been self-inflicted, that the complainer enjoyed the violence as 'part of the love making process' or as an 'unusual form of sexual behaviour'.

In Britain there has been very little research into marital rape apart from Painter's (1991) study undertaken for a television documentary. Among a representative sample of 1007 women in 11 different cities in the UK, she found that one in seven married women said they had been 'coerced' into sex which had had a very detrimental effect on their marriages. This is the same figure that Diana Russell (1982/1990) found in her US study of a random sample of 930 women interviewed in the 1980s, where 14 per cent said they had been raped by their husbands. Studies such as these have concluded that it is far more common for women *not to recognize* being coerced into sex as rape than to 'cry rape' when dissatisfied with sex.

There was no evidence in these studies that women confused the experience of 'bad' sex with rape. Great care in Painter's study was taken to differentiate when women did not really feel like sex and when they clearly refused consent and were raped with violence threatened or used. Women distinguished quite clearly those times when they had sex when disinclined (when tired, uninterested and unwell) from those situations where they had been coerced. Rather than being eager to classify themselves as having been raped, the opposite appeared to be the case. In other words, when they were raped, they were often disinclined to see it as rape. Painter concluded firmly that women are not prone to 'cry rape'. It is important to be clear that consenting to sex, however reluctantly, is conceptually different from being raped.

Painter (1991) also found that divorced or separated women were the most likely to be coerced into sex. One in three divorced women compared to one in seven of cohabiting women had been raped and divorced or separated women were seven times more likely than married women to have violence threatened. Fifty-one per cent of those who had been hit and raped were divorced or separated. Painter calculated that marital rape was seven times as common as rape by a stranger. Ninety-one per cent of women raped by their husbands had never reported or discussed the matter with any official agency such as police, doctor, or Rape Crisis.

The effects of marital rape on women can be devastating. In research I undertook for a television Channel 4 *Dispatches* documentary, *Getting Away with Rape*, one of the respondents described how when she first met him, her partner had come across as a very nice well-mannered young man, the perfect 'gentleman'. However this image soon gave way to a possessive violent brute. This is how she described the effect it had had on her:

> The man was very violent towards me before the rape. He had beaten me up on a number of occasions. He started to attack me physically shortly after I started to have a relationship with him. There was a court order telling him to stay away from me. There was a court order pending. He had broken into my home and was threatening to kill me. Afterwards he said, 'Do you feel like you have been raped?' When he got off me he just sat in a chair and said not to tell anyone, because he had enough problems. I couldn't sleep. I couldn't eat. I had nightmares and anxiety attacks. I was terrified of being left alone. I could smell him all the time. I was too frightened to go out. I wanted to die. I thought everybody was looking at me. I thought I could see on the outside what I was feeling inside. I feel dirty, bathing all the time, needing to be clean.

Background to the marital rape exemption

The marital rape exemption was an extension of the historic domination and control of husbands over wives. The law gave male power over wives an institutional legitimacy, in so far as the law on sexual assault was only significant when it involved the 'property' of a man, usually a virginal daughter or a wife. The exemption had its origins in the following statement by Lord Chief Justice Matthew Hale in 1736: 'But the husband cannot be guilty of rape committed by himself upon his lawful wife, for by their mutual matrimonial consent and contract the wife hath given up herself in this kind unto her husband which she cannot retract' (Hale 1971).

Hale wrote this at a time when marriage irrevocably bound a woman to her husband as his property.

During the eighteenth century the law of rape evolved to protect the theft of female sexual property, not to protect women themselves. Under the law wives could not own property or enter contracts as marriage created a 'unity' in which the husband was supreme and the wife invisible. Rape violated not her bodily integrity, but the patriarchal ownership of her sexuality. Therefore it was not possible for a man to rape his wife as she belonged to him. It was an extension of the historical domination and control of husbands over wives (see Clark 1987).

It was not until the end of the nineteenth century that it became criminal for a husband to beat his wife. A husband was supported by the law in some circumstances even if he kept his wife locked up. In a case decided in 1861 (*R. v. Jackson*) the majority held that a man did not have the right to kidnap his wife when she had left him and did not want to return. However, some of the judges argued that there were circumstances where a husband might rightly keep his wife imprisoned if she had not already left him. Such circumstances included intending to go on a shopping spree and where the husband feared she might spend all 'his' money (Scutt 1993: 204).

What needs explanation is why, when laws giving women substantial rights to the joint property (such as the Married Women's Property Act 1882) and to divorce (the Divorce Act 1857) had long come into force, the rape immunity law proved so difficult to abolish. Estrich (1987: 73), writing of the attempts to revoke the legislation in the US, quotes a commentator who described it as

> one of the most difficult issues to lobby through the state legislatures. People who accept reforms concerning the inadmissibility of evidence of the victim's prior sexual conduct still cannot understand how a wife could charge her husband with rape or sexual assault – unless she was lying, or trying to use a complaint as leverage in divorce or custody litigation.[7]

In England and Wales it was not until 1994 that the marital rape exemption was finally abolished in statute. The House of Lords had precipitated this action by its decision in *R. v. R.* in 1991, in which they declined to apply the generally accepted marital rape exemption.

Rape originated as a crime in common law. The penalty for the crime and the fact that the crime was a felony were referred to in a series of statutes which were consolidated first in the Offences against the Persons Acts (1861) and then in the Sexual Offences Act (1956). A statutory definition of rape was not given until section 1 (1) (a) of the Sexual Offences (Amendment) Act (1976) which expanded on the 1956 Act by providing that 'for the purposes of section 1 of the Sexual Offences Act (1956) [which relates to rape] a man commits rape if he has unlawful sexual intercourse with a woman who at the time of the intercourse does not consent to it.' Where used elsewhere in the 1956 Act the expression 'unlawful' sexual intercourse had been assumed to connote intercourse outside marriage, so it was generally accepted that, by using the word unlawful, Parliament intended at least in some respects to retain the marital immunity (see Law Commission 1992: 4).

Hale's declaration stood untested until a case in 1949, more than 200 years later. This case confirmed Hale's view, but established that there were *exceptions* to this statute law, namely where there were court orders between the couple such as decrees nisi, judicial separation or non-molestation orders. In other words, where the woman had established a status as a separate woman, a husband's indictment to rape was valid. The exception to immunity was limited to husbands living separately under court order as was shown by a case in 1955 where, although the husband and wife were living separately, and the wife had started divorce proceedings, there was no evidence 'to say that the wife's implied consent to marital intercourse had been revoked by an act of the parties or by an act of the courts'.[8] The Criminal Law Revision Committee considered the law should be changed but only in cases where the couple was not cohabiting. According to Jennifer Temkin, Professor of Law at the University of Sussex, speaking on *Woman's Hour* on 3 August 1995, the main reason why this was not enforced was because the legal definition of cohabitation was so contentious that it would have led to cases flooding to the Court of Appeal. A change in the law was therefore rejected by a narrow majority.

In Scotland, the marital rape exemption had been questioned some years before. Hale's view was originally introduced in the Scottish context by Baron Hume's treatise on Scottish criminal law. In April 1989 a woman made legal history by giving evidence against her husband who was accused of rape *while still living with her*. Decisions by the Scottish courts in 1983 and 1984 had established that a husband could be charged with rape of his wife when the parties were not living together. In this case the defendant, Johnston Stallard, was charged with various offences of violence and indecency against his wife, including an allegation that he had raped her. All the offences were said to have occurred at a time when the couple were living together. The judge rejected a preliminary submission by the defence that by the law in Scotland a husband could not be charged with raping his wife while cohabiting with her. The accused appealed to the Court of Sessions, the Scottish Court of Appeal, where the defence counsel warned of the allegedly dire consequences that would flow from a rejection of the appeal. He claimed that if this offence was extended to all marriages, wives would render the possibility of reconciliation more difficult, and this would have an undesirable effect on the institution of marriage itself. Second, counsel warned that, in allegations of marital rape, questions of proof in regard to the absence of consent would be intolerably difficult. Finally, he argued that the very investigation into the sexual relationship in a marriage would be 'highly undesirable'.

The Court of Sessions rejected the suggestion that they were creating a new crime. The law in Scotland already protected a wife from assault by her husband. The court could see no 'plausible justification' for withdrawing that protection merely because the assault culminated in sexual intercourse obtained by force. Rape, the Lord Justice General said: 'has always been essentially a crime of violence and indeed no more than an aggravated assault'. He advanced two reasons why the court should not consider itself bound by Baron Hume's treatise on Scottish criminal law which had articulated Hale's view in the Scottish context. First, if as the court believed, Hume's view was based upon a wife's implied consent to sexual intercourse with her husband as a normal incident of marriage, the court doubted whether this consent ever extended to intercourse against a wife's will and obtained by force. That would amount to an assault. Second, women's status had changed dramatically since the eighteenth century. Husband and wife were for all practical purposes 'equal partners' in a marriage (see Brownlea 1989: 1275).

By treating rape as nothing other that an aggravated form of assault irrespective of the parties' marital state, the Scottish judges undermined the position of those who saw marital rape as somehow less grave and unique than a similar act between parties who are not married. However a report in *The Times* in 1991 concluded that the Crown Office 'can only recall "a handful" of complaints being brought, and no cases involving couples living together have come to trial' (Rodwell 1991).

In July 1990, at the trial of a man in England charged with raping his wife (*R. v. R.*), the question was raised as to whether a wife's consent to sexual intercourse could be revoked, not only by court order or mutual consent, *but also by a unilateral withdrawal from cohabitation*. The wife had moved out of the matrimonial home the previous October, and had gone to live with her parents. The defendant had broken into his wife's parents' house a month later and attacked her. He had ripped her clothing and put his hands around her neck and threatened to kill her. The defendant did not dispute the facts, just the legality of the charge. There was bruising on her throat, a clear sign that he had tried to throttle her by squeezing her neck with both hands. This was accepted as evidence that she had not wanted sex. This case was the first in which a husband was accused of rape where there was no legal separation or court order prohibiting him from molesting his wife.

Mr Justice Owen, in the course of his ruling, accepted that it was not for him to make the law. However, it was for him to state the common law as he believed it to be. He said:

I cannot believe that it is a part of the common law of this country that where there has been withdrawal of either party from cohabitation, accompanied by a clear indication that consent to sexual intercourse has been terminated, that does not amount to a revocation of that implied consent.

Graham Buchanan for the defence said the husband had gone to the house to try to persuade his wife to come back to him. Judge Owen made legal history by sentencing the defendant to three years for attempted rape and 18 months for assault causing actual bodily harm (*The Times*, 31 July 1990). The fact that the defendant had broken into the house of his in-laws (a highly respectable couple) and that two months before the trial a decree nisi was made absolute may well have had a marked influence on the judge's decision. The husband appealed, but before this court hearing another man, who was living under the same roof as his wife, was convicted of raping her.

The abolition of the marital rape exemption

In October 1990 the Law Commission published a working paper reviewing the rule of the common law, that, except in certain particular circumstances, a husband cannot be convicted of raping his wife. The Commission reviewed the way Hale's (1736) proposition had been departed from in a series of cases. On grounds of principle they concluded that there were no good reasons why the whole proposition should not be held inapplicable in modern times, when, for example, sexual intercourse outside marriage would not ordinarily be described as unlawful. In the working paper they reached the conclusion that the rule should be abolished in its entirety.

In February 1991, Lord Lane, the Lord Chief Justice, headed the special five judge Court of Appeal hearing and upheld the *R. v. R.* decision.[9] In doing so the Court overturned 250 years of legal immunity for wife rapists, a decision that was upheld by the House of Lords on 23 October 1991. The House of Lords emphasized that Hale's statement no longer represented the law and that the time has now arrived 'when the law should declare that a rapist remains a rapist and is subject to the criminal law, irrespective of his relationship with his victim':

the status of women, and particularly of married women, has changed out of all recognition in various ways which are very familiar and upon which it is unnecessary to go into detail. Apart from property matters and the availability of matrimonial remedies, one of the most important changes is that marriage is, in modern times, regarded as a partnership of equals, and no longer one in which the wife must be the subservient chattel of the husband. Hale's proposition involves that by marriage a wife gives her irrevocable consent to sexual intercourse with her husband under all circumstances and irrespective of the state of her health or how she happens to be feeling at the time.[10]

In the Court of Appeal too Lord Lane said that to interpret what Hale had said, that the idea that a wife, because she had married, consented in advance to her husband having sexual intercourse whatever her state of health or proper objections, was a fiction and did not remotely represent what was the true position of a wife in present day society. He added, 'This is not the creation of a new offence. It is the removal of a common law fiction which has become anachronistic and offensive.'[11]

The Court of Appeal also took the view that the time had arrived when the law should declare that a rapist remained a rapist subject to the criminal law irrespective of his relationship with his victim. In 1992 the Law Commission report on marital rape was published. It recommended that the abolition of husband's immunity from rape charges should be enshrined in an Act of Parliament. The abolition of the marital rape immunity was finally integrated into statute in June 1994 when the government accepted an amendment to the Criminal Justice Bill that made it a statutory offence for a man to rape his wife. This made sexual intercourse without consent unlawful under any circumstances. Two defendants are nevertheless appealing to the European Court of Human Rights on whether their imprisonment for rape/attempted rape is in breach of their human rights because at the time the assaults were committed they enjoyed the centuries-old immunity from prosecution. The European Commission has ruled it will consider the merits of their complaint which is the first hurdle to bringing a successful case against the government.[12]

There was by no means a consensus regarding the abolition of the marital rape exclusion in society at large. The *Times* leader of 24 October 1991 declared that a 'wave of prosecutions will follow' and Barbara Amiel, speaking from the moral high ground, went so far as to suggest that the marital rape exemption was one of the pillars *holding up the family*. She argued:

since this new ruling on marital rape does not respond to any social need whatsoever, what is the ethos behind it? For some time now the forces of extreme feminism and statism have been agitating to remove any special status or privileges that may exist within the family. I do not for a minute think all supporters of this ruling understand that, but the leading edge of feminists certainly do. They want the removal of any special principle that creates a unique bond within marriage and gives the family some autonomy – an ability to draw a boundary between itself and the state.

Professor Glanville Williams considered that a charge of rape 'is too powerful . . . a weapon to put into the wife's hands'. He considered that assault would be a more appropriate offence with which to charge husbands. In his response in *The Times* (21 February 1991) to the working party, he asked:

> Why is rape an inappropriate charge against the cohabiting husband? The reasons should be too obvious to need spelling it out. We are speaking of a biological activity, strongly baited by nature, which is regularly and pleasurably performed on a consensual basis by mankind . . . Occasionally some husband continues to exercise what he regards as his right when his wife refused him . . . what is wrong with the demand is not so much the act requested but its timing, or the manner of the demand. The fearsome stigma of rape is too great a punishment for husbands who use their strength in these circumstances.[13]

Nor are all judges as enlightened as those who decided *R. v. R.* Sir Frederick Lawton, former Lord Justice who chaired the Criminal Law Revision Committee in 1984, when interviewed in a *World in Action* programme *The Right to Rape* (1989), repeated the argument he had used several years before – that floods of women would rush with complaints to police stations and 'you could not have women running to police stations because of the terrible effect this would have on family life'. Interviewed on 3 August 1995 on *Woman's Hour* and asked again for his opinion in view of the fact that only 12 cases of an alleged rape by a cohabiting husband had reached court in the past five years, he replied that he had not changed his mind at all. He reiterated that, under the Domestic Violence and Matrimonial Proceedings Act (1976), the civil law would have given women protection where the couple were cohabiting. This act introduced non-molestation measures and exclusion orders (which empowered a court if necessary to exclude a man from the family home) for both married and cohabiting couples and gave the police power to arrest a man who broke an injunction (restrictions on having any contact with a wife or cohabitee). This legislation, which was aimed at providing immediate relief for victims of domestic violence irrespective of their marital status, has proved very difficult to implement and the police have not always seen it as one of their priorities (see Dobash and Dobash 1992: 172). As Hester and Radford (1996: 84) point out, the Act has been interpreted conservatively and 'the judiciary rapidly whittled away the scope of the legislation to allow women merely Band-Aid relief from abuse'. In many cases of marital rape the complainants already have injunctions against their husbands, but that this did not give them protection from rape. This indicates that Sir Frederick is complacent about the lack of protection for women in violent marriages and does not regard marital rape as a grave offence, which is associated at the extreme with wife murder.

The question of compelling wives to give evidence

An important change following from the Law Commission report of 1992 involved the contentious issue of the compellability of wives. The Commission recommended that courts should be able to compel wives to testify against husbands charged with any sexual offence against them, including rape, although this compulsion should be administered with sensitivity. The rule compelling wives to give evidence was introduced in 1984 with the intention of protecting domestic violence victims and the commission could see no reason for distinguishing between rape and other violent crimes. This assimilated the rape of wives with other offences. However, compelling wives to give evidence against husbands can render them more vulnerable to assault.

The meaning of the marital rape exclusion

The regulation of sexuality plays an important part in maintaining the institution of the family and in limiting women's sexual rights and autonomy. As we have seen, rape laws were designed to protect male property rights (over wife and offspring) rather than to ensure a woman's right to sexual autonomy or her right to consent. Susan Brownmiller (1976: 380), in her groundbreaking history of rape, was one of the first to point out the meaning of the marital rape exemption:

> The exemption from rape prosecutions granted to husbands who force their wives into acts of sexual union by physical means is as ancient as the original definition of criminal rape, which was synonymous with that quaint phrase of Biblical origin, 'unlawful carnal knowledge'. To our Biblical forefathers any carnal knowledge outside the marriage contract was 'unlawful'. And any carnal knowledge within the marriage contract was, by definition, 'lawful'. Thus, as the law evolved, the idea that a husband could be prosecuted for raping his wife was unthinkable, for the law was conceived to protect *his* interests, not those of his wife.

The change in judicial opinion reflected in R. v. R. is significant but regrettably is not reflected in sentencing policy. The vestiges of patriarchal rights lead judges to take the view that marital rape is less serious than rape by a stranger or acquaintance on the grounds that a husband has certain sexual rights over his wife. The notion that rape is merely an extension of the sexual relationship reflects the myth, strongly contested by survivors and researchers, that rape is an expression of sexual desire rather than sexual power and violence. Judicial condoning of marital rape is due to their reluctance to interfere with the privacy of the family where traditionally 'a man's home is his castle'.

Judicial attitudes also arise from the assumption that marital rape is not 'real rape' and that rapists can be clearly categorized into different types depending on their relationship with the victim. There is little evidence for this. It is possible that some rapists confine themselves to raping strangers and others acquaintances, but many do not. Groth and Birnbaum (1979), in their study of 500 convicted rapists, concluded that

> some offenders assault only their wives, others rape only strangers, and some sexually assault both. However, based on our clinical experience with identified offenders, it makes little difference whether the victim is wife or stranger, the dynamics of the offender are the same.

There is some more recent evidence that many rapists are just as likely to rape their wives as strangers or vice versa. Similarly homicidal rapists sometimes rape and kill both their wives and those they know less intimately. Frederick West, before he committed suicide on New Year's Day 1995, was charged in 1994 with killing 13 women, many of whom were tortured and raped, included his own wife and daughter. John Duffy, a homicidal rapist charged with raping and killing three women in 1990, also raped his wife before they separated. We do not know how many rapists have previously raped their wives but it certainly seems likely that many have. In 1993 Heather Gordon gave evidence that her husband, who was found guilty of raping and attempting to rape two girls aged 18 and 19 in Perth, had viciously raped her some time before.[14] It is therefore wrong to assume that different types of men rape their wives than rape strangers.

Implementing the legislation

In England and Wales, in 1994, only 8.6 per cent of reported rapes resulted in a conviction. This was a drop from 24 per cent in 1985 (Home Office Statistics). Although the number of rapes reported to the police over the past decade has more than doubled, the number of men convicted has remained almost exactly the same. The victim continues to be viewed in court and out of it with suspicion and hostility and facilities to assist her are few and far between (see Temkin 1987, 1993). In the US, too, the courts have been described as a 'disaster' area for rape victims (see Bart and Moran 1993) and in Switzerland it has recently been estimated that only 2 per cent of reported rapes lead to a conviction (see Godenzi 1994). Moreover the closer the relationship between the defendant and complainant, the more difficult it is to gain a conviction (see Grace *et al.* 1992; Gregory and Lees 1996).

In spite of the increased difficulty of gaining convictions in rape cases, it is argued that one significant advance over the past decade is the removal in 1991 of the marital rape exemption. By reviewing Court of Appeal decisions regarding marital rape since its common law abolition in 1991, I examined judges' sentencing practices at the Court of Appeal. These appeal cases represent the longer sentences awarded – men receiving short prison or non-custodial sentences are unlikely to appeal lest their sentences are increased. The Criminal Justice Act (1988) Section 36, also confers power on the Attorney General to refer cases to the Court of Appeal when it appears to him that a sentence imposed in the Crown Court is unduly lenient, but as far as I have ascertained, no marital rape cases were referred during this period.

Sentencing

In 1986 in response to public outrage at lenient sentences imposed by a number of judges in rape cases, Lord Chief Justice Lane issued new sentencing guidelines.[15] He prefaced these by noting that 'the nastiness of rape cases has certainly increased and what would 10 years ago have been considered incredible perversions have now become commonplace'. The guidelines set down five years as the starting-point for contested cases with no mitigating circumstances and a starting-point of 15 years for a campaign of rape. Where there were aggravating features, such as two or more rapists acting together, rape which takes place in the victim's home, rape coupled with the abuse of a position of responsibility, or rape involving abduction and confinement of the victim, the starting-point was set at eight years. The court recognized that young offenders could claim special mitigation and that sentences could be reduced to under five years for pleading guilty or where the victim 'had behaved in a manner which was calculated to lead the defendant to believe that she would consent to sexual intercourse'.

The Billam guidelines have led to an overall increase in length of sentences but the effect of these changes has been exaggerated. The proportion of custodial sentences of at least five years (including life) for the substantive offence of rape rose from 42 per cent in 1985 to 79 per cent in 1987 and for attempted rape from 10 per cent to 40 per cent. Since 1987 however the length of sentences has decreased. According to research conducted by Dr Paul Robertshaw (1994) there appear to be wide discrepancies in sentencing in different parts of Britain. In some places sentences of less than three years or non-custodial sentences are far more likely to be awarded than in other areas. This is contrary to the Billam guidelines that sentences under three years are not appropriate for rape even in cases with one or more mitigating factors.[16] The Court of Appeal regarded such low sentences to be justified only in 'wholly exceptional circumstances' (*The Times*, 14 October 1993). The Home Office does not collect statistics with reference to plea, so it is not possible to know how many of those given low sentences had pleaded guilty. Robertshaw concluded that 'nothing is known of the particular combination of factors in each case, but the statistics suggest at least that in some courts the "wholly exceptional" is fairly frequent'.[17] According to his calculations 40 per cent of sentences in 1991 were of five years or less. He concluded that there were grounds for a thorough monitoring and review of rape sentences and perhaps of the criteria for approving judges for this class of cases.[18]

Although a comprehensive study of the length of sentences for marital rape has not been carried out and would be difficult to undertake, several cases reported by the press indicate that sentences given are at the lower end of the scale. Sentences for marital rape prior to 1991, when marital rape was criminal only when the couple were separated, were frequently lower than in other rape cases. For example, in August 1988 Mr Justice Rougier sentenced a man who terrorized and raped his former lover to two years imprisonment. He justified this on the grounds that: 'I don't think it was such a shock to her as it maybe would be to other women.' The judge described the woman as 'somewhat overemotional'. In a case heard in 1990, Sir Kenneth Jupp gave a man who twice raped his ex-wife a two year suspended sentence, observing: 'This is a rare sort of rape. It is not like someone being jumped on in the street. This is within the family and does not impinge on the public' (Kennedy 1992: 121).

Cases reported since 1991 reflect a similar underestimation of the gravity of marital rape. One of the first rape prosecutions of a man still living with his wife, where the defendant had dragged his wife upstairs, threatened to kill her and then raped her, resulted in a two year suspended sentence. In April 1992 Mr Justice McCullough (see *Independent*, 10 April) sentenced Sean Riley to three years after he had pleaded guilty to raping his wife. The judge made his views of marital rape explicit: 'If you had done this to a stranger the starting-point would have been eight years.' He added that he had found no suitable precedent for the purpose of deciding sentence since the landmark House of Lords ruling in 1991. Riley's wife had decided to leave at the time of the offence but the couple were still living together. The prosecution alleged that Riley hit his wife and then raped her. Minutes later he had held a carving knife to her throat and raped her again. The judge did not appear to think this was life-threatening and commented: 'To be raped by a stranger must be more terrifying and more long lasting in its effect.' Riley's wife Pauline was reported to have said:

That suggests that being raped by your husband is not as awful as being raped by someone you don't know. The judge has got it wrong. Being raped by your own husband is very much worse. Here you are being violated by the man you have loved, trusted and had children with. It's unbelievably terrible and heart-breaking.

(*News of the World*, 19 April 1992)

Court of Appeal decisions

Of the 10 cases which reached the England and Wales Court of Appeal since 1991, five of the appeals on sentencing were rejected (the sentences averaged 5.4 years) and four of the remaining five resulted in the reduction of the sentences which had originally averaged five years. All the cases in which the sentences were upheld involved aggravating features, usually the use of a weapon combined with threats to kill or injuries or, in two cases, theft. In all cases the wife had either decided to separate or had already left, and in all cases there was evidence of previous violence from the husband.

In the first case (R. v. Guy) an estranged husband, armed with a rifle and pistol, broke into his former wife's house and threatened her. She already had a non-molestation order in force. His sentence of six years imprisonment was upheld.[19] In the second case (R. v. Malcolm) the husband had threatened his former partner at knife-point, stolen from her and subjected her to physical violence. His sentence of eight years was upheld.[20] The third case (R. v. Stephen) was the one involving a *cohabiting* married couple in which the sentence was upheld. According to the evidence, they had begun to sleep apart a few days previous to the assault. On the evening of the offence, the wife had told her husband that she was about to leave. The defendant was found guilty of rape, threatening to kill and assault occasioning actual bodily harm and his five year sentence was upheld on appeal.[21] The fourth case (R. v. Henshall) where the sentence of three years was upheld is discussed below.[22]

Upholding these sentences may well represent a shift in sentencing policy as Lord Taylor, Lord Chief Justice, clearly expressed a need to justify upholding the sentences, which are only, however, at the low end of the *Billam* recommendations in spite of the degree of violence involved. The meaning is unclear since there seems to be a contradiction between the sentences being upheld and the suggestion that Taylor said justifications were required, given that they were at the low end of the scale. He argued:

> It should not be thought that a different and lower scale of sentencing attaches automatically to rape by a husband as against that set out in *Billam*. All will depend on the circumstances of the individual case. Where the parties were cohabiting normally at the time and the husband insisted on intercourse against his wife's will, but without violence or threats, the consideration identified in *Berry*[23] and approved in *Thornton*[24] in the passage already cited will no doubt be an important factor in reducing the level of sentencing. Where, however, the conduct is gross and does involve threats or violence, the facts of the marriage, of long cohabitation and that the defendant is no stranger will be of little significance. Clearly between these two extremes, there will be many intermediate degrees of gravity which judges will have to consider case by case.[25]

It does appear that occasionally judges take account of evidence that women are terrorized into withdrawing complaints through fear of retaliation from their husbands. In the fourth case reviewed here (R. v. Henshall) the wife had attempted to withdraw the complaint but the prosecution had gone ahead. The husband was sentenced to three years for twice raping his wife at knife-point. The couple were living together but, after the complainant had spent a night away from the house, the appellant woke her and threatened her with a pair of scissors and raped her. He then rang the police and admitted what he had done. He was arrested and released on bail. Having moved out of the house he returned, threatened her with scissors and raped her again. He remained in the house for several hours and made further attempts to rape her, threatening her on this occasion with a knife. After the appellant had been arrested a second time, the woman indicated that she wished to withdraw her allegation. A pre-sentence report indicated that the attacks were motivated by revenge, and the aggravating features – the use of a weapon, threats to kill, the fact that the man on the second occasion broke in and the protracted nature of the second incident – led the Court of Appeal to uphold the sentence.

Lastly, in the case of R. v. *Haywood*, a five year sentence for rape was upheld where the defendant had also been found guilty of stealing and dishonesty, offences which are clearly taken very seriously by the Court of Appeal and where he had been living with another woman, having abandoned the victim some months earlier.[26]

The main ground for reducing sentences is where there is evidence of contact between the wife, even when estranged, and the defendant. This is usually taken to imply that the couple are reconciled or considering reconciliation rather than to indicate that the wife is terrified of retaliation (involving as we have seen in the Collins case, the danger of murder) when the defendant is released. Yet in extremely serious cases, involving threats to kill and the use of a weapon, evidence that the complainant wishes to withdraw charges leads some appeal judges to reduce sentences. In addition, case law assumes that marital rape is less serious than 'real rape'. Appeal judges sometimes refer to two cases, *Cox* and *Thornton*. In *Cox* Lord Justice Mustill concluded:

> The rape of a former wife or mistress may have exceptional features which make it a less serious offence than otherwise it would be . . . To our mind these cases show that in some instances the violation of the person and defilement that are inevitable features where a stranger rapes a woman are not always present to the same degree when the offender and the victim had previously had a long-standing sexual relationship.[27]

In R. v. *Thornton* the Lord Chief Justice concluded:

> The way in which we view the matter is this. The mere fact that the parties have over a period of nearly two years – 20 months – been

living together and having regular sexual intercourse obviously does not license the man once that cohabitation or sexual intercourse has ceased to have intercourse with the girl willy-nilly. It is however a factor to which some weight can be given by the sentencing court for the reasons which Lord Justice Mustill set out [see above].[28]

In the four cases whose sentences had averaged five years, the average was reduced to 3.4 years. In the remaining case (*Hind*) a 10 year sentence was reduced to six on the grounds that the 'victim had gone a long way to forgiving the defendant' and had written to him and visited him in prison. The details were horrific. When the victim had broken off the relationship the defendant had broken into the house at midnight, tied her hands behind her, undressed her, put a pillow over her head and raped her. He had forced oral sex and put his hands round her throat and squeezed until she became unconscious.[29]

The details of the other four cases where sentences were reduced were as follows. In *R. v. Hutchinson*, a six year sentence was reduced to five as a result of a report that the wife had forgiven him and because she had indicated in committal proceedings that she wished to withdraw the complaint. The couple, who had two children, had been separated and the complainant had obtained an injunction which had not been served. (This is an example of the way injunctions do not always give wives any protection, contrary to Sir Frederick Lawton's assumption.) The defendant had broken into the house and raped her.[30]

Similarly, in *Maskell* the husband pleaded guilty to rape but had not injured his wife although he had threatened violence; the sentence was reduced from four to three years. The Court of Appeal stated that 'he has regular visits from his children and friends and his relationship with his wife is good'. Since they had separated some months prior to the rape as a result of the defendant's heavy drinking, this seemed to be rather unlikely and no evidence was produced in court. (At the trial, defence counsel claimed to have seen letters from her to the defendant.)[31]

In the case of *Collier* the defendant had pleaded guilty to buggery and rape of his cohabitee, with whom he had been living for the previous seven years. Following a quarrel two days before, she had refused sexual intercourse and he had held her face down and raped her in front of their two children. He left the house, returning several days later and was again violent towards her. The Lords of Appeal took into consideration that the assault had been aggravated by the fact that the children had witnessed the incident, but the sentence was still reduced on the grounds that the appellant had pleaded guilty and 'while this was a serious rape, a sentence of three years was appropriate for the offence'.[32]

The fourth case (*Brown*) in which the defendant's sentence was reduced appears to be bizarre. Brown was subject to an injunction, and had broken into his ex-cohabitee's house, raped and badly injured her. He had been sentenced to six years reduced on appeal to five years. Brown had pleaded guilty to unlawfully wounding his former sexual partner by kicking her about the head and body. She had been bleeding badly and had to have seven stitches in her head wound. He was sentenced to two years for unlawful wounding and six years for the rape, to run concurrently. The judge who had sentenced him described him as 'an unreconstructed chauvinist of the first order'. At the appeal, the three Lord Justices reduced the sentence to five years arguing that 'having regard to the previous sexual relationship between these parties, the absence of any injury to Miss B and the absence of any weapon, we regard the sentence of six years on the rape charge as being too long.' This seems a strange argument in view of the conviction for unlawful wounding and the admission by the defence that there was no mitigation.

In the case of couples still cohabiting together, even shorter sentences appear to be the rule. It may well be that few of these cases reach the Court of Appeal as a result of short sentences awarded by Crown Court judges. Some are reduced on appeal, however. In one case, a three year sentence on a man who raped his wife after she told him their marriage had ended was cut to 18 months (*The Times*, 16 December 1994). The husband spent the evening drinking, returned home and raped his wife. He was alleged to have said 'You cannot deny my rights as a husband'. Lord Taylor of Gosforth, the Lord Chief Justice, said that husbands had no absolute right to use their wives for sexual purposes and that imprisonment in such cases was appropriate. However, in this case the man had been living with his wife and sharing her bed at the time of the rape and in his opinion the three year sentence was excessive.

Why some wives resume contact

There are two main reasons why women who have testified against their partners would try to retract evidence or communicate with their husbands in prison. As I have shown, some women who try to leave their husbands are in real danger for their lives. When they have also testified against their husbands this danger is intensified. Yet the threat to their lives is not often taken seriously by the courts and men's possessiveness and violence is still largely condoned by the judiciary. Radford (1993) points out that legal provisions for battered women such as the Domestic Violence and Matrimonial Proceedings Act (1976) and the Domestic Proceedings and Magistrates' Courts Act (1978) are not often enforced and do not guarantee protection for wives.

Second, there is strong tendency for women to minimize the threat to their lives in order to cope with fear which often prevents their escape even when this is possible. This is analogous to the behaviour of victims of disaster and war (see also Symonds 1979). Like battered women, victims of disasters experience reactions of shock, denial, disbelief and fear as well as withdrawal and confusion. Such denial leads to a delay in defining the situation accurately, and leads them to respond with dazed or apathetic behaviour (Browne 1987: 123). Later reactions include suggestibility and dependence where victims may become euphoric and convince themselves that they can rebuild and somehow everything will be all right and that they will wake up and find it was all a horrible dream. Research on victims of rape in particular indicate that they experience acute feelings of powerlessness, vulnerability, loss of control and self-blame (see Burgess and Holmstrom 1974).

Browne (1987: 125) also draws parallels between the principles of brainwashing used on prisoners of war and experiences of women in battering relationships. Key ingredients include

> isolation of the victim from outside contacts and sources of help, humiliation and degradation followed by acts of kindness coupled with the threat of a return to the degraded state if some type of compliance is not obtained. Over time the victims of such treatment become apathetic, sometimes react with despair, and may finally totally submit.

Such reactions, combined with the real threat that their husbands may retaliate on release, explains why wives may agree to communicate with their ex-husbands, but such explanations do not appear to be introduced in court.

Effect of the Children Act (1989)

Recent government concern to encourage contact between fathers and children of divorced or separated women is likely to put wives of violent husbands at even greater risk. The Children Act (1989) (which came into force in October 1991) provides greater rights for fathers and facilitates access to female ex-partners by men who have been violent towards them. According to Hester and Radford (1996), professionals working in this area of family law are misinterpreting child welfare in contact cases and not taking male violence sufficiently seriously. It is not often understood that some men may use the excuse of wanting contact with the children to locate their wives and harm or even kill them. This occurred in Birmingham in January 1996 when a woman living in a refuge was knifed to death by her husband in a frenzied attack at the station after his regular access visit to his 2-year-old son. After the stabbing, their four other children, whom the father had been looking after, were all found dead, three of them in his flat in Bristol (*The Times*, 22 January 1996).

Conclusion

Research into homicides of men killing their wives or cohabitees indicates that there is a connection between marital rape and murder. Both occur where the wife is leaving or has left her husband. Men who rape their wives in such circumstances are highly dangerous and should be recognized as such. All the cases of marital rape which went to appeal between 1991 and 1994 involved women who were trying to escape from violent husbands. In only two cases were the couple cohabiting. In over half the appeal cases, husbands threatened their wives with weapons and in one case the woman lost consciousness when being strangled. She could well have not survived. Five of the 10 sentences were upheld. These averaged 5.4 years and all the cases had involved aggravating factors such as weapons. The other five appeal cases, in which no weapon was involved, were allowed. Sentences averaging around five years were reduced to 3.5 years. With remission, this means that in half the cases the rapists are likely to be released within 2.5 years.

Although marital rape is now recognized as a criminal offence, it is treated less seriously than rape by a stranger or acquaintance. It appears from this chapter, based only on the records of cases reaching the Court of Appeal between 1991 and 1994, that the main ground for allowing appeals is evidence that there has been some contact, however minimal, between the husband and wife. The threat of retaliation is rarely entertained as an explanation for why victims should respond to requests to communicate with their ex-husbands.

Very little has been written about marital rape. An exception is a paper by Naffine (1994), an Australian sociologist, who seeks to explain why it has taken so long in all jurisdictions to abolish the rape immunity law for husbands. She argues that its abolition challenges the view of women as the possessions and passive objects of their husband's desires. Its abolition, therefore, carries the clear implication that a woman does have a right to self-determination or to take an active rather than a passive sexual role. This view, reflecting as it does the idea that acceptable forms of sexuality require the presence of mutual desire and consent, is absent from the definition of sexuality implied in rape trials. Progress has been made, but the courts have to modify their views a great deal further if women are to receive protection from male violence.

Notes

1 *The Guardian*, 9 February 1995, 'Man beat rape claim wife to death'. With remission this should mean Collins would be released in around four and a half years.
2 The reluctance of magistrates to take violence against women seriously was also illustrated in the case of David Jenkins who was twice released on bail, in spite of strenuous police pleas for custody, when charged with assaulting his former fiancée and threatening to kill her. He then proceeded to shoot her as she lay in hospital under treatment for cuts inflicted by him (*The Guardian*, 12 April 1988).
3 See *The Guardian*, 31 January 1996, 'Mother in fear defies court order on children'.
4 In Leeds in 1983, for example, Julie Stead was stabbed to death by her violent lover after numerous attempts to get the police to enforce domestic violence injunctions to protect her. Seven years later, while on parole from imprisonment for her manslaughter, Keith Ward murdered again.
5 The Criminal Justice and Public Order Act (1994) widened the definition to include male rape (penetration of the anus).
6 S1 (2) Sexual Offences (Amendment) Act 1976.
7 Estrich (1987: 134) quotes the case of John Rideout who was charged and acquitted of raping his wife, Greta. The verdict was handed down in December 1978; in January 1979 the couple's reconciliation was widely reported, but their speedy separation and divorce and the husband's continual attacks on his former wife by breaking into her home was given little publicity.
8 *R. v. Miller* (1954) 2 All E. R. 448, 449.
9 (1991) 2 All E. R. 257.
10 (1991) 3 WLR 767, 770E-G in the Law Commission No 205.
11 (1991) 2 All E. R. B 7 al 266.
12 *The Times*, 20 June 1993, Did rape-case husbands really break the law? and *The Times*, 23 February 1994, Marriage rape law challenged.
13 See also *New Law Journal* 10 January and 22 February 1992.
14 *Sun*, 28 April 1993, 'I shopped my rapist husband'.
15 *R. v. Billam* (1986) 1 All E. R. 986.
16 *R. v. Billam* (1986) 82 Cr. App. R. 347.
17 In some courts non-custodial sentences were still awarded, which were always probation or suspended prison sentences, never discharge or fines. Robertshaw considered 655 sentences for rape awarded by courts between 1991–92. He found that almost 70 per cent of sentences passed by courts on the western circuit which covers Truro, Exeter, Bristol and Winchester courts were for less than five years.
18 Robertshaw's research was not well received. One leading member of the legal profession inaccurately described his research as flawed, presumably in order to discredit it.
19 (1993) Cr. App. R. (S.) 642, 28 January.
20 (1994) Cr. App. R. (S.) 26 May.
21 (1992) Cr. App. R. (S.) 30 July.
22 (1994) Cr. App. R. (S.) 388, 28 July.

23 (1988) 10 Cr. App. R. (S.).
24 (1990) 12 Cr. App. R. (S.).
25 W (1992) 12 Cr. App. R. (S.).
26 (1991) Cr. App. R. (S). 28 June.
27 (1985) Cr. App. R. (S.) 422, 6 December.
28 (1990) 12 Cr. App. R. (S.).
29 This case was heard in May 1993.
30 (1993) Cr. App. R. (S.) 718.
31 (1991) Cr. App. R. (S.) 434.
32 (1992) Cr. App. R. (S.) 17 November.

CHAPTER 7

Men getting away with murder: the case for reforming the law on homicide

This chapter focuses on the grounds for the manslaughter verdicts of provocation and diminished responsibility as partial defences for murder. It portrays how sexism continues to dominate a criminal justice system whose official ideology is the rule of law and the equal treatment of individuals. By attending selected murder and rape trials between 1987 and 1990 at the Old Bailey, the Central Criminal Court and by analysing newspaper cuttings in the 1980s, I reveal how lawyers and judges use the law to support a particular cultural convention about how gender relations should be.

No major study of homicide has been carried out in Britain since Blom-Cooper and Morris (1964) conducted their research. While magistrates' courts have been well studied by women researchers (Carlen 1976; McBarnet 1981; Eaton 1986; Allen, H. 1987), before this research only Adler (1987) had studied rape trials. Most of these studies have been undertaken as doctoral research, and were therefore carried out on shoe-string finance. Research foundations tend to exclude criminal law from their remit, so funding is hard to come by. Access is also a problem. Justice has to be seen to be done in most countries and in the UK anyone can gain access to the public gallery. However it is often difficult to hear, space is limited and access cannot be guaranteed, nor notes easily taken, so access to the press seats is essential, which can take a long time to negotiate.

The doctrine that all individuals who stand trial shall stand equal before the law seems clear and unambiguous, but there is considerable grounds for judicial manoeuvre within the law. Legal ideals of impartiality and objectivity, ideals which are so often invoked by the Bench to establish its essential neutrality, may be neither achievable nor desirable goals as they are currently conceived by law. It is, however, important to be clear about the criteria which courts use to differentiate between individuals. My research will show that the law's construction of women is such as to exclude them from the conception of the judicial subject. It shows how in recent murder trials men and women, both as defendants and victims, have been viewed very differently.

The earliest recognition of the limitations of legal rationalism as a critical tool was that the law, which impartially applies to both rich and poor can be, in its very universality, a form of discrimination against the poor and weak. Formal equality at law has severe limitations as a device for the elimination of substantive structural inequalities between people. It may even, as the critical legal theorists argue, consolidate them (see Fitzpatrick and Hunt 1987). Additionally, any universal principle can be formulated in a particularistic way, either with reference to the definition of the actor or to the act. Thus, if all men who commit murder or assault shall stand equally before the law, anyone not defined as a man for legal purposes need not stand in the same relation. Women, children, slaves, non-whites etc. can be treated differently without violating the properties of formal equality as long as the differences in sex or age or whatever are believed to be morally relevant. There is nothing in the formal properties of law itself that provides these criteria with moral relevance. For this reason in the last century, the denial of equality to women co-existed alongside the rule of law. Husbands could legitimately beat their wives for non-compliance whereas similar action by women would be defined as assault. These husbands' rights of coercion weakened during the nineteenth century, though the courts are to this day, for example, still reluctant to concede physical violence as a valid excuse for a woman leaving a marriage (Atkins and Hoggett 1984). The infamous exclusion of marital rape from legal protection gave British husbands the right to rape their wives until as recently as March 1991.

Hilary Allen (1987: 23) records the ambiguity of English law in relation to the 'equality' of men and women. Citing a 1987 decision she documents the official inconceivability of 'a reasonable woman with her sex eliminated'. An invitation to lawyers and judges to interpret what is reasonable is an invitation to them to fall back on their common sense, their culture, their class, race and gender based stereotypes. Thus to decide that what would be reasonable for a man would not be reasonable for a woman, and vice versa, does not breach the requirement of equal treatment. The same rule is being applied – but of course in a different way. So we shall find in the case of murder trials that the law often constitutes gender relations in its discretionary spaces rather than in its explicit rules. Not only does this make these practices difficult to research and uncover, it also renders these practices virtually immune to political action.

In terms of the content of legal statutes concerning criminal behaviour, most historians would argue that the trend has been towards the elimination of particularism and differences in favour of equal treatment for all citizens. As far as women are concerned however, it is still the case that laws are made and implemented overwhelmingly by men and it is male conceptions that have been uppermost. These conceptions serve to keep women in their place and consolidate male domination. It is also why many statutory provisions in the criminal law exhibit an ideology of female passivity, as with rape. However, the ideological vision of female passivity embodied in statutes conflicts with the conception of women as precipitator and provoker that emerges in the court proceedings which are the focus of this study. This contradiction results in women who take an active stance by defending themselves against a husband's violence often being regarded as evil or vengeful. They do not conform to the vision of passivity. Similarly, women who do not fit in with the conventional model of domestic wife and mother are frequently seen as provocative.

Grounds for the commutation of murder to manslaughter, such as the criteria used to establish alternative defences such as provocation, and grounds for mitigating circumstances, bear an uneasy relationship to the rule of law. The advance of law involves the abolition of particularism and exceptionalism in favour of the consistent application of rules. The growth in the use of mitigating circumstances in a legal defence and the widening of defences for murder indicate a recognition that this cannot be done. Justice cannot be achieved by the application of formal rules. It is ultimately a substantive, not a formal, issue. No sooner are formal rules announced than justice requires their modification in particular circumstances or as regards particular categories of people.

The basic difference between the recognition of provocation or self-defence on the one hand and the arbitrary exceptionalism of the pre-legal system on the other, is not a matter of the formal structure of legality. What separates the refusal to try a king for murder, or an underage juvenile or a person regarded as insane, is a question of moral and political convention. Because it is just such a question, those older forms of arbitrariness that have survived the growth of civil and legal rights can find their point of re-entry into the modern legal system through the discretionary spaces embedded in the law, not least those involved in pleas of mitigating circumstances (see also Mitra 1987).

Moral responsibility

This Achilles heel of the modern system of law and right was recognized in essence many years ago by Max Weber (1964). As classically formulated, guilt implies moral responsibility for action and moral responsibility implies the freedom to have acted otherwise. If it can be shown that the person could not have acted other than he or she did in the circumstances, or other than he or she could reasonably have been expected to do, then moral responsibility and hence guilt is negated. It is important to recognize at the outset that the dichotomy of free will versus determinism is one of the central and philosophically unresolved dichotomies of western culture and there is no methodology for identifying whether claims of free will or determinism are valid in particular cases. Thus what are considered valid forms of determinism, forms of constraint on the agent regarded as sufficient to make the exercise of moral responsibility impossible is always conventionally defined. In such situations, predominantly male interests and ideologies will make their presence felt.

Two types of situation in which it might seem that reasonably objective judgements can be made in murder cases are that the killing was the unintended consequence of other actions or was undertaken in self-defence. With unintended consequences, in a typical case of a manslaughter charge (for example where a motorist runs down and kills a pedestrian on an icy road) there has to be some judgement as to whether the motorist was driving with reasonable precautions. But in such cases this affects only the severity of the sentence. The charge of murder legally, if not philosophically, is reserved for cases where intention can be shown.

Killing in self-defence as more clearly associated with intent and the definition of what exactly self-defence involves has been criticized by feminists who have argued that to demand that the danger must be imminent overlooks the disparity of strength between, for example, husbands and wives, where the wife considers she is in imminent danger and kills her husband when he has, for example, passed out with drink or is asleep. The present definition limits the question of to what extent the defendant's life was actually in danger *at the time of the killing* and whether any other evasive action could reasonably have been taken.

Mental illness might seem to be a similar case. If it can be shown through the assumed precision and non-ideological nature of psychiatric evidence that the person was suffering from mental abnormalities sufficient to interrupt the process of rational thought, then a case for non-responsibility for action can be made. This was the conclusion in the Yorkshire Ripper case. The main ambiguities in such judgements centre around the problems of *post facto* psychiatric investigation, coupled with the ever-present danger of tautology, whereby the fact of the crime (for example hideous and multiple murder) is taken as supporting evidence of insanity. The assumption 'no rational person would act thus . . .' is inevitably coloured by conventions which may have a sexual, class or ethnic particularity (see Blumberg 1967; Allen, H. 1987).

Provocation

The UK Homicide Act of 1957 amended the law so that a category of homicide such as murder by shooting and in the furtherance of theft carried the death sentence, but the remainder carried a mandatory sentence of life imprisonment. The death penalty was suspended for murder in 1965 and abolished five years later. All murders were then made punishable by life imprisonment. Under sections 2 and 3 of the Act, the grounds for extenuating circumstances were widened by introducing grounds of diminished responsibility by which murder could be commuted to manslaughter (section 2) and by widening the defence of provocation (section 3). The former depends on medical evidence, but the latter derives its validity from the behaviour of the victim precipitating his or her own death to some lesser or greater extent. Before the Act only limited types of conduct were sufficient to constitute provocation: physical violence or detection of a spouse in the act of adultery were almost invariably required in order to found a case of provocation. The House of Lords in *Holmes* v. *DPP* (1946) stated that, save in circumstances of a most extreme and exceptional nature, a confession of adultery by one spouse to another could not constitute sufficient provocation to justify a verdict of manslaughter if the injured spouse killed his spouse or adulterer (Cross and Jones 1984). Section 3 of the Homicide Act changed this and provided for a manslaughter verdict on the grounds of provocation where there is evidence of a sudden and temporary loss of self-control:

> Where on a charge of murder there is evidence on which the jury can find that the person charged was provoked (whether by things done or by things said or by both together) to lose his self-control, the question whether provocation was enough to make a reasonable man do as he did shall be left to be determined by the jury; and in determining the question, the jury shall take into account everything both done and said according to the effect which in their opinion, it would have on a reasonable man.

Juries must therefore take into account first, the events which have happened (anything done or said, or a combination of acts and words, will suffice), and second, the relevant characteristics of the defendant which may result in loss of self-control. The difficulty with these guidelines is that both the jury's view of the events which happened and the relevant characteristics of the defendant are often ambiguous. As Edwards (1985: 138) comments:

> Whilst provocation might well appear as a relatively clear legal category bound by rules and procedures, what precise forms of action, behaviour, mannerisms, speech and situation, and relevant characteristics a jury may consider constitutes provocation, is both arbitrary and ambiguous.

The concept of provocation is, as Atkins and Hoggett (1984: 129), authors of a legal textbook, suggest, 'the most insidious of all to emerge from cruelty cases'. It is at best a very fluid and difficult defence. Is provocation being used as a psychological or as a moral factor? The difficulty of any hard and fast rules for the use of provocation in murder trials derives, first from the fact that a large number of murders could be described as crimes of passion which from the subjective standpoint of the defendant are the result of intolerable provocation. The question for the court to decide is whether the action is a justifiable response to its antecedents; whether any set of reasons could be construed as justifiable homicide. Within this framework ideological conceptions of 'normal behaviour' will inevitably be bought to bear.

Sexist assumptions and prejudices colour these conceptions of normality in at least two respects, first, in what is considered legitimate behaviour for women. Studies of rape trials, for example, have shown how evidence relating to the prostitute status of a victim, as a construction of the latter's promiscuity, is frequently allowed in cross-examination in the formation of verdicts. Similarly, any prior relationship between the victim and the accused is used to argue tacit consent to rape on the part of the victim (Edwards 1981: 58; Adler 1987). The sentencing of women to prison has been shown to be more dependent on their non-marital status or unconventional lifestyle than the gravity of the actual offence. Pat Carlen (1983) found that women who resisted the oppression of their gender role were particularly at risk of imprisonment. Women who resist being beaten up by their husband by attacking him as he sleeps, or women who take to alcohol, could find themselves in danger of a prison sentence if charged with quite petty offences.

Similar constructions of legitimate (i.e. non-provocative) female behaviour surfaces in the murder trials that I observed. Here evidence that the victim was seeking a divorce or unsubstantiated evidence that she was in any way promiscuous, is cited and frequently accepted as grounds for provocation. Part of what is considered as legitimate behaviour on the victim's part in these cases is derived from a view of the responsibilities of the normal wife. Similarly, as we shall see, when battered women kill in self-defence after years of brutal beatings, they generally face much harsher treatment by the criminal justice system than men who kill in jealousy or in response to marital difficulties (see Browne 1987; Jones 1991). Without a doubt, it can be said that if the men in these cases had achieved a 'reputation for promiscuity' and this had been cited by defence counsel for their wives where the latter were on trial for the murder of their husbands, the court would not have given it a moment's consideration.

The second criterion of normal behaviour involves an evaluation of whether the behaviour was 'exceptional' for the defendant (i.e. atypical compared with past behaviour). This is brought to bear as evidence for whether or not the murder was an understandable response to provocation. As Mary Eaton (1983) points out in her study of magistrates' courts, pleas of mitigation invoke a consensual social world in which the defendant's relationship to the family is presented as the benchmark of normality. The family is therefore at the centre of the model of social normality that is used to differentiate 'real criminals' from others. A good family member is not really a criminal but criminal behaviour on the part of an individual with an unconventional lifestyle is unsurprising. An independent woman is just not acceptable (Eaton 1986: 44). Where the woman is a victim, likewise, in the Old Bailey trials that I watched, the lack of conventional behaviour is taken as evidence for her provocation. Whether a victim or defendant in trials where women are involved, it is therefore a woman's reputation that is focused on. In my earlier research on adolescent girls, as we have seen in Chapter 1, the only security against verbal insults and a bad reputation was for girls to confine themselves to the 'protection' of a male partner. The law can be seen as an extension of processes of control that affect all girls and women in their everyday lives.

For Asian women appearing in murder trials in the UK, there is an added dimension. *Izzat* is the notion whereby women are seen as the upholders of honour and tradition of their family and in-laws. *Izzat* is a concept in all major Asian religions and is central to keeping women under control and within the confines of the family. If a woman deviates from the accepted norms by, for example, choosing her own partner in marriage, marrying outside her caste or religion, or separating from her husband, she commits the ultimate crime, dishonours her family, culture, religion and will be labelled as not respectable (Wilson, A. 1978). If she steps outside her prescribed role, she is considered tainted, promiscuous and treated with contempt. She is seen as coming under the corrupting influence of immoral western values. No wonder that she is regarded as doubly unconventional should she be involved in a court case. Even as in the case of Kiranjit Ahluwalia (see postscript) where she killed her husband, the reasons that led to her crime are irrelevant; it is the action itself that is the focus.

In cases where men are on trial for murder, a major problem is that the woman is dead and therefore cannot answer false allegations that may be presented by the defence. The defence counsel can therefore paint a picture of the deceased that is far from the truth. It is possible for the prosecution to present evidence 'in rebuttal' of allegations (to refute them) but in the cases analysed this rarely occurs. Therefore, entirely false allegations can be presented without anybody contesting them.

Feminist philosophical considerations

The history of modern philosophy appears disproportionately obsessed with establishing rules by which mind, reason, self and will can legitimately control the body, the emotions, the external world and desire.

(Gould 1984: 56)

During the past 10 years, feminist philosophers have proposed that sex should be the variable of interest in the scientific examination of such human characteristics as rationality (Harding 1983; Ruddick 1990). Genevieve Lloyd (1984), for example, traces the history of the double association between reason and masculinity and emotion and femininity. She shows how this association has taken different forms from the seventeenth century onwards, but that rationality has been seen as a way of controlling emotions and passions. Masculinity and rationality were also seen to be closely connected. Philosophers such as Descartes distinguished the sensuous, imaginative and emotional from the rational and argued that women were somehow lacking in respect for rationality. The idea that rationality could be attained by training which involved gaining control over emotion and imagination led to the perverse argument that since women were incapable of rationality, they should be educated differently. Such discriminatory ideas about women's education were expressed by Rousseau in his tract *Emile* (1762/1974: 328):

> To be pleasing in his sight, to win his respect and love, to train him in childhood, to tend him in manhood, to counsel and console, to make his life pleasant and happy, these are the duties of woman for all time and this is what she should be taught while she is young.

Lloyd (1984) argues that faith in the 'victory of reason' has declined now that threats to humanity can no longer be said to be posed by the forces of unreason rather than by having their source within reason itself. Nevertheless the same ideas are still embedded in the legal process.

Alison Jagger (1989) agrees that from Plato until the present, with a few notable exceptions, reason rather than emotion has been regarded as the indispensable faculty for acquiring knowledge. She too argues that the rational has been contrasted with the emotional and linked to other dichotomies, such as that between masculinity and femininity. It appears that there are different conceptions of rationality, which may be determined partly by the social and gendered background and experiences of individuals as well as the really different possibilities which exist for men and women. Thus the most rational action for a woman may well indeed be different from the most rational action for a man, even if they could be imagined to be in apparently similar circumstances.

Feminist sociologists have also attacked the neutrality of scientific rationality (see MacKinnon 1987; McNeil 1987; Smith 1988) and have argued that objectivity is little more than male subjectivity. Whether women are regarded as the same or different from men, the standard by which women are judged is male. As MacKinnon (1987: 84) comments: 'Gender neutrality is thus simply the male standard, and the special protection rule is simply the female standard, but do not be deceived: masculinity or maleness, is the referent for both.'

Feminists do not claim a feminine point of view that is objective, abstract or universal – far from it. They recognize that women's perspective will vary under different political systems and that bias is inevitable. They reject the ascendance of the universal, abstract point of view. What feminists do argue however is that the human rationality has been defined from a distinctively masculine perspective which is not only one-sided but also in some respects perverse (Gould 1984: 44).

It is important to examine these arguments and conceptualizations in order to understand our present legal system and the extent to which it rests on a male standpoint and on male interests. The evidence suggests that conceptions of rationality underpinning legal definitions protect patriarchy and condone male violence. This chapter demonstrates that, first, our traditional masculine conceptions of humanly rational belief must be revised; and second, that the dichotomy between conceptions of emotion and rational behaviour needs to be questioned.

My research at the Old Bailey

Between September 1987 and October 1990 I attended 14 murder trials at the Old Bailey, the Central Criminal Court. Newspaper cuttings for the years 1985–89 were analysed. Women kill far less frequently than men; the ratio of men killing women to women killing men is about eight to one. Between 1982 and 1989, the numbers of women indicted ranged between four and 14 a year, compared with 80 to 109 a year involving men who were indicted for killing their wives, ex-wives or lovers (Hansard 1991 quoted in Radford 1993: 182). In case after case the most frequent remark recorded by male defendants is 'If I can't have her, no one else can'. The jealous husband kills either the wife or her alleged lover.

The judge's direction

Judges normally begin their summing up with a statement such as, 'You must put your emotion aside', implying that sympathy will disrupt the 'rational' process of decision making. He or she then goes on to direct the jury that in cases of provocation there must be two elements; the defendant must lose their self-control and the provocation must have been such as to make a reasonable man (or woman) lose their self-control. Justice Pain described this as follows:

> You have to look to see if there was a complete loss of self-control to the extent to which you really do not know what you are doing. Simple anger is not enough. Then you have to consider if the provocation would have made a reasonable man lose his self-control.

You apply the test of a person of similar age in a similar situation. Rational people do irrational things. The prosecution has to show that this was murder. You might be satisfied that this was a case where there was no provocation. Then there is no problem. You might be satisfied that this was a case where there was provocation. Again there is no problem. If you are not sure then he is entitled to the benefit of the doubt and you return a verdict of manslaughter. To argue that rational people do irrational things, and that simple anger is not enough, is to suggest that there are certain emotional responses that are out of control of the rational person.

(my transcript, Old Bailey, 1 March 1988)

However, irrationality is a relative rather than an absolute concept. Studies of some alien categories show them to be culture specific interpretations of apparently irrational beliefs, and to 'make sense' in the context of culture specific views. What is regarded as irrational behaviour by judges may be little more than the judge's failure to acknowledge the reality of male violence as a means of social control and domination over women. To prove the crime of murder there has to be two features, the act of killing and the intent to kill. It is, however, argued in trials that if the intent to kill is irrational, murder is commuted to manslaughter. Evidence of intention is therefore sometimes overruled when the judge does not regard the act as rational.

The problem is how to draw the line between an angry response that involves elements of intention and an angry response that is uncontrollable. It is debatable whether any violent response is ever uncontrollable in the way judges suggest. The examples English judges often use in their summing up to juries to describe provocation are of the soldier, returning either from the Falklands or Northern Ireland, to find his wife *in flagrante delicto* (in this case, in bed with another man). This example is curious as judges sometimes point out in contradiction that in Britain we do not have a legal category of crimes of passion. In reality, such cases are extremely rare, but giving such examples provides a rationale for the whole defence. Once the jury has accepted the idea of provocation where a man is beside himself on confronting his wife in bed with someone else, then they are more likely to accept the idea of provocation for bad housekeeping or insubordination. It is a slippery slope. It could be argued that it is not rational to kill someone under any circumstances except self-defence, or for some nefarious gain. The rational action on confronting your partner in bed with someone else would seem to me to discuss it together over a cup of tea. Not so according to British justice. In this way almost any behaviour can be seen as provocative. The most common scenario in murder trials is where the woman is seeking a separation or divorce, does not wish to continue living with her husband, does not wish to have sexual relations with him, yet this very wish is presented as grounds for provocation of murder. Legally, it is regarded as grounds for the defence of provocation.

Second, the whole rationale for the defence is debatable. The law provides a legitimation for men to behave violently in the face of insubordination or marriage breakdown. Can a man be driven 'beyond his senses' to kill someone and then return unscathed to the 'rational' human being he was before? If he can't take her nagging any more why doesn't he just leave? This way of resolving marital difficulties is never considered. Stark contradictions emerge in the way that violence is regarded in court cases. As Lee Ann Hoff (1990: 125) points out, if women have violence used against them and fail to leave, they lack self-respect. If men are stressed by non-violent behaviour (e.g. nagging) their use of violence is justified as necessary. This reasoning presupposes the traditional belief that a man's self-respect depends on the use of violence in such a case.

Male reason v. female unreason

There are profound objections to the way the defence is allowed to operate. Different criteria are applied to male and female behaviour. For provocation to be argued in aid of a woman who has killed her partner, the man must be persistently violent; in the reverse situation, women need only be insubordinate. Such criteria reflect a double standard. 'Rational' men are able to avoid their responsibility by pointing to sexual or irrational behaviour, 'woman trouble' or other feminine influences which can be used to blame the victim. The unfairness, and the untold distress caused to victims' relatives, will continue as long as the courts allow pleas of provocation to open the door to unverifiable allegations which are neither sought to be proved by the defence nor rebutted by independent evidence. Libel laws do not cover the deceased so relatives are not able to seek redress from false allegations made in homicide trials of men who kill their partners. Violence from wives is met with a quite different response, as shown in the following case.

Susan Goddard-Watt shot and injured her husband with a Magnum revolver as he was finally leaving her (*The Guardian*, 15 July 1986). The evidence of provocation (that he was leaving for good) and the absence of any long-term injuries did not save her from an eight year prison sentence. Her husband, an RAF serviceman younger than her, described how he was 'duped into marrying her, lured by steamy sex sessions and snared by lies'. Four months after their wedding day, 'she had imposed a sex ban. She had satisfied her appetite for me'. Described as a trained markswoman, she had 'loaded her Magnum and blasted his car' as he drove past with a friend after he had walked out on her for good. They were injured but had both made a full recovery. As a trained markswoman and by marrying a man younger than herself, she hardly fitted into the conventional feminine stereotype.

Plea bargaining

As we have seen, women kill far less often than men and the vast majority have been subjected to previous violence. Men who kill, on the other hand, should surely bear more responsibility for their actions since killing usually occurs when other forms of control have broken down and the woman has decided to leave or has already separated. Instead many of the cases do not even reach court as the prosecution accepts a plea of manslaughter in return for a guilty plea. Often relatives are not even informed that the case is not going to trial. In the case of Caroline Schofield, for example, her mother was not told that plea bargaining had reduced the charge of murder of her daughter to manslaughter until two days before the trial. Caroline Schofield was found battered and strangled at their house in Gloucestershire, shortly after she had finally split up with her husband. She had started a new business and had wanted to start a new life.

The murder charge was dropped and Richard Schofield pleaded guilty to a lesser charge of manslaughter on the grounds of diminished responsibility and received a sentence of only four years. None of the evidence of his previous violence came out in court. Where plea bargaining is accepted, the prosecution evidence is not heard, and the family have no chance to speak. The hearing only took an hour, during which five psychiatric reports were read out. Her mother commented after the trial:

> It left me feeling as though my daughter had committed a crime. After her death I discovered that when she had left Richard a few years ago, she had taken out an injunction against him on the grounds of violence. That did not emerge, nor did we have any say in whether or not there should be a trial. Because he spent nine months on remand, Richard could be out at the end of the year with good behaviour. I just cannot believe it.
>
> (Driscoll 1990)

The law, in its rules of evidence, in its exercise of prosecutorial discretion, condemns such victims and their families to carry responsibility for their own deaths. In so doing it establishes that non-compliant women are beyond its effective protection.

What should be done?

How can it be argued that it is reasonable to murder your wife or husband if they wish to leave, are unfaithful, let you down, fail to be a 'good' partner or nag you? We may all have murderous feelings, but this has nothing to do with the immorality of actually committing murder. It is not rational to argue that men cannot control their anger, and are not responsible for killing women. To argue that men kill their wives because they cannot help it, are driven beyond their senses, are provoked into it by insubordinate behaviour, is a convenient way to condone male violence. It also fails to address the prevalence of violence against women in the home which serves the function of maintaining women's subordination. It fails to take into account the women who are killed in the process of divorce proceedings where violence is the main grounds for the breakdown of the relationship. The defence of provocation should be abolished. Originally designed to protect men and women who were 'provoked' by being attacked, it is now used to condone men for murdering wives who are often seeking a divorce in response to years of violence.

There are three ways in which violence is condoned. First, judges frequently sympathize with the male assailant. This sympathy for the murderer even extends to cases where the wife has not been unfaithful, contemplating divorce or allegedly failing in her wifely duties. Bochnak makes a similar point in regard to the sympathy judges show for men who have committed violence against women:

> The man's act while not always condoned is viewed sympathetically. He is not forgiven, but his motivation is understood by those sitting in judgement upon his act since his conduct conforms to the expectations that a real man would fight to the death to protect his pride and property . . . the law however has never protected a wife who killed her husband after finding him with another woman. A woman's husband simply does not belong to her in the same way that she belongs to him.
>
> (Bochnak 1981: 14)

Second, when a husband uses violence against his wife, it is regarded by the judiciary as a random irrational act or, in the final analysis, the woman's fault. That the men use violence when they are fully in control of their senses to prevent women from leaving, getting a divorce, through jealousy, or to coerce them is not on the agenda. The power they hold over women, the fact that they may have motives, financial and other, for getting rid of them is often hidden, denied and rationalized away. The feminist analysis which sees male domination as a crucial factor contributing to the maintenance of wife abuse is disregarded. As Radford (1987) has suggested, the law is concerned with defining the limits of violence appropriate for the control of women. Even after a conviction for murder, the 'irrationality' of the act can be used to excuse it.

Third, implicit within the context of the defence of provocation is that male violence is *uncontrollable* and therefore men cannot be held fully responsible for it. In this way male violence is condoned by the judiciary. Anger is a reasonable response when displayed by men but only rarely when shown by women. We have already seen in the case of Susan Goddard-Watts how her aggression was treated harshly by the judge.

Provocation as a defence for women who kill

Provocation is also successful as a defence for women, but only in certain circumstances as we shall see in the next chapter. Since the Maw sisters were imprisoned in 1980 for three years for the manslaughter of their violent father who had subjected them and their mother to years of violence, there has been some move in Britain to take into account cumulative provocation (*The Times*, 18 November 1980; see also Edwards 1985). This typically involves a course of cruel or violent conduct by the deceased, lasting over a substantial period of time which culminates in the victim or someone acting on his or her behalf intentionally killing the tormentor (Wasik 1982). An example of such a case occurred in November 1986 when Valerie Flood, described as a devoted wife, killed her husband after years of drunken beatings, and was found guilty of manslaughter rather than murder on the grounds of provocation (*The Guardian*, 12 November 1986). The court heard how she had been frequently beaten, hit with hammers, cut on the legs with a machete, had her nose broken several times and had been burnt with cigarettes. She finally snapped when he tried to strangle her and attacked her with a carving knife, which she snatched from him and then used against him. Though in this case provocation was used as a defence, I would argue that this was much more a case of self-defence than provocation. He was attacking her and she snatched the actual knife that he was using against her. Had self-defence been successfully argued, she would of course have been acquitted rather than found guilty on a reduced charge. It seems that provocation may work against women even when used in their defence. So does the law constitute and reward 'appropriate' gendered behaviour by policing the inappropriate?

The unacceptability of anger

If anger is not regarded as an acceptable response on the part of women how then is it conceptualized? Since a woman is never regarded as really reasonable, it is not possible for her to lose her reason. In law, therefore, it does not appear that a 'reasonable' woman can be driven 'beyond her senses' and remain 'reasonable' unless she is suffering from premenstrual tension (PMT) and is, as Dr Katherine Dalton put it, 'at the mercy of her hormones' (Dalton 1989). This fits in with the idea that non-conformity in women is due to biological imbalance rather than rational choice. She is either suffering from diminished responsibility, which means she is then confined, usually for an indefinite period, to a mental hospital, or she is deemed to be suffering from PMT, or she is acting in revenge and is guilty of murder. This implies that, unlike a man, she can never be 'provoked' into violence and remain a reasonable person (see the case of Kristina English, described in the next chapter).

The unacceptability of female anger as a response to provocation is mirrored by the lack of understanding about the predicament of victims of violence. Bochnak, in her study of women subjected to male violence in the family, found judges often failed to understand what living under the threat of attack involves. As one of the trial judges commented:

> Given your domestic troubles, which I find were present but are not to be accepted in their entirety, *the law itself is not without remedy and was not without remedy to you. There are friends; there are relations; there are community and Church and other avenues of advice; there are policemen; there are Chamber Magistrates; there are solicitors; there are means of protection in the community.*
> (Bochnak 1981: 33; emphasis in original)

All the evidence suggests that these forms of protection are in fact not widely available in the community and that it is very difficult for women to get help. In the UK, the women's refuge movement, rape crisis centres and victim support schemes provide some skeletal service, but this is underfunded and rudimentary. Extensive financial support would be needed to provide the kind of help judges assume exists.

The concept of provocation embodies the idea that murder is precipitated by the victim; in effect the victim is to blame for her death. The arguments used in court by the prosecution reflect a strong gender bias that not only allows some men to go free or be leniently punished but also serves to condone violence against women. This sympathy for male defendants is not confined to homicide cases. The idea that sympathy for the victim can distort judgement, whereas sympathy for the defendant does not, arises from an identification of male judges with male defendants.

There is a dichotomy between the understanding of reason and emotion in the law and practice of homicide and rape trials. It parallels the dichotomy between masculinity and femininity, where rationality is associated with men and emotionality with women. Not only has reason been contrasted with emotion, but it has also been associated with the mental, the cultural, the universal, the public and the male whereas emotion has been associated with the irrational, the physical, the natural, the particular, the private and the female. Both Plato and Freud considered that women had a lesser moral sense than men. To quote Freud (1925: 257–8):

> I cannot evade the notion (though I hesitate to give it expression) that for women the level of what is ethically normal is different from what it is in men. Their super-ego is never so inexorable, so impersonal, so independent of its emotional origins as we require it to be in men . . . They show less sense of justice than men . . . they are less ready to submit to the great exigencies of life . . . They are more often influenced in their judgements by feelings of affection or hostility.

Although Freud did emphasize that he was talking about the construction of femininity, he still clearly considered that for whatever reason, women were not able to think 'rationally' to the same extent as men, that their views were too easily coloured by their emotions, that they employed less abstract categories. Philosophers on the whole agree with Freud's views that emotions and personal feeling are an impediment to thought. In contrast, Susan Sherwin (1989) argues that feminists who consider direct personal experience an important component of truth, pay particular attention to the emotional content of thought. It is certainly true that consciousness-raising has used emotional experience as a starting-point from which to move to a more abstract analysis of personal experience. But is talking about personal experience the same as talking about emotions? And what are philosophers saying when they argue that emotions interfere with rationality?

Surely this is a false dichotomy in that there is no such entity as 'raw' feeling which is not constructed by cognitive categorization. We learn to label certain emotional sensations in the same way that we label physiological sensations, such as hunger, thirst and pain. This involves a cognitive process that is dependent not only on cultural concepts but may also be gendered. Feminists grasped this many years ago in pointing out that sometimes cognitive categories did not exist to describe their emotional experiences. We spoke of the 'silencing' of women's experience and the lack of vocabulary to describe it. Friedan (1963) talked of 'the problem that has no name' and terms such as 'sexual harassment' were coined and have now passed into everyday usage. The lack of language to express experience may well lead to women sounding incoherent, and being dubbed irrational as a result.

The distinction made between reason and emotion is fundamental to the law on homicide. Where men behave violently, their behaviour is often seen as being 'uncontrollable', and it is argued that their 'rationality' is *temporarily* overcome usually as a result of some kind of provocation from the woman. After this, they return to their natural state of reason. It is posited in law that, under provocation, it is reasonable for men to behave in a violent or irrational way. This is based on the assumption that men are temporarily not in control of their emotions if sexually aroused or aroused by jealousy or insubordination. Violence in such circumstances is seen as a *temporary aberration* rather than the responsibility of the perpetrator. This shifts the responsibility from the man to the victim who is seen as provoking her own death or her own assault. It is the woman's reputation which is the focus of both homicide and rape trials. It is often said that it is she who is on trial, even after death.

When a woman is on trial for murder however, provocation is rarely successful as a defence unless she is physically attacked immediately before the killing. This fails to take into account that such women often kill when they believe their life or the lives of their children are in danger and that there is no other way of escape. In view of the difference in their strength they may only be able to retaliate by waiting until the abuser is, for example, sleeping. Women also successfully plead diminished responsibility, especially on the grounds of premenstrual tension, but this only colludes with the ideology of femininity as resting on an emotionality divorced from 'rational' behaviour. Lawyers in their defence of clients collude in the ideology of gender bias and the law itself perpetuates gender inequality.

The defence of provocation illustrates the way the rules for establishing appropriate relationships between mind and body, reason and the emotions, are geared to male interests. We have seen that in homicide trials, the concept of provocation rests on a certain conception of rationality which denies that men can rationally use violence to control their wives. This is not to say that they always intend necessarily actually to kill their wives. However, the definition of murder embraces not only intention to kill but also intention to do some serious harm, and there is little doubt that in most of the cases where provocation is presented as a defence, evidence exists that this second intention was present. By regarding violence as irrational or provoked, men avoid responsibility for their violence and retain their so-called rationality unsullied. Thus male irrationality, as far as the law is concerned, is temporary and understandable, whereas female irrationality is biologically given and so always immanent and never available to male comprehension. The dichotomy between emotion and rationality, and connection with dichotomies of femininity and masculinity, results in a denial of emotionality and desire as important determinants of human conduct and has far-reaching and perverse consequences. Lawyers have to work within the framework of these interpretations of the law.

Feminist standpoint philosophers argue that there is a need to redefine reason and restructure its priorities. They argue for an alternative moral and epistemological vision that would not only question the condoning of violence in the family but also call for a different vision. Nancy Hartsock, for example, has developed and transformed the Marxist notion of a privileged political and epistemological standpoint. A standpoint is an engaged vision of the world opposed and superior to dominant ways of thinking. As a proletarian standpoint is a superior vision produced by the experience and oppressive conditions of labour, a feminist standpoint is a superior vision produced by the political conditions and distinctive work of women, such as is involved in caring (see Hartsock 1983; Ruddick 1990: 129). Conversely, a male standpoint when embedded in the law and supported by myths of universality, constitutes women as *properly* vulnerable to male strategies of domestic control – even to the point of murder.

Rights of Women (1992) in their *Submission to the Royal Commission: Proposed Amendments to the 1957 Homicide Act* put forward two recommendations. They advocate a redefinition of 'reasonable' in a way that makes sense for women as well as the 'reasonable man' and put forward the idea of a new defence of 'self-preservation'. In regard to the former, they argue for a subjective criterion for reasonableness, based on honest belief. Quoting the case of Yvonne Wanrow, a US Indian woman who shot and killed a known child abuser who had broken into her house at night and made advances towards her child, they cited the following extract:

> The impression created – that of a five foot four inch woman with a cast on her leg and using a crutch must, under law, somehow repel an assault by a six foot two inch intoxicated man without employing a weapon in her defence. Unless the jury finds her determination of the degree of danger to be objectively reasonable, constitutes a separate and distinct misstatement of the law and, in the context of this case violates the respondent's right to equal treatment of the law. The respondent [Wanrow] was entitled to have the jury consider her actions in the light of her own perception of the situation, including those perceptions that were the product of a nation's 'long and unfortunate history of sex discrimination'. Until such time as the effects of that history are eradicated, care must be taken to be sure that our self-defence instructions afford women the right to have their conduct judged in light of the individual physical handicaps which are the product of sex discrimination.
>
> (Gillespie 1989: 117)

Second, they argue that the new defence of self-preservation should be a partial defence, similar to provocation resulting in a manslaughter verdict, in recognition that taking a person's life is never justified, yet is a very different situation from that worthy of a finding of premeditated murder. This defence would be open to a person who has been subjected to continuing sexual and or physical abuse and intimidation combined with psychological abuse to the extent that 'they honestly believe that they have reached a point in which there is no future, no protection and no safety from the abuse and believe it is a question of only one of them being able to survive' (Rights of Women 1992).

Postscript: June 1996

Since this article was written four years ago, there has been some progress in gaining recognition of the effects of cumulative provocation on women who kill their husbands. After a long campaign, three women, Emma Humphreys, Kiranjit Ahluwalia and Sara Thornton, all of whom were originally found guilty of murder, have had their convictions reduced to manslaughter on appeal. In only one case, however, was the manslaughter verdict clearly based on provocation rather than on diminished responsibility, although both grounds were put forward by the prosecution. The defence of diminished responsibility (or battered woman syndrome as it is usually argued in such cases) gives the impression that the woman's retaliation was abnormal and mentally disturbed rather than the result of provocation, so does not represent a widening of the legal grounds as recommended by Rights of Women, a pressure group of radical women lawyers who publish a quarterly bulletin and put forward recommendations for reforming the law (see Rights of Women 1992; Lloyd 1995: 105).

The cases of Emma Humphreys, Sara Thornton and Kiranjit Ahluwalia

Emma Humphreys had become a child prostitute aged only 13 and four years later was given a life sentence for killing her drunken boyfriend to stop him raping her. She had already served 10 years in prison when her appeal was heard in June 1995. The Court of Appeal allowed evidence of cumulative provocation, but still required evidence of a triggering event.

The other two cases of women who had killed their husbands attracted the most media coverage. At their first trials Kiranjit Ahluwalia in 1989 and Sara Thornton in 1990 were both found guilty and sentenced to life imprisonment (Rights of Women 1991: 2–5). Kiranjit Ahluwalia had poured petrol onto her husbands' bed when he was sleeping and set fire to it. She had been married for 10 years and had experienced constant abuse and humiliation. She had been slapped, kicked, punched, beaten, raped, tortured with knives and hot irons and frequently suffered death threats. She had made several attempts to escape. At her first trial the violence she had experienced was trivialized and represented by the prosecution as 'being knocked about a bit' although on the night she retaliated, her husband had both beaten her viciously and put a hot iron against her cheek. After the murder verdict, Crawley Women's Aid and Southall Black Sisters set up a campaign and soon after, in Leeds in 1990, Justice for Women was formed (see Bindel *et al.* 1995). The campaign led to Kiranjit Ahluwalia winning an appeal hearing.

At the appeal hearing, her lawyers argued that the present definition of 'reasonable man' in the defence of provocation was not applicable to a woman. The appeal judges rejected this, arguing that

> the reasonable man referred to . . . is a person having the power of self-control to be expected of an ordinary person of the sex and age of the accused, but in other respects sharing such of the accused characteristics as [the jury] think[s] would affect the gravity for the provocation to him, and that the question is not merely whether such a person would in like circumstances be provoked to lose his self-control, but also whether he would react to the provocation as the accused did.
>
> (p. 13 *R. v. Ahluwalia*, quoted in Rights of Women 1993: 10)

Instead the Court of Appeal judges ordered a retrial, arguing that, although at her first trial there had been evidence that Ahluwalia had suffered violence, there had not been any medical evidence that she suffered from post-traumatic stress disorder or battered woman's syndrome. At the new trial on 25 September 1992, the prosecution announced that it was prepared to accept psychiatric reports which indicated that she had been suffering from mental illness which impaired her responsibility. She was sentenced to the time she had served, and was immediately released.

Sara Thornton had also endured repeated and violent attacks from her husband, an ex-police officer, and had approached numerous agencies for support, her local church, her GP, Alcoholics Anonymous, social services and the police. This is not unusual. Women who have been subjected to violence often have made vain attempts to seek help and support to escape violence, yet our judiciary assumes that easy escape routes do exist. At her trial she was too traumatized to give evidence in her defence of her lover's brutality (*Observer*, 1 February 1994) and she was found guilty.

In 1991 the Court of Appeal turned down her appeal (on the grounds that she had been provoked) by supporting a narrow definition of provocation, arguing that at the moment of the fatal blow, the accused must have lost her self-control which was previously exercised. This did not fit the details of her crime where, although her husband was alleged to have threatened to kill her and her daughter, Louisa, aged 13, on the night in question, she had run into the kitchen to find his truncheon for self-defence, but instead picked up a knife and sharpened it. She said he had continued to mock her, and threatened to kill her in her sleep. She then stabbed him in the stomach.

In August 1993 an application for a second appeal was lodged on the basis that lawyers had not had access to all the evidence of abuse and psychological trauma she had undergone and new reports regarding her husband's alcoholism. The Home Secretary, Michael Howard, rejected a second Appeal Court hearing. In January 1994, Thornton's lawyer submitted new eyewitness accounts of the violence inflicted on her and finally in 1995 an appeal hearing was agreed.

The Court of Appeal did not, however, accept that there was evidence of provocation. They continued to accept a narrow definition of provocation and held that at the moment of the fatal blow, the accused must have lost self-control which was previously exercised. It rejected the argument of Lord Gifford, Counsel for Sara Thornton, that this defence as commonly accepted is 'apt to describe the sudden rage of a male, but not the slow burning emotion suffered by a woman driven to the end of her tether'. In other words that there is an important difference between the way women react to long-term cumulative violence and the way a man might reach to a single provoking event. The judges still held to the position that case law indicates that an accused must have acted from a 'sudden and temporary loss of self-control' caused by the words or acts of the victim. This fails to take into account the reality of cumulative provocation resulting from a history of abuse and the physical vulnerability of women.

The Court of Appeal quashed the murder conviction and ordered a retrial after her lawyers had argued that she had been suffering from battered woman syndrome as a result of her husband's repeated violence (*Independent*, 31 May 1996). On 30 May 1996 at her retrial at Oxford Crown Court, psychiatric evidence indicated that she suffered from a condition called dissociation, which caused her to react inappropriately to events. She was acquitted of murder and found guilty of manslaughter. Mr Justice Scott Baker Press, sentencing her to five years which she had already served, said 'that the outcome was the result of evidence that she was suffering from a severe personality disorder rather than a question of provocation'. He told Thornton 'I sentence you on the basis that your responsibility for killing your husband was diminished by your abnormality of mind'. She was given a sentence commensurate with the time she had already served. Press coverage was not, however, sympathetic. The *Daily Mail* (31 May 1996) pictured her with a glass of beer in her hand and a broad grin on her face under the headline 'Judge denies killer wife her day of triumph'.

Battered woman syndrome has also been used as an argument for reducing sentences on appeal for manslaughter. For example, Janet Gardner was found guilty of manslaughter at Winchester Crown Court in November 1991 and sentenced to five years' imprisonment for killing her violent former partner. He had terrorized her over a number of years, causing her to be hospitalized twice. She had sought injunctions and reported him to the police on numerous occasions. At the Court of Appeal in 1992 her sentence was reduced to two years' probation on the grounds that she was suffering from battered woman syndrome (a state of hopelessness and depression following unrelenting physical and verbal attacks) which had not been presented at the trial (*The Times*, 30 October 1992).

The Rights of Women (1993: 11–12) expressed severe reservations about labelling the various ways women react to violence as a 'syndrome', at the same time as recognizing the need to resort to short time strategic use when it serves the interests of individual women. A particular shortcoming referred to is the way there is an inevitable subjectivity in the way decisions as to which women are considered as suffering from the syndrome and which are not. Another weakness of the concept of 'syndrome' defences is that women's reactions to domestic violence are medicalized, which can lead to colluding with the categorization of women by perpetuating notions that certain women are sick, anti-social or in some way inadequate.

The law is still fundamentally unsatisfactory and both men and women face a lottery in terms of conviction and sentencing. There is still a great deal of inconsistency and women who appear to have similar cases to the above are still not given leave to appeal. Josephine Smith, for example, whose husband was violent and made her enact scenes from pornographic films, was refused leave to appeal against her murder conviction in 1994 (*The Times*, 31 May 1996). For men, the leniency with which they are often treated reflects and reinforces the condoning of violence against women. For women, the harshness with which some are still treated is a consequence of a law which fails to recognize the effects that continual violence have on women and how difficult it is to get away. The law on provocation and self-defence still needs to be clarified and resources need to be made available to enable women to escape from violent relationships.

Finally, it should not be forgotten that some women retaliate against their attackers in different ways. Britain does not have a Mrs Bobbitt, the American woman renowned for cutting off her husband's penis in 1993 in retaliation for years of violence inflicted on her. However, in 1989 a mother of four poured boiling water over the genitals of Lee Roberts, the man who raped her 5-year-old daughter, and was jailed, along with her husband and son, for 30 months at Exeter Crown Court. The judge, Sir Jonathan Clarke, told her: 'I accept your feelings of anger and justification. I have asked myself if there is any way I could have avoided sending you to prison. I am afraid there is not.' Uncharacteristically, the *Sun* newspaper organized a campaign which led to an early appeal and their release.

CHAPTER 8

Naggers, whores and libbers: provoking men to kill

An meanwhile rest of t'Sutcliffes
spent up their Fleet Street brass
an put their boot in Sonia
'Job's all down to t'lass

'Our Pete were nivver a nutter,
E'd allus a smile on t'face
that Sonia nagged im rotten
till a killed ooors in er place

'Cos that's the rub wi women,
they push us blokes too far
till us can't be eld responsible
for being what we are.

(Blake Morrison, 'The Ballad of the Yorkshire Ripper', 1987: 34;
Sonia is Peter Sutcliffe's wife)

Peter Sutcliffe, the Yorkshire Ripper, who murdered 13 women and at-tempted to murder another seven, had been interviewed nine times by the police before he was fortuitously arrested on 2 January 1981 for having false number plates on his car. Thousands of police had been searching for the so-called Yorkshire Ripper for five years. The question of why he evaded arrest for so long should have been the focus of a formal invest-igation. Yet few enquired as to why the police were so utterly ineffective. The most convincing explanation was that Sutcliffe was simply not what the police expected. They were searching for a maniac, dominated by his mother, a stranger to the area. As it turned out Peter Sutcliffe had been brought up in the area, from an 'ordinary' working-class family. His atti-tudes to women were not so far removed from the woman-hating attitudes prevalent in the community. Even after his arrest much attention has focused on his wife, Sonia, a local teacher. Could she have provoked these horrendous attacks? One senior Ripper squad detective thought exactly this, and apparently said, 'I think when Sutcliffe attacked his 20 victims, he was attacking his wife 20 times in his mind'. The *Daily Mirror* commented, 'Sonia, shy and frail to the world outside, would often become the nagging wife'. Yet Peter's marriage was not the cause of his violence but an attempt to contain it (see Smith, J. 1989: 112–51, for an excellent analysis of why the investigation lasted five years and led to so many unnecessary deaths).

This chapter focuses on the way the defence of provocation in homicide trials serves to perpetuate the condoning of male violence. In rape trials it is often argued that women 'precipitate' the rape by arousing the man's desire and then withdrawing consent. Similar allegations of precipitation are more blatantly embedded in the defence of provocation. Here the assumption is that the woman, usually a wife or lover, drives a man to take temporary leave of his rationality and kill her. My research, conducted at the Central Criminal Court, was partly instigated by a television documentary *No One Speaks for the Dead*, shown in August 1986 produced by L. A. Lever. Men's violence leads not only to the death of women lovers and wives in particular, but also to the death of their male friends and acquaintances. In case after case the most frequent remark recorded by male defendants is 'if I can't have her, no one else can'. The jealous husband kills either the wife or her alleged lover. In some cases the allegations of infidelity are completely unfounded.

The press gives wide coverage to killers like Dennis Nillsen, a homosexual civil servant who strangled to death 16 young men between 1978 and 1983, and Peter Sutcliffe, the Yorkshire Ripper, who murdered 13 women and attempted to murder another seven, and keeps us up to date with every development of the Myra Hindley case (the notorious 'Moors Murderer' who in the 1960s, with Ian Brady, tortured and murdered children on the Yorkshire moors) but it rarely mentions the murderers who are known to the victims. This leads to a conception that the typical murderer is a psychopathic killer. In fact, according to a Home Office analysis, of 2839 murders committed between 1984 and 1988 only 14 per cent of women were killed by strangers (Cowdry 1990).

A jury has to decide between five alternative verdicts in British murder trials, a choice that can be confusing. First, the defendant can be found guilty of murder, which carries a mandatory life sentence. Second, he or she can be found not guilty: the defendant did not do it, or did it accidentally. Third, the defendant can be found not guilty on the grounds of self-defence. Fourth, he or she can be found not guilty of murder but guilty of manslaughter on the grounds of provocation. Last, he or she can be found guilty of only manslaughter on the grounds of diminished responsibility where, according to Section 2 of the Homicide Act (1957), the defendant must be shown to have suffered from an abnormality of mind arising from an injury, a sickness or a developmental problem which substantially impaired her or his responsibility at the time of the killing. Such a diagnosis must be supported by two psychiatrists.

A defence counsel does not necessarily confine himself or herself to arguing only one of these alternatives. If the defendant pleads not guilty to murder (on the grounds, for example, that there is doubt whether in fact the defendant knifed the victim or whether the victim fell on the weapon), the defence counsel can suggest alternative verdicts to the jury: that the defendant acted in self-defence, was provoked or even was not guilty at all. It is often difficult for a defence counsel to present several grounds for defence simultaneously. The complexity of the alternatives is often too much for jurors to contend with, resulting in some bizarre verdicts. For example, in the case of *McDonald* v. *the Crown* (1988) a young woman was charged with the murder of her lover, who had beaten her up in the past. She was heard by two witnesses to say, 'I've knifed him, I've knifed him', and they gave evidence that she held the murder weapon in her hand. She said she saw the defendant coming towards her with a look in his eye that he had had before when he attacked her. But the jury found her not guilty of murder rather than not guilty on the grounds of self-defence (my transcript, Old Bailey, March 1988).

In murder verdicts the judge has no discretion and life imprisonment is mandatory. In manslaughter verdicts, by contrast, the judge has wide discretion. Sentences range from life imprisonment to absolute discharge. Provocation and diminished responsibility have functioned as grounds for commutation of murder to manslaughter, with the result that judges have allowed men who killed their wives or lovers to walk free from court. That this tendency has increased is suggested by the fact that the number of life sentences for murder dropped from 169 in 1979 to 114 in 1984, in spite of an increase in the number of homicides from 546 to 563 during the same period. A study conducted by the Bedford College Legal Research Unit found that manslaughter sentences between 1957 and 1968 were between three and six years (Ashworth 1975: 75–9). Christopher Nuttall, director of Research and Statistics at the Home Office, who analysed 1071 killings of wives by husbands or lovers that took place between 1983 and 1991, found that 62 per cent of men were found guilty of manslaughter, of whom 47 per cent used the defence of diminished responsibility, 32 per cent provocation and 21 per cent no intent to kill. He reported that 73 per cent of the men convicted of manslaughter received a prison sentence, the average sentence being 56 months (around four and a half years). Only 12 per cent of men were given probation or a suspended sentence (Nuttall 1993). These figures do not take into account the fact that a considerable proportion of sentences may well be reduced on appeal and with remission, four years can be reduced to two. Another factor that does not appear to be taken into account is that some sentences are suspended, as I discuss later (see the cases of Bisla Singh and Roy Geech, pp. 172–3) so that in fact the man does not actually serve a sentence unless he reoffends. More recent statistics are not available, but the pattern in the cases cited below is sentences in the region of three to six years (a third of which is remitted with good behaviour).

The defence of provocation

We saw in the last chapter how the law on provocation is defined and what kind of grounds are considered legitimate. Courts have been more willing to excuse a man for killing his wife's lover than a woman for killing her rapist. The man's act, while not always legally condoned, is viewed sympathetically. He is not forgiven, but his motivation is understood by those sitting in judgement upon his act since his conduct conforms to the expectations that a real man would fight to the death to protect his pride and property. A comparison of two cases, Mumtaz Baig, a man who killed his wife, and that of Pamela Megginson, a woman who killed her lover, heard at the Old Bailey in September 1987 illustrates the way the law excuses the man but blames the woman even when the facts suggest greater intentionality on the part of the man. I attended the case of Mumtaz Baig myself and obtained information about the case of Pamela Megginson from press cuttings.

The case of Mumtaz Baig

Mumtaz Baig was charged with murdering his wife Rohila, by strangling her with a piece of rope that he said she used for tying up a rubber plant. This was refuted by Rohila's sister, a witness for the prosecution, who in her evidence said that she had frequently visited and that her sister had used knitting wool to tie up the plant.

They had married in 1980. Mr Baig returned to Pakistan shortly before the birth of their second son in 1982, following what he described as arguments with his in-laws. His pregnant wife had returned to her parents after her husband had beaten her up. He admitted hitting her but described it as 'not hard – I swear I was never violent towards her'. Nonetheless she obtained a transfer of the house to her name and a legal separation. Between 1982 and 1986 his only contact with the family was to send birthday and Christmas cards. It was not until four years later in January 1986 that he returned to England and moved back into the house which was in her name. According to the prosecution, Mrs Mumtaz had not wanted him back and had made it clear that she wanted a divorce. He killed her in December. His defence of provocation rested on his unsupported allegation that she had been unfaithful with a friend of his called Ibrahim. In his evidence he stated that after making love on the day of her

death, he had asked why she looked so happy and she had replied: 'I have
a friendship with Ibrahim. You're doing well but he has a really big thing'.
Ibrahim was called to the witness box and vehemently refuted these allegations. He maintained that he had never been alone with Mrs Baig, let
alone had a sexual relationship with her. The unlikelihood of any woman,
let alone a devout Muslim, making such a comment was not raised nor the
horror with which her family would have reacted to such an allegation. As
Baig's English was poor all his written statements were translated and he
had an interpreter in court. He did, however, use colloquial English idioms
but not quite correctly, as in, 'I was not in my senses', which sounded as if
it might not have been his own phrase. In his evidence, on the other hand,
he also stated explicitly: 'Because she wanted to take away the children.
I intended to kill her.'

The contradiction between these two positions was not taken up. The
defence counsel, in summing up, asked, 'Is there any evidence that he was
anything but a gentle husband and father?' With good reason, he was
confident that the evidence of his violence, his four year absence, his own
admission that he intended to murder his wife and his failure to contribute
anything to the household would be disregarded. The prosecution did comment weakly : 'You've only heard one side of the story. No one knows what
Rohila Baig would have said.' But this did not prevent the jury from finding him not guilty of murder on the grounds of provocation. He was sentenced to six years for manslaughter (my transcript, Old Bailey, September
1987).

The case of Pamela Megginson

Compare this case with the one of Pamela Megginson, aged 66, who in
September 1983 killed her 79-year-old self-made millionaire lover, with
whom she had lived for the past 13 years. He was rendering her homeless by taking another lover. In evidence she said the only thing that had
excited him sexually was hitting her, and although she had not wanted sex
on the night in question, she had agreed to try in order to persuade him
to change his mind. After he hit her she lost control and hit him over the
head with a champagne bottle, which killed him. She pleaded not guilty
of murder but guilty of manslaughter on the grounds of provocation. She
was, however, found guilty of murder and given a mandatory life sentence
(Old Bailey Court Record, 1984).

In both these cases the murder victim was planning to break up the relationship, although in the Baig case it had really ended four years before.
Nonetheless, the jury in the Baig case took the view that the man was
provoked by his wife's desire to continue to live on her own with the
children. The lack of corroboration to his allegations of her infidelity and

the absurdity of his description of their bedtime talk made no difference. Nor indeed did the evidence that he contributed little if anything to the marriage, had been violent in the past, and had admitted that he intended to kill her, lead the jury to reject his plea of provocation. With remission he would have only served three or four years, little redress for a cold blooded, premeditated murder of a defenceless woman.

In the Megginson case, though the evidence appeared to point to an unpremeditated, unintentional and accidental death occurring in the course of sexual sado-masochistic activity initiated by the victim, the jury found the defendant guilty of murder. Neither the context of the actual killing nor the threat of the loss of her home and relationship were regarded as grounds for provocation. The alleged infidelity of a woman, even if uncorroborated, is accepted as grounds for provocation, but the man's infidelity is no grounds. The very wording of the law – 'a reasonable man' – excludes a woman.

In one of the few summaries made of murder trials (occurring between 1957 and 1962) criminologists Terence Morris and Louis Blom-Cooper conclude that 'one factor emerges very clearly from these homicide cases and that is that the area of heterosexual relationships is one exceptionally fraught with potential violence whether within marriage or outside it' (1964: 322). The close relations between love and hate, the intense feelings of possessiveness and passion raised by close relationships are widely accepted. What is, however, less accepted is that possessiveness that leads to violence is almost always male and is widely condoned not merely by the populace but by the law and its enforcement agencies. Criminologists have failed to investigate possessiveness and to question the acceptability of male violence in the privacy of the family.

According to the 1991 Home Office statistics 108 wives/cohabitees and only 13 husbands/cohabitees were recorded as victims of homicides where the chief suspect was their spouse. Studies indicate that femicides are the tip of the iceberg of male violence against women. Female violence however, when it occurs, is often a response to years of battering and mental cruelty.

Review of cases where manslaughter was used by a defence for femicide

In the following cases provocation or diminished responsibility, two of the main grounds for manslaughter, were used as a defence for murder. They illustrate the way the law encourages male possessiveness even to the point of condoning murder. In all the cases which follow the relationship between the defendant and the victim had been under strain or it was alleged that infidelity had occurred. Corroboration for the allegations was not considered necessary.

The case of Gordon Asher

In 1981 Gordon Asher was charged with murdering his wife at a party where he claimed she had danced with another man. He said he had asked her where she had been and she replied 'nowhere'. Calling her a bloody liar, he had grabbed her round the neck and carried her out of the house. According to one of the guests she looked as though she had been knocked cold but it is likely she was already dead. Asher drove six miles to a chalk pit where he buried her body. He was arrested a week later and the body of his late wife was recovered. In court he was portrayed as a model husband and father, whereas his wife was described as a 'two timing flirt'. After leaving court with a six month suspended sentence for manslaughter he said: 'It is marvellous. I am a really happy man', adding that if he married again: 'It would have to be someone very special' (see Lever 1986; Radford and Russell 1992: 253–66).

The case of Peter Wood

Mary Bristow, aged 36, a librarian in Winchester, was of above average intelligence with an IQ said to be 180. She worked in a pub once a week and was an active member of CND. According to her nextdoor neighbour, Bruce Murphy, who was not called to give evidence at the trial, she was a generous, compassionate and respected member of the community. In 1976 she bought a small house and Peter Wood, who was unemployed, moved in as a lodger. They had at one time been lovers. Between 1976 and 1981 Mary asked him to leave a number of times and in 1981 eventually forcibly moved him out. He continued to pester her. Two weeks before her murder he broke into the house and bored holes in her bedroom ceiling and had taken to spying on her from the loft. Her friends advised her to go to the police, but she said that he needed a doctor, not the police. Ten days before her death the ground floor was gutted by fire. The evidence in fact all pointed to premeditated murder; Mary was clubbed to death with a meat tenderizer, smothered with a pillow and strangled. Wood pleaded both provocation and diminished responsibility.

Psychiatrists appearing for the prosecution and defence were in almost total accord about Wood's state of mind before the murder. He was depressed, they agreed, though the only evidence for this diagnosis was his own statement that he had been drinking heavily and was currently out of work. Interviewed on the Thames television programme *No one Speaks for the Dead* (Lever 1986), Wood talked of losing Mary's 'emotional support': 'I had become so emotionally dependent, I was in danger of collapsing'. The wheeling in of psychiatric evidence on spurious grounds is a common feature of murder trials and the success of pleas of diminished responsibility rest primarily on the skill of the defence counsel to muster psychiatric support. The trial lasted four days. The judge, in summing up, placed great weight on what he referred to as Mary's unconventional lifestyle and her unorthodox pattern of living:

> It may be that the conventions which surround sex however much some people may think them old hat are there to prevent people from burning themselves. You may think it rather difficult to imagine any set up more plainly calculated to lead to precisely the kind of disaster which followed. Talk about playing with fire.

There was no evidence to suggest that Mary was either irresponsible or promiscuous so this is an extraordinary statement for the judge to make. He appears to regard it the duty of any woman who has sex with a man to be responsible for him for the rest of his life! In this case there is no evidence that Mary was even having another affair. This did not stop the judge from launching into a sermon:

> Mary Bristow was a rebel from her middle-class background. She was unorthodox in her relationships. The cleverest people are not always very wise. Those who indulge in sexual relationships should realize that sex is one of the deepest and most powerful of human motivations. If you are playing with sex, you are playing with fire.

Such statements reflect the subtle condoning of the use of violence in sexual relationships, where the responsibility for violence is subtly shifted onto her, even in the event of her death (see Lever 1986; Radford and Russell 1992).

The case of Stephen Midlane

In January 1989 Stephen Midlane, aged 30, was charged with strangling and cutting up his wife Sandra, aged 23, by whom he had two children. Officers toiled for weeks looking for her remains on an Essex rubbish tip and found everything except one leg. Stephen Midlane was not even charged with murder. The Crown Prosecution Service accepted his plea of guilty to manslaughter of Sandra and attempted murder of the couple's two sons, aged 4 and 5. Judge Neil Denison QC sentenced him to five years (which with full remission, amounts to only three).

In mitigation, the defence claimed that Sandra had been unfaithful and that he had attacked her in the middle of an argument over her infidelity, accidentally hitting the vagal nerve on her neck. The manslaughter plea ensured a number of critical statements made to detectives by friends and family were never put to the judge. These statements outlined the breakdown of the marriage due to mutual incompatibility, the increasing amount of violence used by Midlane against Sandra and her hospital treatment for broken bones at the Charing Cross Hospital, their separation and her determination to divorce, his threats of further violence – in all, a picture indicating premeditation for the attack, a picture very different from that given by the defence. Debby Jennings, aged 24, and Sandra's closest friend when interviewed by Terry Kirkby of the *Independent* (20 January 1989) said:

> I told police how she was scared that Stephen was going to kill her. He had begun to beat her up in the last few months, and had started breaking into her flat late at night and demanding to stay. She told me that he had once tried to strangle her and had once tied her up. Two weeks before he killed Sandra, he hit her so badly her jaw fractured. That was how she was identified from her remains on the tip.

The case of Peter Hogg

In March 1985 (after her body had been discovered) Peter Hogg was charged with having murdered his wife in 1976 and disposing of her body in the Lake District. His case was given wide coverage in the press. His past record as a war hero was given prominence as indeed was his murdered wife's alleged promiscuity. *The Times* (9 March 1985) reported her 'to have a reputation for promiscuity which stretched back to her teenage years although her marriage in 1963 appeared to have a calming effect. It was not long before she began to show an interest in the friends of her husband'. It was not suggested that they might also have shown an interest in her. When her husband, an airline pilot, was abroad flying she was said to spend hours on the phone running up bills which he had to pay. In October 1976 Mrs Hogg went for a week's holiday with her lover, Mr Graham Ryan, a banker whom she had been seeing since 1973. When she returned Hogg said: 'I just lost control and grabbed her throat with both hands and squeezed until she stopped screaming.'

During the night he dragged the body outside, put it in the boot of the car, and put into action an intricate plan to dispose of the body. He rang the head of the public school where his son was a pupil and drove to the school saying he was spending the night there. Instead he drove with a rubber dinghy to the Lake District, dumped the body using a concrete bar to weight it, and then drove back to Taunton. He spread the story that his wife had walked out, reported her as missing to the police and filed for a divorce, which was granted in October 1977. Hogg's derisory 15 months in prison was justified on the basis of his wife's alleged infidelity. On his release in June 1986 Hogg said: 'Locking me up didn't achieve a thing. What had happened had happened. Nothing could put the clock back. Nothing could bring my wife back.'

The case of Nicholas Boyce

In the Nicholas Boyce case at the Old Bailey, tried in October 1985, murder was commuted to manslaughter through a combination of arguments involving provocation and unintended consequences. He was tried for the murder of his wife, Christabel, by head banging and strangulation. He had dismembered her body in the bath, cooked parts of it to disguise them and dumped the pieces in plastic bags. By a unanimous verdict, he was acquitted of murder and found guilty of manslaughter on the grounds of provocation. Although he was sentenced to six years, in February 1989 he was released on parole – having served little more than four years of his sentence.

Boyce had been a student for six years at the London School of Economics and Christabel had been the sole breadwinner for two years when her husband's postgraduate grant had finally run out. She had worked as a full time senior social worker at the London Hospital as well as taking the main responsibility for looking after the couple's two children. At the time of her death, she had decided to seek a divorce.

The jury apparently accepted that Boyce had been the subject of, to quote his defence counsel, 'a non-stop form of humiliation and degradation which drained every bit of self-respect from a grown man. He used to sneak home terrified of his life'. The defence counsel continued that Boyce had been subjected to a regime of 'rules' by his wife that had included no sexual relations; he was not even allowed in the marital bed, irrespective of whether or not his wife was there at the time. He could not even take a bath at home. Add to this the constant abuse and accusations allegedly screamed at Boyce by his wife, and is it surprising that 'he finally broke down in circumstances in which an ordinary man might also have done' (judge's summing up)?

Two important assumptions underlie this statement: first, there are limits to the degree of 'nagging' that a man can take and murder is a reasonable response to this behaviour – rather than walking out or perhaps listening to the reasons why a woman is 'nagging'; and second, that the ordinary man cannot be expected to put up with insubordination on the part of a wife, particularly if it involves the withdrawal of marital relations. The fact that Christabel wanted to leave after years of an unsatisfactory marriage is not considered relevant by the recorder, who in his judgement said:

> I will deal with you on the basis that you were provoked. You lost your self-control, and that a man of reasonable self-control might have been similarly provoked and might have done what you did. Not only did you kill her but you came to your senses and took meticulous steps to ensure her death would never be discovered. You got rid of her body, you cleaned up the flat the best you could, you cut her up and boiled her skin and bones. You bagged up the pieces and over the next two days, disposed of her body. Later, to your credit, you gave yourself up.

The judge expresses the opinion that 'a man of reasonable self-control could calmly cut up his wife'. One would have expected such evidence to be brought forward to show Boyce's insanity and lack of responsibility for his action. Instead, it is used as evidence of his sanity and his wife's provocation. As the defence counsel, Mr Michael Wolkind, put it: 'Boyce took the job as a cleaner to satisfy his nagging wife's demands'. In actual fact, at the age of 37 Boyce had never had a steady job. Mr Woldkind went on: 'She constantly bullied him and remorselessly ground him down until he finally snapped and strangled her with an electric flex. What he wanted, all he ever wanted was some peace and time to spend with his children' (court transcript).

The whole trial revolved round the assumed character of the victim, which opened the door to all sorts of unverifiable allegations. Journalist Maureen Cleave, writing in the *London Standard* after the trial, reported that Christabel had moved to Lavenham with the two children but had agreed to spend Christmas with her husband. She had written to her aunt, however, saying she feared Boyce was planning to kill her. She reported that two close friends of Christabel, who had asked to give evidence at the Old Bailey but were never called, had a different story:

> They would have told the court how worried they had been about Christabel, how they had begged her to spend Christmas with them, how their telephone conversations would abruptly end when apparently Nicholas came into the room; how she was frightened; how she had brought her few possessions to them in a box for safe keeping because he had begun to break things that were special to her, beginning with her watch; how he had been reading books about criminal law.
> (Smith, J. 1989: 5)

The case of Leslie Taylor

Leslie Taylor appeared at Aylesbury Crown Court in May 1987, charged with knifing his wife to death after he discovered she had been kissing another man at a wedding reception. He had spent the night drinking and then went to his mother-in-law's in Islington, where she had gone, and stabbed his wife eight times in front of their 12-year-old son. He claimed his wife had been unfaithful to him during the previous two years of their 16 year marriage. He said he 'felt totally humiliated at what she had done in front of my family' and 'could not sleep' so after phoning his wife to say he was coming, he took a knife round to the house. Normally this would imply intention, but a manslaughter verdict ensued, on the grounds of provocation, with a six year sentence.

The case of Thomas Corlett

In February 1992 at Southwark Crown Court Thomas Corlett, a higher executive officer at the Department of Employment, was charged with killing his wife to whom he had been married for 25 years. It was reported that he liked to have his mustard on one side of his plate and the newspaper on the other, but his wife had moved them around. According to the *Daily Mirror* report (9 July 1987: 7) Corlett told the police: 'I removed the tube of mustard, and I was about to open the paper to the crossword page when my wife picked up the mustard and put it heavily down where it was before. She said to me 'That's where I want it and that's where I will put it'. He had leapt to his feet and strangled her. Afterwards he had allegedly told the police that it was 'her fault'.

At his trial where he was charged with murder, in mitigation Corlett testified that he did most of the housework because his wife was a bad housekeeper. He complained that after cutting his toenails she would leave clippings on the carpet and after doing embroidery leave threads on the sofa. His defence counsel called two psychologists who supported the claim that he had suffered from diminished responsibility when he strangled her. Their reports said that he suffered from 'obsessionality' – preferring rigid routines and was easily upset by minor changes. Miss Margaret Hilton, one of the psychologists, said that pent-up rage was a common cause of domestic violence and testified that Corlett had displayed 'obsessional traits akin to those of an excessively proud housewife' (*The Times*, 10 July 1987). Judge Gerald Butler, QC, described him as 'a hardworking, conscientious man, normally of placid disposition who acted wholly out of character. He was acquitted of murder and sentenced to three years for manslaughter on the grounds of diminished responsibility.

Can women successfully plead self-defence?

It is the acceptability of male violence as a response to any form of insubordination from the woman which is at the core of the acceptance of the plea of provocation. When a woman is attacked by a man, on the other hand, and attacks him back, the argument of provocation is only successful in circumstances where the accused entertains a reasonable, or generally speaking, any kind of belief that her life is in danger. In such circumstances self-defence would be a more reasonable defence, but it is rarely successful. Bel Mooney (1981), in an article in the *The Times* entitled 'Has the woman the right to fight back?', reports the following case of *R. v. Maguire*, heard before Judge Stanley Price at York Crown Court on 17 July 1981, as follows:

> On the night in question, the victim started to walk home after securing her pony and missing the last bus. The accused, aged 24, was being driven home when he saw her walking along a lane. After being dropped off at home, he ran back over one mile and confronted the girl, pretending to be a policeman. He dragged her into a field and

told her he was going to kill her. The 'victim' although clearly terrified, managed to pull out a small sheath knife which she used to cut open bales of hay and 'stuck it into the defendant's neck'. The jury found him guilty of threatening to kill her. The judge, who felt that the defendant had already been punished enough, in passing a twelve month suspended prison sentence remarked: 'This lady inflicted a very considerable punishment on you'.

The judge, in other words, allowed a man guilty of an appalling attack – of attempted murder – to go free because his victim protected herself.

Two trials I attended provided some grounds for optimism that provocation and self-defence at least in some circumstances are becoming more acceptable as defences for women charged with murder.

The case of Janet Clugstone

The case of Janet Clugstone in September 1987 was described as 'a beacon of hope for victims of rape' (*The Guardian*, 6 October 1987) when she was found not guilty of murdering her rapist, Stephen Cophen, on the grounds that she had acted in self-defence. The case was heard by a judge, now deceased, known to be progressive, Judge John Hazan. The facts of the case were as follows.

In October 1986 Mrs Clugstone, aged 38, met Stephen Cophen, aged 24, on her way to a discotheque. The night ended at 2 a.m. in a friend's flat where the electricity had been disconnected; she alleged that she had been forced to enter it and that he raped and buggered her repeatedly. Mrs Clugstone could not cry out because her larynx had been removed owing to cancer. She found an open penknife on the floor and stabbed Cophen with one wound that killed him. She then gave herself up to the police. Her account was supported by medical and forensic evidence and by a woman police constable, who described it as the worst case of sexual abuse and degradation she had ever encountered. The transcripts of the trial reveal several significant differences from cases in which the defendants are male.

First, in summing up Judge Hazan bent over backwards to emphasize that 'the issue is not to blacken the character of a man who isn't here to speak for himself'. He documented corroboration for the allegations with great care, showing how they were supported by witnesses, evidence of previous criminal offences, and medical and forensic evidence.

Second, the question of whether Janet Clugstone acted in self-defence or for revenge rested on whether or not Cophen had withdrawn his penis at the time of the attack rather than on whether repeated rape was a terrifying, life-threatening experience. To quote Judge Hazan's directions to the jury:

> The question is did she kill him after he'd withdrawn, kill him in reasonable self-defence or stop him raping and assaulting her? In lawful

self-defence you should acquit. If she's not telling the truth – why isn't she? Is she a lady killing a young man in circumstances she's unwilling to reveal after he's withdrawn in revenge for the rape? That is not a lawful killing. She should then be found guilty of murder – an unprovoked and unlawful killing with intent to cause death or serious injury.

(my transcript, 28 September 1987)

It is penetration that is all-important in assessing her motivation – not whether she was terrified for her life, humiliated and pushed 'beyond her senses' but simply whether or not she killed him when he was penetrating her. This absurd distinction obscures what is the reality of rape as experienced by the victim.

Third, much of the trial was concerned with assessing whether or not Janet Clugstone was a 'decent woman'. In the middle of the most sensitive cross-examination about the details of the rape, she was asked: 'Have you had sex with other West Indians?'

In a rape trial this question could have been disallowed on the grounds that questions relating to the past sexual history of the victim can only be raised at the discretion of the judge (see section 2 of the Sexual Offences (Amendment) Act of 1976). The prosecution counsel should certainly have objected to the following question, too. Janet Clugstone was asked by the defence: 'Do you get on well with West Indians and other races on the council estate where you live?' Judge Hazan ended by warning that his verdict should not be seen as a charter for victims of serious crimes to kill their attackers.

The case of Trevor Virgo

The importance of contesting irrelevant probes into the reputations of women subjected to violence emerges graphically from the testimony of the main prosecution witness Julia Wolton in the case of Trevor Virgo, whose attack on her resulted in the miscarriage and death of her unborn child. After having to recount the appalling detail of Virgo's attack on her – he forced her to undress in the snow near a motorway – Julia Wolton was subjected to the following cross-examination by the defence counsel:

DC: You're quite a lot older than the defendant. You have had wider experience than him?
JW: Yes.
DC: Wider sexual experience than him?
JW: Is this relevant?
Judge: Very good question.
JW: I think you are trying to stereotype me.

(transcript, 21 September 1987)

Julia Wolton was perfectly right; the defence was trying to stereotype her. This is the most common ploy that is used to discredit women subjected to male violence. Evidence that this ploy is common practice not only in England but elsewhere comes from an Australian study of women who had killed cohabitees or husbands. In all but three cases the woman had been assaulted by the man in the past, in some cases beaten up over a period of 20 years. Thirteen out of 16 women interviewed said they had killed their husbands or cohabitees to protect themselves from physical assault. In court the image of the women presented was of a cold-blooded and premeditating murderer rather than a woman provoked beyond endurance by a man's violence. Research into battered women indicates, on the other hand, that women who have lived for years in a battering relationship reach a point where they reasonably believe that if they do not kill their husbands they will be killed. Bacon and Lansdowne (1982: 97) concluded:

> The images of women as victims, neurotics and provocateurs, and the ideology of privacy which surrounds the institutions of sexuality and the family, play a role in perpetuating the domination and violence experienced by these women. The same ideologies and myths pervade the criminal justice system and prevented the actual circumstances of these homicides emerging in the court process which judge and sentenced them.

Conclusion

This study of the use of partial defences of provocation or diminished responsibility shows that, in cases where wives are on trial for the murder of their husbands, they are treated differently from husbands murdering their wives or children. It is almost permissible and by definition 'reasonable' for a husband to kill his wife (or even his children) for insubordination. Similarly, a man is more readily excused for killing his wife's lover than a woman for killing her rapist after an attack.

The acts of men and women are subject to a different set of legal expectations and standards. As we have seen, in most cases where provocation is alleged by men it is the character of the victim, if a woman, rather than the defendant's that is up for trial. When the victim is a man, allegations about his sexual infidelity would just not be taken seriously, and it is doubtful whether they would even be raised. Where the victim is a woman, her reputation is regarded as crucial to the questions of the defendant's guilt. If infidelity is alleged, let alone proved, provocation is usually allowed. As a friend watching the Boyce trial commented, 'Christabel was on trial, not Nick'. Since the victim is not there to tell her side, the defendant can give an account that is unchallengeable.

In theory, the prosecution counsel can call witnesses to counter the defence, but in practice this is rarely done. Part of the problem lies in the assumption that the Crown counsel's role is one of impartiality and that it should not be concerned with defending the victim. In the US, Canada, and Australia the prosecution insists that evidence in rebuttal should be brought when allegations about a murdered victim are made. The main distinction between murder and manslaughter revolves around whether the killing is premeditated or not. 'Malice aforethought' or intention to kill, is murder. If someone kills by accident or through negligence, or is provoked, then it is manslaughter. However, we have seen that there was clear evidence in a number of cases cited above that the murder was planned and therefore intentional. In practice, if allegations about the woman victim are accepted, evidence of prior intention is disregarded. In both the Baig and the Boyce cases there was evidence of prior intention. However, in cases of women who kill, any evidence of prior intention precludes arguing self-defence.

Case studies allow us to make a detailed investigation of empirical reality. We then can see how the court ascribes specific roles to men and women that are used as evidence of whether the crime is 'reasonable'. The defence of provocation reflects the defendant's relationship to the social world. As Mary Eaton (1983: 387) states: 'Should this relationship follow an acceptable pattern it will be used to show that the defendant is not really a criminal since the social identity in question is basically conformist. Criminal activity will be presented as a temporary aberration.' If the victim's behaviour is considered unconventional, on the other hand, this is presented as reacting to intolerable pressure. The victim is then presented as the real culprit in having pushed the man to violence. Sexist concepts about the nature of men and women's roles in the family, and about the acceptability of male violence as a reaction to any behaviour deemed to be insubordinate to male authority, legitimize the violence the laws purport to protect women from.

The problem is not so much with the individual behaviour of judges as with the system, which serves to entitle men to behave violently in close relationships. During the last few years women killers of men who had subjected them to persistent violence have successfully pleaded cumulative provocation, although the defence may not be allowed if a woman is seen to be acting in revenge. In many of these cases self-defence would seem to be the more relevant plea, which if successful would result in a not guilty verdict rather than a conviction for manslaughter.

On the other hand, anger is discounted as an acceptable response to frustration on the part of a woman. In law it does not appear that a reasonable woman can be driven beyond her senses and remain reasonable unless she is suffering from premenstrual tension (PMT). This fits in with the idea that non-conformity in women is due to biological imbalance rather than rational choice.

In line with the idea of women offenders as neurotics dominated by their ovaries or as Katherine Dalton (1989) put it, 'at the mercy of their raging hormones', the only foolproof mitigating circumstances that have been used by women convicted of murder relate to postnatal depression and premenstrual tension, epitomizing the tendency to treat female conforming behaviour as healthy and non-conforming behaviour as sick or mad. In 1981, for example, Mrs Kristina English killed her lover by driving her car at him after he had told her that he was going out with another woman. She claimed that something had snapped when he had made a V-sign at her. Medical and psychiatric evidence diagnosed her as suffering from PMT on the basis of PMT pointers: following pregnancy she had suffered from postnatal depression; she had been sterilized; and she had not eaten for some hours before the attack. It is alleged that failure to eat in PMT sufferers produces hypoglycaemia, which causes a predisposition to aggressive uncontrollable behaviour. Her plea to diminished responsibility was accepted. She was banned from driving for a year and given a one year conditional discharge (see Luckhaus 1986). As Bel Mooney argued:

> The courts did not give her a reduced sentence because her boyfriend was a cad ... she was conditionally discharged because she convinced the court that PMT had led to diminished responsibility – even though she had threatened to run the boyfriend over earlier in the day, which might have been taken as evidence of premeditation.
>
> (*The Times*, 18 July 1981)

When women express anger at men, men often accuse them of 'being emotional' so denying the reasons for their anger.

More recently in March 1987 Miss Linda Hewett, aged 31, walked free out of the Old Bailey after being convicted of attempted murder. The judge had given her three years' probation for stabbing her sleeping lover, with whom she had become reconciled after a short separation. Mr Justice Leonard's reasons for the sentence were that Hewlett had become depressed after the birth of her twins, and that she had become irritated by her lover's lack of interest in her obstetric complications. 'I could not face another day of him saying, "Have you done the vacuuming, have you dusted?" ' The judge accepted that she was suffering from postnatal depression heightened by PMT (*Today*, 28 February 1987).

Third, in April 1988 Anna Reynolds, a 19-year-old girl who had killed her 61-year-old mother with a hammer and had been found guilty of murder and sentenced to youth custody at Northampton Crown Court, won her appeal on the grounds that PMT and postnatal depression had impaired her sense of responsibility. The Court of Appeal judges substituted a verdict of manslaughter through diminished responsibility and put her on probation for two years with a condition that she seek psychiatric treatment (see Benn 1993: 165).

A woman is therefore deemed either to be suffering from diminished responsibility – which means she may be confined, usually for an indefinite period to a mental hospital – or to be suffering from PMT, or to be acting in revenge and to be guilty of murder. This implies that, unlike a man, she cannot be 'provoked' into violence and remain a reasonable person in the way a man can by asserting that he was acting 'beyond his senses' but has now returned to his senses. Clearly the whole basis for a provocation defence is entirely spurious and should be abolished.

The reluctance of the judiciary adequately to protect women is part of the general condoning of male violence in marriage. As far back as 1962 one judge commented on the danger of husbands using provocation too often as mitigation. Justice Thesiger at the Essex Assizes, in finding Kenneth Burrell not guilty of murder but guilty of manslaughter on the grounds of provocation by his wife, who was in bed with a lover, commented:

> The accused undoubtedly had very severe provocation but on the other hand the large number of divorces do indicate that this sort of situation, though not quite in such a dramatic form, is apt to arise and it would be a terrible thing if all people who commit misconduct while their husbands are away were subjected to a violent attack like this.
>
> (Morris and Blom-Cooper 1964: 155)

Such reservations are rare and provocation is often accepted far too readily without any evidence that the woman has even been unfaithful.

Criminologists have been no more enlightened than the judiciary, at least in the past. The summary chapter of the main textbook on homicide cases, *A Calendar of Murder* (Morris and Blom-Cooper 1964: 322), states:

> Few people, it might be argued, die simply because they have been careless, promiscuous, avaricious, or vain and while it is relatively easy to say that a man has lost his belongings through his own fault, it is much more difficult to say that a man has lost his life through his own fault. For one of the most permanent qualities attributed to the victims of murder is that of innocence. Even a cursory reading of the thumbnail sketches of homicide printed in this book will show that this is often misplaced generosity, for some of the victims might well have been capable of killing either by provocation in words or deeds, or by incessant nagging, that they clearly precipitated their own death.

Nagging, according to these criminologists, is a reasonable provocation to murder. In other words, women have only themselves to blame for male violence. Prostitutes, and even young girls, are also 'asking for it' as they suggest on the next page:

While understandably, little sympathy attaches in the public mind to the prostitute victim of homicide, the same is not true of other victims of sexual murders particularly when they are young ... While little girls cannot be classed directly with adult prostitutes by no means all of them are lacking in sexual curiosity ... It is invariably a drive they dimly perceive but one which may draw them into situations where they may become victims of crime.

(Morris and Blom-Cooper 1964: 323)

These statements cannot be regarded as objective. Male lawyers and criminologists are unaware of the degree to which they take a male stance and fail to grasp the viewpoint of the woman, even in the face of her death or rape, which all on the face of it regard with horror. In regard to the issue of the marital rape exclusion, we can recall the words of Professor Glanville Williams, cited in Chapter 6 (p. 119). He argued: 'A charge of rape is too powerful ... a weapon to put into the wife's hands' (*The Times*, 21 February 1991). By the same token presumably a charge of murder is too strong a weapon to inflict on a man who has killed his wife.

The cases of Joseph McGrail, Bisla Singh and Roy Geech

During the five years since this was written, men have continued to be treated with unwarranted sympathy by judges in spite of having far less excuse for the violence they have inflicted on their wives than the women mentioned above who have suffered such terrible violence themselves. Men who kill their wives are still sometimes not only given their freedom but are showered with sympathy by judges. The following three cases indicate that killing a wife is treated with blatant leniency by many judges and such judgements are accepted with complacency by the press and wider society.

In the first case, it was argued that his wife's drinking drove Joseph McGrail to murder, a mere two days after Sara Thornton's failed appeal in 1991. The court heard that on 27 February 1990 McGrail said that on returning home and finding his wife drunk and demanding more to drink, he had kicked her to death. She died from internal bleeding. Malcolm Morse, for the prosecution, said 'It was a sudden temporary loss of control'. Mr Justice Popplewell, in awarding a mere two year suspended sentence, said of the victim, 'This lady would have tried the patience of a saint' (*Independent*, 1 August 1991).

For Bisla Singh, it was his wife's 'nagging' which had led him to kill her – 'to shut her up'. According to the defendant, the nagging consisted of a two hour stream of abuse which he had first tried to stem by throttling his wife with his bare hands. He had then strangled her with a cord. He told police, 'I didn't mean to hurt her – I just wanted to shut her up'. The court heard that Mrs Singh shouted and swore at her husband. Judge Denison said:

> You have suffered through no fault of your own a terrible existence for a very long time. You bore it better probably than most people would have done until, finally, your self-control snapped and you did what you always admitted doing. I do not see that sending you to prison is going to do you any good.

His plea of manslaughter by provocation was accepted and he received an 18 month sentence suspended for a year (see *The Times*, 30 January 1992).

In the third case, the grounds for the defence of diminished responsibility was an alleged affair. On 23 February 1994 Roy Geech, aged 58, walked free from the court after being found guilty of manslaughter of his wife of 30 years. The court heard that he had stabbed his wife 23 times with a kitchen knife after apparently discovering that she was having an affair. David Poole, QC, defending, described Mr Geech as a 'man of gentleness'! Geech walked free from the court when the Manchester Recorder, Judge Rhys Davies, QC, gave him a two year suspended prison sentence and told him 'Your mind was so affected that your responsibility for what you did was very considerably diminished. You have not only been a man of good character but you are also a good man' (*The Guardian*, 22 February 1994). For a judge to describe a man who has murdered his wife for whatever reason as good is surely symptomatic of patriarchal justice. It would be inconceivable for a woman who had killed her husband to be described as good.

An anomaly criticized in the following terms by Glanville Williams, Professor of Law, is the way that judges justify their leniency on the grounds that prison would not benefit the perpetrators:

> A critic might say that prison sentences are rarely given or expected to do the offender good, otherwise than by deterring him from repeating the offence, of which there was no risk in this case, the source of the provocation being dead. What a prison sentence might have done would have been to reaffirm the principle that husbands cannot strangle their scolding wives (however intolerable their wives may be) without expecting a prison sentence for it.
>
> (Williams 1992: 381)

This is the heart of the issue. The leniency with which male violence is treated reinforces the condoning of violence against women and is an important factor in maintaining patriarchal power over women. Judges are allowing men to walk free after murdering their wives, who are often desperate to get away from them. They do not ask defendants why they do not leave or seek help for marital disharmony rather than kill, but instead extend sympathy to them. Violence is seen as a legitimate way to behave, even when it results in the death of over two wives a week (around 40 per cent of women killed by men are killed by husbands, cohabitees or lovers or have had such a relationship in the past). Domestic violence accounts for 25 per cent of recorded crime in Britain (see Labour Party 1995) and leads to untold suffering of women and children and, indeed, of men who are relatives of the deceased.

CHAPTER 9

In search of gender justice: sexual assault and the criminal justice system

(with Jeanne Gregory)

Within the feminist movement, there is profound scepticism about the value of research into the workings of state institutions, particularly the legal system. When feminists engage with the law, it is argued, they invariably concede too much; the rules of engagement are drawn in a way that contains the feminist challenge while reaffirming the power of law (Smart 1989). It is not difficult to find examples in the history of feminist campaigns which support this position, documenting the disillusionment of feminist activists who have abandoned attempts to reform the legal system and instead promote their objectives by means of non-legal strategies.

Yet in view of the complex and contradictory ways in which the legal system operates, there is room for a variety of approaches to reform, which are not necessarily mutually exclusive, nor in conflict. The use of legal and non-legal strategies in combination constitutes a safeguard against being 'co-opted' by the law. To abandon legal strategies altogether would be no solution at all; rather, it would be to concede defeat, leaving the law unchallenged, our silence taken to imply that we had no criticisms to make. In developing such a critique, it is important to go beyond an analysis of legal discourse, in order to understand the law in action and its impact on women (Dahl 1987). Only then can we avoid the trap of accepting changes to the legal system which deliver the appearances but not the reality of reform.

In practice, feminist researchers and activists across the world have directed a barrage of criticisms at the failure of the law to deliver justice to women who have been sexually assaulted. They have challenged the dominant discourse that regards rape as an expression of sexual desire, arguing instead that it is an expression of sexual power intended to humiliate. This is confirmed by the way in which rape becomes a weapon of war, used with cruel effect to demoralize an enemy by inflicting permanent physical and psychological wounds on the female members of the 'enemy' community (Brownmiller 1976). Yet in non-war situations the typical rape trial is conducted on the basis of apportioning blame and it is the character and behaviour of the woman that is placed under the severest scrutiny. Researching the law in action reveals that for many women the trial procedures are almost as traumatic as the initial attack; they describe the experience as a second rape. The outcome of this ordeal is that in two-thirds of the cases that reach court the man is acquitted and his behaviour thereby condoned.

In attempting to develop a feminist politics from such an analysis, the dilemma is the perennial one so often encountered by feminists: given that it is not possible to stage a revolution and implement the feminist agenda in toto, what piecemeal reforms will achieve at least marginal improvements for some women and can this be achieved in a way which leaves us free to work for the longer term agenda?

In some situations, feminists have been able to enter into a dialogue with sympathetic governments while lacking a power base from which to ensure that their agenda is fully implemented and not jettisoned. For example, feminists working for Women's Aid in the 1970s were able to play a major role in the drafting of the Domestic Violence Act (1975). They were not able to prevent the restrictive judicial interpretation of its key provisions, combined with an initial unwillingness on the part of the police to play their role fully. Nor have they been able to stop the subsequent cutback in resources for Women's Aid with the steady erosion of any political will to make the law work effectively (see Edwards 1989).

A more promising scenario occurs when feminists are able to create a power base inside state institutions, developing a 'femocracy', i.e. a bureaucracy with a feminist agenda. The question then becomes how to move forward without selling out and how to retain the links with grass-roots feminist movements. The severing of these links can lead the femocrats to compromise on important matters of principle, believing that they are acting in the best interests of the women although they have ceased knowing what these interests are (Watson 1990). In Canada, the presence of feminists in high places has had a beneficial impact in a number of areas of the law. Yet the failure of the legislators to accept that men and women have very different notions of consent meant that the new sexual assault law passed in 1983 continued to endorse the right of men to define women's sexuality (Los 1990). In the absence of a successful challenge to this male prerogative, the impact of the legal reforms was limited.

Campaigning from the margins in the hostile political climate of the 1990s, there are obstacles to having any voice at all. The first task is to break through the official rhetoric, which unreservedly condemns acts of sexual violence, by demonstrating the extent to which the current legislation is failing to bring the perpetrators of such acts to justice. The maximum penalty for rape or attempted rape is life imprisonment and for serious sexual assault, 10 years (Sexual Offences (Amendment) Act 1985).

The availability of such harsh penalties provides the illusion that the state has taken appropriate action to control rapists, although in practice the maximum penalties are almost never used. This illusion is compounded by a deeply rooted complacency emanating from the judiciary, conveying the belief that the system delivers justice to the small number of women deemed worthy of protection at the same time as protecting men from the hordes of women who make false allegations. The occasional expression of public outrage when the media report a particularly lenient sentence or an offensive and insensitive judicial comment is greeted with expressions of pained surprise and has no lasting impact on subsequent cases.

If the judges seem impervious to criticism, a chink has appeared in the armour of the criminal justice system, at a point more responsive to public pressure than the judiciary. The police service, in adopting new policies and practices in its treatment of women reporting domestic violence, rape and sexual assault broke ranks with the dominant discourse, producing tensions within the institutions of the state and opening up the possibility of change. It was the appearance of this ideological fracture and the potential it provided for creating new alliances that provided the inspiration for our research. The timing of the project also enabled us to assess the impact of the formation of the Crown Prosecution Service (CPS), a major new state institution, established in 1985 to take over from the police the task of prosecuting offenders.

Devising the research plan

Our interest in researching rape and sexual assault arose from the disturbing findings of previous research, including our own earlier involvement in this area. Our concern was triggered by evidence of extremely high rates of attrition in cases of rape and sexual assault; at each stage of the criminal justice process, cases were falling away in large numbers, which meant that only a tiny proportion of cases reported to the police were resulting in a conviction. As the vast majority of women who have been sexually assaulted do not even take the initial step of reporting to the police, those who do report are merely the tip of the iceberg and yet this tip is further decimated as the criminal justice system runs its course. It appeared to us that this evidence stood in sharp contrast to the rhetoric of the politicians and of the media, who gave the impression that more women were coming forward to report sexual attacks and that more men were being convicted and receiving their 'just deserts' in the shape of longer sentences. Under these influences, the tide of public opinion was beginning to turn, caught up in the quite legitimate concerns precipitated by a number of well-publicized cases of miscarriages of justice, mostly occurring in another area of the criminal law altogether. The old myth that allegations of rape may be very easy to make and very difficult to refute reasserted itself in the popularity stakes.

There was indeed some statistical evidence that more women were reporting rape and sexual assault, either because of an actual increase in the incidence of this crime, or because they had been encouraged to expect a more sympathetic reception at the hands of the police. A documentary television programme about the Thames Valley police transmitted in 1982 (BBC Police Series 1982; see also Dunhill 1989) had drawn attention to the harsh treatment meted out to women complaining of sexual assault and this, together with a report on Violence against Women published by the Women's National Commission (WNC 1985) had provided the impetus for a fundamental shift in the way that complaints were handled.

Our research plan was developed on the basis of three major objectives: first, to investigate the impact of the innovations in police practices on women reporting sexual offences, to see whether they were satisfied with the way their complaints had been handled; second, to take a new look at the rates of attrition (the process by which cases are dropped) to see whether these had declined as a result of the new policies; third, to assess the role of the CPS in terms of its impact on service delivery and attrition rates. In order to accomplish these objectives, we required access to police records and we also needed to interview complainants, police officers and other professional people working in this area (see Lees and Gregory 1993; Gregory and Lees 1996).

Gaining access to state institutions

There is very little research on the workings of the legal system in the area of violence against women. There are two main obstacles: gaining access to records, court officials and courts and obtaining funding for the research. Gaining access requires time, patience and energy. Officials employ a variety of delaying tactics, in the hope that researchers will give up and go away.

When we first approached local police stations, we were fortunate enough to be put in contact with a woman deputy chief superintendent who was extremely supportive. We also had to clear the research with Scotland Yard and this proved to be more difficult. By the time this period had elapsed, the deputy chief superintendent was on sick leave and a new chief superintendent had been appointed; he felt unable to grant us the access to police records which we believed we had already negotiated. After several more months of negotiation and a number of intimidating interviews, a compromise was agreed. The police were anxious that they should not be required to shoulder the blame for any shortcomings in the system alone and we were able to assure them that we were interested in examining multiagency responses to the problem of sexual assault. An agreement to that effect was signed by all parties. It was also agreed that two women police officers would be seconded to obtain information from the police records according to our instructions.

We had certain reservations about this arrangement, as we would have no way of telling whether data were being withheld for some reason, perhaps in order to present the police in a more favourable light. In the event, however, because of the commitment and enthusiasm of the policewomen who were seconded to this task, we were able to obtain better quality information than if we had been given permission to undertake it ourselves. Many record forms, particularly when cases are still ongoing, are not filed but have to be tracked down and may even be held at a different police station. A combination of determination, inside knowledge and personal contacts enabled the women officers to achieve a much higher success rate in the data collection than we could ever have hoped to achieve. In response to our requests, they collated crime report forms held at two police stations relating to a two year period (September 1988 to September 1990) and presented us with detailed information on 301 reported cases of rape and sexual assault.

Criminal justice professionals have their own concerns and agenda for change. In deciding whether or not to grant access to outside researchers, they have to weigh the possibility that the findings will be critical rather than supportive against the possible adverse consequences of non-cooperation. It may be more desirable from their point of view to grant at least partial access, in the hope of retaining some control over the shape and direction of the research. Not all the gatekeepers of different parts of the criminal justice process necessarily resolve this dilemma in the same way. In our research, there was a marked difference between the reaction of the police who, after some initial hesitation, cooperated fully with the project, and the Crown Prosecution Service, who retained a defensive stance throughout, blocking our access to the front-line lawyers with the most experience of handling rape and sexual assault cases.

Instead, after a considerable delay, we were offered an interview with the branch crown prosecutor. He cancelled the first appointment and attempted to cancel the second, but the notification did not reach us and we presented ourselves at the offices of the CPS. The interview did go ahead but the prosecutor chose his words with extreme care, constantly referring to the Code for Crown Prosecutors and adding very little of significance. He did suggest that if there was any specific information we needed, we should write to him yet again, but by that time our research was in its final stages and the delaying tactics had proved effective, in so far as we did not pursue this line of inquiry any further.

The search for funding

Obtaining funding for the research, without relinquishing control of the research design or the research output, presents a second major obstacle. The funding councils, such as the Economic and Social Research Council, while fully respecting the need for academic autonomy, are exercising an increasing influence over the type of projects that receive funding. They do this by allocating a substantial proportion of the available money to specific research initiatives for which researchers are invited to bid. The problem then is to persuade them that, at a time of shrinking budgets and tighter controls, research into violence against women should be regarded as a priority area.

If funding is sought directly from the state, rather than via the research councils, the issues of priority and autonomy both have to be addressed. The controllers of the purse strings have to be persuaded that the project is worthwhile and also that it is not in their interests to censor or suppress the findings, however controversial. We made several approaches to the Home Office, which was about to publish the findings of its own in-house research into attrition rates in rape cases. This was a study conducted in 1985, prior to the setting up of the Crown Prosecution Service (Grace *et al.* 1992). It is possible that this study will be repeated for the period since 1985, but it seems unlikely that it will be contracted out to independent researchers. Certainly, our negotiations have so far proved fruitless. Most Home Office research in this area is conducted in-house; the only commissioned project of which we are aware is a psychological study of convicted rapists (Grubin and Gunn 1990). Presumably psychological profiling, in which the focus of attention is on individuals who rape, is seen as less threatening to the state than a more statistical and sociological study which places state practices under the spotlight.

It was the local state, in the shape of Islington council's Police and Crime Prevention Unit, that provided us with funding, after more than a year of negotiation through the Department of the Environment's Inner Cities programme. The Islington Police Committee has been at the forefront of a number of crime prevention research initiatives, beginning with the Islington Crime Survey, the first local crime survey to investigate the extent of violence against women (Jones *et al.* 1986), and more recently, the Domestic Violence Project (Mooney 1993). The Police and Crime Prevention Unit reacted positively to our initial proposal. Islington has a high proportion of women councillors, many of whom take an active part in promoting safety for women and their support through the Women's Committee was supportive. It was a unique combination of an imaginative Police and Crime Prevention Subcommittee and some central government funding for inner city projects that enabled this research to go ahead, not to mention our persistence.

Ethical considerations

For feminist researchers, ethical considerations are paramount, particularly when working in such a sensitive area as sexual assault. Confidentiality is particularly important where issues of violence against women are involved. Since we did not have access to the women's addresses, our letter asking whether they would be willing to be interviewed about their experiences was sent out by the police. This might have led to some confusion as to the identity of the researchers. Two women contacted assumed it was the police, although our letter specifically stated that we were independent researchers. Their confusion is understandable, since the letter was written on police headed note paper and this may have deterred some women from replying. Only 40 women responded, some 12 per cent of those to whom the letter was sent. Thirty women wrote to say they were willing to be interviewed; two of those contacted cancelled the appointment on three occasions and failed to answer a letter inviting them for another interview. Therefore 28 women were interviewed, two on the telephone, as they indicated that they would have found a face to face interview too distressing. Despite the small size of the sample, it did include women from different racial and ethnic groups. Two of those interviewed were African Caribbean, one was Asian and the rest were white, two from Ireland and one from France.

Ten women who were not prepared to be interviewed wrote to tell us that they would have found it too painful. Most of them had gone to court and the suspect had been found not guilty. The reasons they gave for not speaking to us are a moving testimony to the pain they had experienced and wanted so desperately to forget. It is significant that none of the defendants in these cases had been convicted and several cases had been 'no-crimed', in other words, not recorded as offences. The following are typical of the replies:

> I just try to forget what happened. (from a woman who had gone to court and the defendant, an acquaintance, had been found not guilty of rape and actual bodily harm)

> I am just getting over the assault and do not wish to discuss the matter, because it is still too painful to do so. (from a woman allegedly raped by her ex-boyfriend who was found not guilty at the Crown Court)

We can only guess at the pain and anguish and destroyed lives that lie behind the silence of the women who chose not to respond.

The findings

Service delivery to complainants

Three-quarters of the women interviewed were satisfied with the way they were treated by the police; they appreciated the increase in the number of female officers dealing with cases of sexual assault and some were surprised that the police treated their complaint so seriously and sympathetically. On the other hand, several women commented on the poor flow of information on the progress of their case; many received no information whatsoever. There appears to be a serious communication gap occurring across the spectrum of case outcomes, although we have no way of knowing whether there was a similar pattern of experiences among the women who declined to be interviewed. It is possible that the most dissatisfied group were the least willing to come forward, especially as our letter was sent to them by the police.

The medical examination was described by almost all the women as a horrific endurance test and several described it as utterly degrading. One woman even said it was as bad as the rape itself. Only one woman interviewed described her medical examination positively. Some doctors appear to have been callously unsympathetic. Others may not have been deliberately heartless but do not appear to have appreciated the acute sensitivity of women whose bodies have been bruised and denigrated. Doctors need specialized training in how to examine sexual assault survivors, so that they are taught to avoid humiliating women who have already faced appalling degradation. One woman described how she was made to feel like an object, rather than a human being:

> I looked down at myself with this sheet wrapped around me and he [the doctor] turned to the woman police officer and said: 'Cover her up will you?' I felt like a piece of something on a slab – cover that up, we should not be looking at that.

These findings suggest that forensic requirements are put into effect with little flexibility. It is questionable whether a full medical was really necessary in the case of one woman, whose bedroom was broken into by a man with a knife and who had not in fact been raped: 'They did the whole bit – spit in the tube and swabs for this and swabs for that. It was all very degrading. They didn't explain what they were doing it for.'

Women experienced going to court as an ordeal in itself. The prospect of coming face to face with the man or men who attacked them was universally dreaded. They described the appalling inadequacies of court facilities where there was often no heating, sparse furnishing and poor canteen arrangements. Having to share this space with the suspect understandably unnerved a number of complainants. As one woman put it:

> I would have liked not to have to sit where he had to sit. I don't see why I had to sit in the same room. It's the same kind of personal space invasion, so the perpetrator should have to sit in a separate room. I've never seen him again, thank goodness. I'm not sure what I would do if I saw him again.

Research has shown that women who have been raped and sexually assaulted suffer from what has been called 'rape crisis syndrome' (Holmstrom and Burgess 1978), which involves symptoms such as sleeplessness, panic attacks, unreasonable fears, horror of smells associated with the rape, disinterest in sex and depression. All the women we interviewed who had been subjected to attacks, even of a relatively minor kind (such as being touched over clothing) experienced some anxiety. Those who had experienced serious injury suffered from sleeplessness, nightmares, fear of going out alone or of being alone. Our findings were also in line with earlier research in that such symptoms often did not appear immediately, which indicates the importance of long-term counselling for the survivors of sexual attacks.

In London we found there were two main organizations that aimed to provide some form of counselling for the survivors of sexual assault. Rape Crisis was predominantly a telephone helpline set up by rape survivors and provided some counselling, mainly over the telephone. In London, the training of volunteers was regarded as a priority but limited funding meant that the centre was unable to provide face to face counselling and operated one telephone line for only a few hours a day. Victim Support was a nationwide service partly funded by the Home Office and provided help to victims of all types of crime. Unlike Rape Crisis, it did not specialize in sexual assault cases. It provided some face to face counselling, but the service varied from one local authority to another. In Islington a special attempt was made to provide counselling for the survivors of sexual assault and the feedback from these women was more positive than from those living outside the borough, although some said they would have liked more intensive counselling. Most recently, in October 1996 the Rape Crisis Federating Project was launched in Manchester to coordinate rape crisis centres across Britain and lead to an improvement and standardization of services throughout the country.

Researching the role of the police

Once the research was underway, regular contact was maintained with the two women officers assigned to research and collate the records on our behalf. Meetings were held with the two chief superintendents at crucial points in the study; both of them were fully supportive of the research and allowed free access to their officers as required.

All the officers seemed willing to talk to us and were very keen to describe the transformation that had taken place in recent years in the treatment of women reporting rape and sexual assault. Many made reference to the 'bad old days' depicted so vividly in the aforementioned 1982 television documentary programme on the Thames Valley police, which showed a woman complainant undergoing a harsh interrogation (BBC *Police Series* 1982). Since the furore generated by that episode, the police have operated under a clear instruction that no one reporting a serious sexual assault is to be disbelieved. As an example of this policy in action, one of the detective inspectors related a case in which a woman reported that she had been raped by a taxi driver but at the same time admitted that she may have dreamt it. The inspector acknowledged that in the past 'she would have been laughed out of the station', but in accordance with the new policies, the complaint was treated seriously. Semen found on her sheets matched with samples obtained from the taxi driver and he was convicted.

Current police practice in this area is to assign a female officer who has completed the training programme on sexual offences investigation techniques to a case from the outset and she assumes responsibility, as far as possible, for all communication with the complainant. Although a detective inspector (most of whom are male) takes overall charge of the investigation, it is the female officer who takes the complainant's statement, accompanies her to the rape examination suite where most medical examinations in such cases now take place, provides her with information and support and, should the case reach court, will accompany her. If it seems unlikely that the case will go to court, the officers are required to emphasize that what happened was not the woman's fault and that it was just a problem of evidence.

At one level, the police officers seemed committed to making the new policies work. The female officers interviewed were particularly impressive; they were attempting to provide some support for complainants, despite the tendency for the rest of their work to pile up while they did so and they were genuinely concerned that so few cases went to court. At another level, it is important to realize that old attitudes die hard and also that the police are subjected to conflicting pressures. On the crucial question of false allegations, for example, it was apparent from the interviews that many officers believed these to be a frequent occurrence. They gave hypothetical examples of mischievous reports of rape, such as the woman who has had a row with her boyfriend, the prostitute who has not been paid, the young woman who becomes pregnant or stays out all night and wishes to escape parental wrath. One inspector commented that the last three rapes he had dealt with were not rapes at all, and a female inspector believed that 50 per cent of the rapes reported were probably false allegations.

Apart from that particular inspector, women officers were less likely to express such scepticism. In view of the roles they as policewomen are expected to perform and their concentration in the junior ranks, women officers find themselves on the front line in rape and sexual assault cases. It is this hands-on experience which dispels the myth of false allegations; the female inspector quoted above was part of the dominant culture, operating at one remove from complainants and had served her time in the lower ranks before the new 'sympathetic' policies were adopted.

It is indicative of the fragile nature of the changes in police policies that by the end of the 1980s they had had no noticeable impact on the practice of 'no-criming' cases, i.e. not recording them as crimes. This is a long-standing police practice, justified as a way of avoiding wasting time on 'hopeless' cases and previously encouraged because it produced a higher clear-up rate in the official statistics. Home Office circulars produced during the 1980s, directing the police to handle sexual assault complaints more sympathetically, also established new guidelines for the practice of 'no-criming'. Cases of serious sexual assault were only to be placed in this category if the complainant withdrew the allegation and admitted that it was false. Yet our findings indicated that during the two year period covered by our study 38 per cent of the reported cases (116 out of 301) were treated as 'no-crimes' and that the reasons given for classifying them in this way fell outside the official guidelines.

Cases in which there was some kind of a relationship between the complainant and the suspect were much more likely to be 'no-crimed' than stereotypical 'stranger' attacks. These were also the cases least likely to be taken up by the Crown Prosecution Service or to result in a conviction. In 'no-criming' such a high proportion of cases in which there was some kind of prior acquaintance or even intimacy between the complainant and the suspect, the police are anticipating outcomes at later stages in the criminal justice process. They are 'screening out' those cases in which the complainant will not be seen as a credible witness by the CPS or by a jury.

As the police attempt to resolve this dilemma, the tensions are likely to be accentuated rather than reduced. On the one hand, they informed us that there had been a further tightening of the 'no-criming' procedures since the two year period covered by our research; on the other hand, they are being encouraged to pass to the CPS only those cases with a reasonable prospect of resulting in a conviction. This leaves them with an ever-increasing number of cases on file that cannot be resolved, particularly as more women are coming forward to report sexual attacks now that they can expect a sympathetic hearing. The police are themselves being subjected to stringent performance criteria, so that the tension between the conflicting demands of service delivery to complainants and demonstrated success at solving crimes is likely to increase.

Another reason for attrition is the downgrading of cases by the police

at a later stage through plea bargaining. It appears that the police sometimes downgrade cases of attempted rape to indecent assault. Nineteen
cases were downgraded to reflect a less serious offence; two reports of rape
and six reports of attempted rape were reclassified as indecent assault. One
case of indecent assault became indecent exposure and in the remaining 10
cases the sexual aspect of the crime was removed altogether. Clearly, it is in
the interests of the victim to reduce the charge if there is insufficient evidence to proceed with the more serious charge and such decisions have to be
made on the basis of experience and judgement. However, some of the cases
in which the sexual classification was removed altogether are rather puzzling.
They include a case classified simply as robbery, although the suspect had
squeezed the victim's breast and put his hand on her inner thigh, and a
charge of grievous bodily harm (GBH) in which the attacker had ripped
off the victim's T-shirt and bra and put a finger in her vagina, slashing her
breasts while threatening to cut them off. In another case classified as common assault, the victim regained consciousness to find the suspect urinating
on her.

In several of the cases where the complainant was interviewed, the description of the attack appeared to suggest attempted rape but it was classified as indecent assault. The distinction between rape and indecent assault
was often unclear and it is debatable what should constitute the difference.
How exactly is intention to rape to be measured? Is it genital contact and
if so, what kind of contact, or is verbal expression of intent sufficient?
Does throwing a woman on the ground or on a bed, trying to remove her
knickers and then being fought off constitute intention to rape?

Several of the women interviewed described attacks which had been
classified as indecent assault but appeared to be as serious as other cases
classified as attempted rape. If the woman is knocked off her feet, pinned
down, and kissed or groped, this should surely be classified as attempted
rape. Consider the following case of Lizzie (not her real name):

> I was attacked in the lobby of a block of flats where I used to live as I
> came home quite late at night. It was about 2 a.m. in the morning. I
> was just about to get into the lift when suddenly a man appeared wear-
> ing just a shirt, nothing else and he started moving towards me and he
> actually had an erection and was masturbating. My first instinct was
> just to kick. I aimed for his groin and I missed and the next thing I
> knew he'd thrown me around against the wall and I obviously screamed
> very loudly but he then covered my mouth and my nose so I couldn't
> breathe. After a few minutes of struggling we ended up on the floor
> and I managed to get his hands off my mouth and I decided to talk to
> him. I told him that I was two months pregnant and that my husband
> was waiting for me upstairs – and said 'Please, please, let me go'. He
> released his grip and I managed to get out and ran into the street. I was

looking for a phone and couldn't find one even though if I'd thought about it I knew where one was. I stopped a taxi and got him to take me round the block and asked the taxi driver to come in with me. I phoned the police as soon as I got in.

It transpired that the suspect lived in the same block of flats and over the next few weeks Lizzie kept sighting him and was terrified of coming face to face with him. She eventually moved from her flat as she was so terrified of running into him. After seeing him she alerted the police and he was arrested. She spent a day in the police station picking him out of an identification parade. The assailant was already on a suspended sentence for another sexual offence and had since attacked two other women, who had also picked him out of an identification parade. Yet he was not charged with attempted rape but with indecent assault. He was found guilty of two counts of indecent assault (both which appeared to be attempted rapes) and received only an 18 month sentence to be served on top of the 18 months of his suspended sentence. Lizzie had been terrorized and suffered from nightmares and panic attacks. It appears that if a woman fights back and gets away from her assailant he is unlikely to be charged with attempted rape even if masturbating, has an erect penis, is half naked, and is pinioning a woman down with his hand over her mouth.

The only case where a woman had reported her separated husband shows how indecent assault cases are often difficult to prove even when the charge is combined with actual bodily harm (ABH). Una described what happened:

> I was married for 17 years. I took a lot over the years for the sake of the children. But you get to the point when you think, 'that's it'. You can't explain the kind of pressure I was under when I left, phone calls and hassle. I had an injunction as well to keep him away. But he just flipped. I thought he was going to kill me. I'd never seen him like that. He said 'Sleep with me and I'll give you some money'. Then he tried to rape me. I fought and he beat me up. My daughter was in the house and she heard everything. The police arrested him for indecent assault. I said I wanted him arrested for attempted rape. He got off for indecent assault but was found guilty for ABH. I would rather he had been found guilty on the indecent assault than the ABH charge.

It is interesting to consider why the police would wish to downgrade the seriousness of cases in this way. One senior policewoman helped to throw light on this question when she recounted how, on returning to the station from other duties at the end of 1988, she had taken a statement from a rape victim who did not wish to proceed with the case. In accordance with previous practice, she had 'no-crimed' the report and was reprimanded for doing so. She was informed that the new guidelines related to rape reports only and was asked if the report could be downgraded to indecent assault, in which case it could then be 'no-crimed'.

The role of the CPS and the courts

The third main point of attrition is the CPS whose lawyers decide whether cases that the police regard as sound go to court. The CPS only recommend cases for a hearing if they consider there is a good chance of conviction. The code of practice asserts that for prosecution to occur, all cases must have a realistic prospect of conviction. Since few reported rapes result in a conviction, the CPS are unwilling to take cases to court which they think will result in an acquittal. (Informally in rape cases police refer to the CPS's 50 per cent rule for rape.)

Less than a third of the cases originally reported to the police went forward to the Crown Prosecution Service, that is, 88 out of 301 cases. Despite this Draconian sweep of 'weak' cases, the CPS took no further action in 17 of those referred, so that 71 cases proceeded to a prosecution. In 41 of these a conviction was secured, although one of these was quashed on appeal. Three offenders were detained under the Mental Health Act and in the remaining 27 either the proceedings were discontinued at some point or the suspects were found not guilty.

In only 29 cases were custodial sentences given, ranging from one month to life imprisonment and in only five of these cases had there been a prior acquaintance between the offender and the complainant; the rest were all stereotypical stranger attacks. All five of the 'acquaintance' cases involved a considerable degree of violence; in two cases, this included buggery as well as rape and in three cases there was an age gap of some 25 years between the woman and her attacker. In other words, although more women are being encouraged to report assaults by men they know, these assaults are not being recognized as such by the criminal justice system. The fact that the police deal sympathetically with these women and accept their account as true is important in helping their recovery, but in failing to convict all but a handful of the men responsible for the assaults, the criminal justice system is condoning their actions and encouraging them to attack again.

The way forward

As our research focused mainly on the work of the police and was conducted on behalf of a local authority, it was easier for us to make recommendations for further improvements in service delivery than to tackle the underlying problem of the attrition rate. The recommendations included strategies for improving the flow of information between the police and complainants and for reducing the trauma of the court appearance; also for the development of a much more comprehensive and sensitive medical service, including advice and support in relation to pregnancy, venereal disease and HIV testing and for ensuring the availability of long-term counselling. We also recommended a fundamental review of police recording procedures, in order to yield a more objective picture of precisely why cases fail to proceed and the abolition of the 'no-criming' category altogether. The local police seemed receptive to our suggestions for further reform and recognized the need to monitor how the changes were working in practice. We were subsequently invited to speak to the Sexual Offences Steering Committee at New Scotland Yard, who were equally receptive, while rightly pointing out that the key to solving many of the problems we had identified lay elsewhere, in the courts and in the wider society. Detective inspectors, police superintendents and senior medical officers expressed frustration with the practices of the judicial system and agreed that changes were overdue.

One of the dominant themes of official discourse concerns the rights of individuals, encouraged to demand high standards of service delivery in various walks of life, whether as patients, passengers, or victims of crime. Yet as these 'charters' proliferate, each in turn meets the stumbling block of scarce economic resources and the criminal justice system is no exception. On the one hand, there is a new official concern with 'witness care' and users' groups are being established in a number of Crown Courts. On the other hand, the CPS is under pressure to reduce the number of jury trials by extending the practice of plea-bargaining. In relation to rape and sexual assault cases, this could mean even more men accused of serious sexual crimes pleading guilty to indecent assault, a crime which can be disposed of in the magistrates' court with the imposition of a light sentence, such as a fine or community service order. Unlike police officers, CPS lawyers have no direct contact with complainants; their main concern is to reduce time delays, improve conviction rates and keep costs under control. Their current strategy for achieving these goals is to anticipate judicial decisions rather than challenge them.

Conclusion

Within the police service, the dominant discourse which holds that women complaining of rape or sexual assault frequently make false allegations is under attack. It is caught in a pincer movement between senior policy-makers, who instruct officers to deal with complainants as though they believed them, and the junior officers most closely involved with the cases who really do believe them. Despite these powerful pressures, there is a real danger that the police, believing themselves to be isolated, may take the line of least resistance and retreat from the advances they have made. In order to prevent this occurring, it is essential to sustain attacks as enshrined in judicial pronouncements and in the trial itself. Support for such a campaign can be found within the media. Recent television programmes have highlighted lenient sentences in rape cases (*Panorama* 1993) and the scandal of serial rapists who escape justice only to rape many times again (*Dispatches* 1994). The CPS has been criticized for dropping too many cases, particularly when complainants then go on to pursue a successful civil action (*London Programme* 1993). Such anecdotal evidence is confirmed by Home Office statistics, which show that between 1985 and 1991 the conviction rate for crimes of rape and sexual assault fell from 24 per cent to 14 per cent (Home Office 1993).

Whether legislative reforms are introduced from within, by femocrats or sympathetic politicians, or by a less sympathetic government implementing its own agenda, their impact in the courtroom will be minimal until sexual offence cases are heard by judges, including Court of Appeal judges, who have been carefully screened and received intensive training from counsellors experienced in dealing with the survivors of sexual assault. It is time to challenge the simplistic notion that the only 'politically correct' stance for anyone on the left is to side with the defendant against the state. As James Garvie (1993) perceptively argues, it is possible to develop a radical position with regard to the role of the prosecution and the needs of the victim, without attacking the civil liberties of the defendant.

At present, the balance in rape trials is very much in favour of the defendant. His sexual history and past criminal record are protected even if he has attacked the character of the complainant. He also has his own highly paid legal representative, whose main task is to destroy the credibility of the complainant. She, by contrast, has no lawyer specifically to represent her interests, nor to protect her when her version of events is challenged and her good character and past sexual behaviour are called into question. Until this imbalance is corrected, the attrition rate in cases of rape and sexual assault will remain high, leaving the perpetrators of these crimes free to attack again.

Note

This article was written together with Jeanne Gregory, Professor of Criminology at the University of Middlesex and appeared in *Feminist Review* No. 48, Autumn 1994. She assisted in the design of the questionnaire used on the *World in Action* programme on marital rape (*The Right to Rape*, shown on 25 September 1989).

Bibliography

Abrams, D. (1991) *Aids: What Young People Believe and What They Do*. Canterbury: University of Kent.

Adler, Z. (1987) *Rape on Trial*. London: Routledge.

Adler, Z. (1992) Treatment of male victims of rape, in G. Mezey and M. King (eds) *Male Victims of Sexual Assault*. Oxford: Oxford University Press, pp. 116–31.

Allen, H. (1987) *Justice Unbalanced*. Milton Keynes: Open University Press.

Allen, I. (1987) *Education in Sex and Personal Relationships*. London: Policy Studies Institute.

Allen, J. (1990) *Sex and Secrets: Crimes Involving Australian Women Since 1980*. Oxford: Oxford University Press.

Allport, G. (1954) *The Nature of Prejudice*. London: Addison Wesley.

Arnot, M. (1984) How shall we educate our sons? in R. Deem (ed.) *Coeducation Reconsidered*. Milton Keynes: Open University Press.

Ashworth, A. J. (1975) Sentencing in provocation cases. *Criminal Law Review*, 1: 3–46.

Atkins, S. and Hoggett, B. (1984) *Women and the Law*. Oxford: Basil Blackwell.

Atwood, M. (1988) *Cat's Eye*. Toronto: Seal Books.

Bacon, W. and Lansdowne, R. (1982) Women who kill husbands: the battered wife on trial, in C. O'Donnell and J. Craney (eds) *Family Violence in Australia*. Melbourne: Longman Cheshire.

Bart, P. and Moran, E. (eds) (1993) *Violence Against Women*. London: Sage.

BBC *Police* Series (1982) The Thames Valley Police interrogation of rape victim covered in this programme (January) is referred to in C. Dunhill (1989) *The Boys in Blue*. London: Virago.

Benn, M. (1993) Body talk: the sexual politics of PMT, in H. Birch (ed.) *Moving Targets*. London: Virago, pp. 152–72.

Beynon, J. (1989) A school for men; an ethnographic case study of routine violence in schooling, in L. Barton and S. Walker (eds) *Politics and the Processes of Schooling*. Milton Keynes: Open University Press, pp. 191–217.

Bindel, J., Cook, K. and Kelly, L. (1995) Trials and tribulations – Justice for Women: a campaign for the 1990s, in G. Griffin (ed.) *Feminist Activism in the 1990s*. London: Taylor & Francis, pp. 65–77.

Blom-Cooper, L. and Morris, T. (1964) *Calendar of Murder*. London: Michael Joseph.

Blumberg, A. (1967) *Criminal Justice*. New York: New Viewpoints.

Bochnak, E. (1981) *Women's Self Defence Cases: Theory and Practice*. Melbourne: Mitchie Company.

Bordo, S. (1993) Feminism, Foucault, and the modernization of patriarchal power, in I. Diamond and L. Quinby (eds) *Feminism and Foucault: Reflections of Resistance*. Boston, MA: Northeastern University Press, pp. 61–86.

Box-Grainger, J. (1986) Sentencing rapists, in R. Matthews and J. Young (eds) *Confronting Crime*. London: Sage.

Brah, A. and Minhas, R. (1985) Structural racism and cultural difference: schooling for Asian girls, in G. Weiner (ed.) *Just a Bunch of Girls*. Milton Keynes: Open University Press, pp. 14–26.

Brandes, S. (1981) Like wounded stags: male sexual ideology in an Andalusian town, in S. Ortner and H. Whitehead (eds) *Sexual Meanings*. Cambridge: Cambridge University Press, pp. 216–40.

British Youth Council (1992) *The Time of Your Life: The Truth About Being Young in '90s Britain*. London: British Youth Council.

Brown, B., Burman, M. and Jamieson, L. (1993) *Sex Crimes on Trial: The Use of Sexual Evidence in Scottish Courts*. Edinburgh: Edinburgh University Press.

Browne, A. (1987) *When Battered Women Kill*. New York: Free Press.

Brownlea, I. (1989) Marital rape: lessons from Scotland. *New Law Journal*, 22: 1275.

Brownmiller, S. (1976) *Against Our Will*. Harmondsworth: Penguin.

Burgess, A. and Holmstrom, L. (1974) Rape trauma syndrome and post traumatic stress response, in A. Burgess (ed.) *Research Handbook on Rape and Sexual Assault*. New York: Garland, pp. 46–61.

Cain, M. (1989) Introduction: feminists transgress criminology, in M. Cain (ed.) *Growing up Good*. London: Sage.

Cain, M. (1990) Towards transgression: new directions in feminist criminology. *International Journal of the Sociology of Law*, 18 (1): 1–18.

Carlen, P. (1976) *Magistrates' Justice*. London: Routledge.

Carlen, P. (1983) *Women's Imprisonment*. London: Routledge.

Carlen, P. (ed.) (1985) *Criminal Women*. Cambridge: Polity.

Carlen, P. and Worral, A. (eds) (1987) *Gender Crime and Justice*. Milton Keynes: Open University Press.

Chambers, G. and Millar, A. (1986) *Prosecuting Sexual Assault*. Scottish Office Central Research Unit, Edinburgh: HMSO.

Channel 4 (1995) *Till Death Do Us Part*, 11 October.

Clark, A. (1987) *Women's Silence, Men's Violence: Sexual Assault in England 1770–1845*. London: Pandora.

Connell, R. W. (1987) *Gender and Power*. Cambridge: Polity Press.

Connell, R. W. (1995) *Masculinities*. Cambridge: Polity Press.

Coward, R. (1984) *Female Desire*. London: Paladin.

Cowdry, Q. (1990) Half women murder victims killed by husband or lover. *The Times*, 14 April.

Cross, R. and Jones, P. (1984) *Introduction to Criminal Law*. London: Croom Helm.

Dahl, S. T. (1987) *Women's Law: An Introduction to Feminist Jurisprudence*. Oxford: Oxford University Press.

Dalton, K. (1989) *The Menstrual Cycle*. London, Penguin.

Daly, M. (1979) *Gyn/Ecology: The Metaphysics of Radical Feminism*. London: Women's Press.

Davidoff, L. and Hall, C. (1987) *Family Fortunes: Men and Women of the English Middle Class 1780–1850*. London: Hutchinson.

Davies, B. (1989) *Frogs and Snails and Feminist Tales: Preschool Children and Gender*. Sydney: Allen & Unwin.

Dispatches (1994) *Getting Away with Rape*, Channel 4 TV, First Frame, 16 February.

Dispatches (1995) *Male Rape*, Channel 4 TV, Platinum Productions, 17 May.

Dobash, R. and Dobash, E. (1992) *Women, Violence and Social Change*. London: Routledge.

Dobash, R. P., Dobash, R. E. and Gutteridge, S. (eds) (1986) *The Imprisonment of Women*. London: Blackwell.

Dollomore, G. (1989) Live Births in 1988. *Population Trends*, 57: 20–6.

Douglas, M. (1966) *Purity and Danger*. London: Routledge & Kegan Paul.

Doyal, L. (1983) Women, health and the sexual division of labour. *International Journal of Health Services*, 13 March.

Driscoll, M. (1990) Family of dead wife seeks rights in court. *Sunday Times*, 28 January.

Dunhill, C. (1989) *The Boys in Blue*. London: Virago.

Eaton, M. (1983) Mitigating circumstances: familiar rhetoric. *International Journal of the Sociology of Law*, 11: 385–400.

Eaton, M. (1986) *Justice for Women? Family Court and Social Control*. Milton Keynes: Open University Press.

Eder, D. with C. Evans and S. Parke (1995) *School Talk: Gender and Adolescent Culture*. New Brunswick, NJ: Rutgers University Press.

Edwards, S. (1981) *Female Sexuality and the Law*. Oxford: Martin Robertson.

Edwards, S. (ed.) (1985) *Gender, Sex and the Law*. London: Croom Helm.

Edwards, S. (1989) *Policing 'Domestic' Violence*. London: Sage.

Enloe, C. (1988) *Does Khaki Become You?: Militarization of Women's Lives*. London: Pandora.

Estrich, S. (1987) *Real Rape*. Cambridge, MA: Harvard University Press.

Ettorre, E. (1992) *Women and Substance Use*. London: Macmillan.

Evans, G. (1980) Those loud black girls, in D. Spender and E. Sarah (eds) *Learning to Lose*. London: Women's Press, pp. 183–93.

Farrell, C. (1978) *My Mother Said: The Way Young People Learned About Sex and Birth Control*. London: Routledge & Kegan Paul.

Fine, M. (1988) Sexuality, schooling and adolescent females: the missing discourse of desire. *Harvard Educational Review*, 58: 29–53.

Finkelhor, D. and Yllo, K. (1982) Forced sex in marriage: a preliminary research report, *Crime and Delinquency*, 34: 29–39.

Fisher, N. (1995) *Best Guide to Sex*. Harmondsworth: Penguin.

Fitzpatrick, P. and Hunt, A. (eds) (1987) *Critical Legal Studies*. Oxford: Blackwell.

Foley, M. (1994) Professionalising the response to rape, in C. Lupton and T. Gillespie (eds) *Working with Violence*. London: Macmillan.

Ford, N. (1992) Aids awareness and the sexual behaviour of young people. *Journal of Adolescence*, 15 (1): 393–413.

Ford, N. and Morgan, D. (1989) Heterosexual lifestyles of young people in an English city. *Journal of Population and Social Studies*, 1 (2): 40.

Foucault, M. (1980) Two lectures, in C. Gordon (ed.) *Michel Foucault: Power/ Knowledge, Selected Interviews 1972–77*. Brighton: Harvester Press.

Foucault, M. (1990) *The History of Sexuality*, vol. 1. London: Penguin.

Foucault, M. (1991) *Discipline and Punish*. London: Penguin.

Francome, C. (1986) *Abortion Practice in Britain and the United States*. London: Allen & Unwin.

Freud, S. (1925) Some psychical consequences of the anatomical distinction between the sexes, in *Standard Edition of the Complete Psychological Works of Sigmund Freud*, vol. 21. (ed. by J. Strachey) London: Hogarth Press.

Friedan, B. (1963) *The Feminine Mystique*. New York: W. W. Norton.

Garvie, J. (1993) In defense of the prosecution. *Guardian*, 31 August.

Giddens, A. (1992) *The Transformation of Intimacy*. Cambridge: Polity Press.

Gillespie, C. (1989) *Justifiable Homicide: Battered Women, Self Defence and the Law*. Columbus, OH: Ohio State University.

Gillespie, T. (1996) Rape crisis centres and 'male rape', in M. Hester, L. Kelly and J. Radford (eds) *Women. Violence and Male Power*. Buckingham: Open University Press, pp. 148–66.

Godenzi, A. (1994) What's the big deal? We are men and they are women, in T. Newburn and E. Stanko (eds) *Just Boys Doing Business? Men, Masculinities and Crime*. London: Routledge.

Gould, C. (ed.) (1984) *Beyond Domination: New Perspectives on Women and Philosophy*. Totowa, NJ: Rowman & Littlefield.

Grace, S., Lloyd, C. and Smith, L. (1992) *Rape: From Recording to Conviction*. London: Home Office Research and Planning Unit Papers.

Gregory, J. and Lees, S. (1996) Attrition in rape and sexual assault cases. *British Journal of Criminology*, 36 (1): 1–18.

Griffin, G. (ed.) (1995) *Feminist Activism in the 1990s*. London: Taylor & Francis.

Groneman, C. (1994) Nymphomania: the historical construction of female sexuality. *Signs*, 19 (2) winter: 337–67.

Groth, A. and Birnbaum, H. (1979) *Men Who Rape: The Psychology of the Offender*, New York: Plenum Press.

Grubin, D. and Gunn, J. (1990) *Imprisoned Rapists and Rape*. London: Home Office Research Unit.

Hale, Sir M. (1971) *The History of the Pleas of the Crown*, 1. London: Professional Books LVIII.

Hall, L. (1991) *Hidden Anxieties*. Cambridge: Polity.

Hansard (1991) 'Domestic homicide statistics' in written answer 361 to John Patten, 19 October, London: Home Office.

Harding, S. (1984) Is gender a variable in conceptions of rationality? A survey of issues, in C. Gould (ed.) *Beyond Domination, New Perspectives on Women and Philosophy*. Totowa, NJ: Rowman & Littlefield, pp. 43–64.

Hartsock, N. (1983) The feminist standpoint: developing the ground for a specifically feminist historical materialism, in S. Harding and M. Hintikka (eds) *Discovering Reality: Feminist Perspectives on Epistemology, Methodology and Philosophy of Science*. Boston, MA: D. Reidel.

Heidensohn, F. (1985) *Women and Crime*. London: Macmillan.

Heilbron Committee (1975) *Report on the Advisory Group on the Law on Rape*, Cmnd 6352. London: HMSO.

Hester. M., Kelly, L. and Radford, J. (eds) (1996) *Women, Violence and Male Power*. Buckingham: Open University Press.

Hester, M. and Radford, L. (1996) Contradictions and compromises: the impact of the Children Act on women and children's safety, in M. Hester, L. Kelly and J. Radford (eds) *Women, Violence and Male Power*. Buckingham: Open University Press.

Hicks, E. (1993) *Infibulation: Female Mutilation in Islamic North Eastern Africa*. New York: Transaction Publishers.

Hite, S. (1988) *Women and Love: A Cultural Revolution in Progress*. New York: Knopf.

HMSO (1992) *Health of the Nation*. London: Department of Health.

Hoff, L. A. (1990) *Battered Women as Survivors*. London: Routledge.

Holland, J., Ramazanoglu, C. and Scott, S. (1990) Managing risk and experiencing danger: tensions between government Aids education policy and young women's sexuality. *Gender & Education*, 2 (2): 125–47.

Holmstrom, L. and Burgess, A. (1978) *The Victim of Rape: Institutional Reactions*. New York: Wiley.

Home Office Statistics (1985–1993) Available from the Home Office Statistics and Research Department. London: Home Office.

hooks, b. (1989) *Talking Back*. London: Sheba Feminist Publications.

Howe, A. (1994) *Punish and Critique: Towards a Feminist Analysis of Penality*. London: Routledge.

Hudson, D. (1987) You can't commit violence against an object, in J. Hanmer and M. Maynard *Women, Violence and Social Control*.

Hudson, F. and Ineichen, B. (1991) *Taking It Lying Down, Sexuality and Teenage Motherhood*. London: Macmillan.

Jagger, A. (1989) Love and knowledge: emotion in feminist epistomology, in A. Garry and M. Pearsall (eds) *Women, Knowledge and Reality*. London: Unwin: 129–57.

Jamieson, L. (1994) 'The social construction of consent revisited'. Paper presented at BSA Annual Conference, Sheffield. March.

Jones, A. (1991) *Women Who Kill*. London: Victor Gollancz.

Jones, T., Maclean, B. and Young, J. (1986) *The Islington Crime Survey*. London: Gower.

Kelly, L. (1988) *Surviving Sexual Violence*. Cambridge: Polity.

Kelly, L. (1992) Not in front of the children: responding to right wing agendas on sexuality and education, in M. Arnot and L. Barton (eds) *Voicing Concerns: Sociological Perspectives on Contemporary Education Reforms*. London: Triangle.

Kennedy, H. (1992) *Eve was Framed: Women and British Justice*. London: Chatto & Windus.

Kenway, J. (1995) Masculinities in schools: under siege, on the defensive and under reconstruction? *Discourse: Studies in the Cultural Politics of Education*, 16 (1): 58–79.

King, M. (1992) *Male Rape in Institutional Settings*. Oxford: Oxford University Press.

Kinsey, A. C. (1948) *Sexual Behaviour in the Human Male*. Philadelphia, PA: Saunders.

Labour Party (1995) *Peace at Home*. London: Labour Party.

Law Commission (1992) *Criminal Law on Rape Within Marriage*. Law Commission No. 205. London: HMSO.

Laws, S. (1991) Issues of blood. *Trouble and Strife*, 20, Spring: 45–51.

Lee, C. (1983) *The Ostrich Position*. London: Readers & Writer Publishing Company.

Lees, S. (1986) *Losing Out: Sexuality and Adolescent Girls*. London: Unwin.

Lees, S. (1989a) Blaming the victim. *New Statesman and Society*, 24 November.

Lees, S. (1989b) Trial by rape. *New Statesman and Society*, 1 December.

Lees, S. (1993) *Sugar and Spice: Sexuality and Adolescent Girls*. Harmondsworth: Penguin.

Lees, S. and Gregory, J. (1993) *Rape and Sexual Assault: A Study in Attrition*. London: Islington Council Crime Prevention Unit.

Lees, S. (1996) *Carnal Knowledge: Rape on Trial*. London: Hamish Hamilton.

Leonard, D. (1980) *Sex and Generation*. London: Tavistock.

Lesbian and Gay Youth (1988) *Report on High Schools: A Study Prepared for the Coalition for Lesbian and Gay Rights in Toronto*. Toronto: Ottawa Hill.

Lever, L. A. (1986) *No One Speaks for the Dead*. Thames Television, August.

Lloyd, A. (1995) *Doubly Deviant, Doubly Damned: Society's Treatment of Violent Women*. London: Penguin.

Lloyd, G. (1984) *The Man of Reason: 'Male' and 'Female' in Western Philosophy*. Minneapolis: University of Minnesota Press.

Los, M. (1990) Feminism and rape law reform, in L. Gelsthorpe and A. Morris (eds) *Feminist Perspectives in Criminology*. Milton Keynes: Open University Press, pp. 160–73.

London Programme (1993) *The Crown Prosecution Service*. Thames Television, 13 August.

London Rape Crisis Centre (1989) *Strength in Numbers*. London: London Rape Crisis Centre.

Luckhaus, L. (1986) A plea for PMT in the criminal law, in S. Edwards (ed.) *Gender, Sex and the Law*. London: Croom Helm.

Mac an Ghaill, M. (1991) Schooling, sexuality and male power: towards an emancipatory curriculum. *Gender and Education*, 3 (3): 291–309.

Mac an Ghaill, M. (1994) *The Making of Men: Masculinities, Sexualities and Schooling*. Buckingham: Open University Press.

McBarnet, D. (1981) *Conviction: Law, the State and the Construction of Justice*. London: Macmillan.

MacKinnon, C. (1987) *Feminism Unmodified: Discourses on Life and Law*. Cambridge, MA: Harvard University Press.

MacKinnon, C. (1989) *Towards a Feminist Theory of the State*. Cambridge, MA: Harvard University Press.

McMullen, R. J. (1990) *Male Rape: Breaking the Silence on the Last Taboo*. London: Gay Men's Press Publishers.

McNeil, M. (1987) *Gender and Expertise*. London: Free Association Books.

McRobbie, A. (1991) *Feminism and Youth Culture*. London: Macmillan.

Messerschmidt, J. (1995) From patriarchy to gender: feminist theory, criminology and the challenge of diversity, in N. Rafter and F. Heidensohn (eds) *International Feminist Perspectives in Criminology*. Buckingham: Open University Press, pp. 167–89.

Mezey, G. and King, M. (1989) The effects of sexual assault on men: a survey of 22 victims. *Psychological Medicine*, 19: 205–209.

Mezey, G. and King, M. (eds) (1992) *Male Victims of Sexual Assault*. Oxford: Oxford University Press.

Mies, M. (1983) Towards a methodology for feminist research, in G. Bowles and R. Klein (eds) *Theories of Women's Studies*. London: Routledge & Kegan Paul.

Mirza, H. (1992) *Young, Female and Black*. London: Routledge & Kegan Paul.

Mitra, C. (1987) Judicial discourse in father–daughter incest appeal cases. *International Journal of Sociology of Law*, 15 (2): 121–48.

Mooney, B. (1981) Has the woman the right to fight back? *The Times*, 21 July.

Mooney, J. (1993) *The Hidden Figure: Domestic Violence in North London*. London: Islington Council.

Moore, S. and Rosenthal, D. (1991) Condoms and coitus: adolescent attitudes to Aids and safe sex behaviour. *Journal of Adolescence*, 14: 11–27.

Moore, S. and Rosenthal, D. (1993) *Sexuality in Adolescence*. London: Routledge.

MORI (1991) *Young Adults: Health and Lifestyle Report*. London: Health Education Authority.

Morris, T. and Blom-Cooper, L. (1964) *A Calendar of Murder*. London: Michael Joseph.

Morrison, B. (1987) *The Ballad of the Yorkshire Ripper*. London: Chatto & Windus.

Moxon, D. (1988) *Sentencing Practice in the Crown Court*. Home Office Research Study, No. 103. London: HMSO.

Naffine, N. (1990) *Law and the Sexes*. Sydney: Allen & Unwin.

Naffine, N. (1994) Possession: erotic love in the law of rape. *Modern Law Review*, 57 (1): 10–37.

Nardi, P. (1992) *Men's Friendship*. London: Sage.

Nuttall, C. (1993) Courts regard female killers as no deadlier than the male, *Sunday Times*, Style Section, 9 May.

Painter, K. (1991) *Wife Rape, Marriage and the Law*. Manchester: University of Manchester Press.

Panorama (1993) *The Rape of Justice*. BBC 1, July.

Phillips, A. (1993) *The Trouble with Boys*, London: Pandora.

Phillips, A. and Rakusen, J. (eds) (1989) *Our Bodies Ourselves*. Harmondsworth: Penguin.

Public Eye (1992) *Hidden from View, Hidden from Justice*. BBC 2. February.

Radford, J. (1987) Policing male violence – policing women, in J. Hanmer and M. Maynard (eds) *Women, Violence and Social Control*, London: Macmillan, pp. 30–46.

Radford, J. (1989) When legal statements become pornography. *Rights of Women Bulletin*, autumn.

Radford, J. (1991) When legal statements become pornography: an update. *Rights of Women Bulletin*, autumn.

Radford, L. (1993) Pleading for time: justice for battered women who kill, in H. Birch (ed.) *Moving Targets*. London: Virago, pp. 172–98.

Radford, J. and Russell, D. E. H. (eds) (1992) *Femicide: The Politics of Woman Killing*. Buckingham: Open University Press.

Ramazanoglu, C. and Holland, J. (1993) Women's sexuality and men's appropriation of desire, in C. Ramazanoglu (ed.) *Up Against Foucault*. London: Routledge, pp. 239–65.

Rights of Women (1991) Sentenced to life imprisonment for resisting male violence: man made law denies justice for women. *Rights of Women Bulletin*, autumn.

Rights of Women (1992) *Submission to the Royal Commission: Proposal Amendments to the 1957 Homicide Act*. London: Rights of Women.

Rights of Women (1993) 'We'll be freeing all the women': the struggle continues into 1993. *Rights of Women Bulletin*, spring: 9–12.

Robbins, D. and Cohen, C. (1978) *Knuckle Sandwich*. London: Penguin.

Roberts, C. (1989) *Women and Rape*. London: Harvester Wheatsheaf.

Robertshaw, P. (1994) Sentencing rapists: first tier courts in 1991–92, *Criminal Law Review*: 343–5.

Rodwell, L. (1991) Will truth be the victim of marital rape? *The Times*, 25 October.

Roiphe, K. (1993) *The Morning After*. New York: Little Brown.

Rose, D. (1996) *In the Name of the Law: The Collapse of the Judicial System*. London: Jonathan Cape.

Rousseau, J. J. (1762/1974) *Emile*. London: Dutton.

Rowland, J. (1986) *Rape: The Ultimate Violation*. London: Pluto.

Ruddick, S. (1990) *Maternal Thinking: Towards a Politics of Peace*. London: Women's Press.

Rush, F. (1990) The many faces of the backlash, in D. Leidholdt and J. G. Raymond (eds) *The Sexual Liberals and the Attack on Feminism*. Oxford: Pergamon Press.

Russell, D. (1990) *Rape in Marriage*. Indianapolis, IN: Indiana University Press.

Sanday, P. R. (1990) *Fraternity Gang Rape: Sex, Brotherhood and Privilege on Campus*. New York: New York University Press.

Scully, D. (1990) *Understanding Sexual Violence: A Study of Convicted Rapists*. London: Unwin Hyman.

Scutt, J. (1993) Women and law, in C. Kramarae and D. Spender (eds) *The Knowledge Explosion*. London: Harvester Wheatsheaf.

Seabrook, J. (1990) Power lust. *New Statesman & Society*, 27 April.

Sex Education Forum (1992) *A Framework for School Sex Education*. London: National Children's Bureau.

Sharpe, S. (1994) *Just Like a Girl*. Harmondsworth: Penguin.

Sherwin, S. (1989) Philosophical methodology and feminist methodology: are they compatible? in A. Garry and M. Pearsall (eds) *Women, Knowledge, and Reality*. London: Unwin Hyman, 21–37.

Shuttleworth, S. (1990) Female circulation; medical discourse and popular advertising in the mid-Victorian era, in M. Jacobus, E. Fox and S. Shuttleworth (eds) *Body/Politics*. London: Routledge.

Skeggs, B. (1991) Challenging masculinity and using sexuality. *British Journal of Sociology of Education*, 12 (2): 343–58.

Skelton, C. and Hanson, J. (1989) Schooling the teachers, in S. Acker (ed.) *Teachers, Gender and Careers*. London: Falmer Press, pp. 109–23.

Smart, C. (1989) *Feminism and the Power of Law*. London: Routledge.

Smart, C. (1990) Law's power, the sexed body and feminist discourse. *Journal of Law and Society*, 17: 194–210.

Smart, C. (1995) *Law, Crime and Sexuality: Essays in Feminism*. London: Routledge.

Smith, D. E. (1988) *The Everyday World as Problematic*. Milton Keynes: Open University Press.

Smith, J. (1989) *Misogynies*. London: Faber & Faber.

Smith, L. (1989) *Concerns about Rape*. No. 106. London: HMSO.

Social Trends (1990) Vol. 20. London: HMSO.

Sousa, C. (1991) Dating violence intervention project, in B. Levy (ed.) *Dating Violence: Young Women in Danger*. Seattle, WA: The Seal Press, pp. 223–32.

Spender, D. (1980) *Man Made Language*, London RKP.

Squirrell, G. (1989) Teachers and issues of sexual orientation. *Gender and Education*, 1 (1): 17–35.

Stanworth, M. (ed.) (1987) *Reproductive Technologies: Gender, Motherhood and Medicine*. Cambridge: Polity.

Steketee, G. and Austen, A. (1989) Rape victims and the justice system: utilization and impact. *Social Service Review*, 63 (2): 285–303.

Stiglmayer, A. (1993) The rapes in Bosnia Herzegovina, in A. Stiglmayer (ed.) *Mass Rape: The War against Women in Bosnia-Herzegovina*. London: University of Nebraska Press, pp. 82–169.

Sumner, C. (1983) Rethinking deviance: towards a sociology of censures. *Research in Law, Deviance and Social Control*, 5: 187–204.

Summers, C. (1975) *Damned Whores and God's Police*. Sydney: Penguin.

Symonds, A. (1979) Violence against women: the myth of masochism. *American Journal of Psychotherapy*, 33: 161–73.

Szirom, T. (1988) *Teaching Gender*. London: Allen & Unwin.

Tannen, D. (1992) *You Just Don't Understand: Men and Women in Conversation*. London: Virago.

Temkin, J. (1987) *Rape and the Legal Process*. London: Sweet & Maxwell.

Temkin, J. (1993) Sexual history evidence – the ravishment of section 2. *Criminal Law Review*, 1: 3–19.

Thomson, R. (1994) Moral rhetoric and public health pragmatism: the recent politics of sex education. *Feminist Review*, 48 autumn: 40–61.

Thomson, R. and Scott, S. (1991) *Learning About Sex: Young Women and the Social Construction of Sexual Identity*. London: Tufnell Press.

Ussher, J. (1991) *Women's Madness*. London: Harvester Press.

Vines, G. (1993) *Raging Hormones: Do They Rule Our Lives?* London: Virago.

Walker, J. (1988) *Louts and Legends: Male Youth Culture in an Inner City School*. Syndey: Allen & Unwin.

Walkowitz, J. (1980) *Prostitution and Victorian Society*. Cambridge: Cambridge University Press.

Wasik, M. (1982) Cumulative provocation and domestic killing. *Criminal Law Review*, 30 (1): 29–37.

Watson, S. (1990) *Playing the State: Australian Feminist Interventions*. London: Verso.

Weber, M. (1964) On bureaucracy, in H. H. Gerth and C. Wright Mills (eds) *Essays from Max Weber*. London: Routledge & Kegan Paul.

Weeks, J. (1977/1983) *Coming Out: Homosexual Politics from the 19th century to the Present*. London: Quartet Books.

Williams, G. (1992) Domestic provocation and the ivory tower. *New Law Journal*, 142, 20 March: 381–2.

Willis, P. (1977) *Learning to Labour: How Working Class Kids Get Working Class Jobs*. London: Saxon House.

Wilson, A. (1978) *Finding a Voice*. London: Virago.

Wilson, D. (1978) Sexual codes and conduct, in C. Smart and B. Smart (eds) *Women, Sexuality and Social Control*. London: Routledge.

Woman's Hour (1995) Marital rape five years on, 3 August.

Woman's National Commission (WNC) (1985) *Violence Against Women*. London: Women's National Commission.

Wood, J. A. (1984) Groping towards sexism: boys' sex talk, in A. McRobbie and M. Nava (eds) *Gender and Generation*. London: Macmillan, pp. 54–84.

World in Action (1989) *The Right to Rape*. Thames Television, 25 September.

Wright, R. (1984) A note on attrition in rape cases. *British Journal of Criminology*, 24 (4): 339–400.

Wyre, R. and Swift, A. (1990) *Women, Men and Rape*. London: Hodder & Stoughton.

Young, A. (1990) *Femininity in Dissent*. London: Routledge.

Index

THEORISING HETEROSEXUALITY
TELLING IT STRAIGHT

Diane Richardson (ed.)

Little attention has traditionally been given to theorising heterosexuality. Heterosexuality tends to be taken for granted, as something that is 'natural' and 'normal'. *Theorising Heterosexuality* questions this assumption and demonstrates how much of our understanding of ourselves and the social worlds we inhabit is based upon unquestioned assumptions about the nature of heterosexuality.

- In what ways does heterosexuality encode and structure everyday life?
- How does heterosexuality shape our sense of identity?
- What is the nature of heterosexual desire?
- What is the relationship between heterosexuality and feminism?

In addition to addressing these questions, the contributors to *Theorising Heterosexuality* provide a critical examination of recent debates about heterosexuality, in particular within postmodern, feminist and queer theory.

Well written in a clear and lively style, this book brings together leading authors in the field, who represent a variety of differing approaches and viewpoints. Heterosexuality is theorised in terms of its institutionalisation within society and culture, as practice and as identity. The result is an impressive and exciting collection, whose insights invite a radical rethinking of many of the concepts we use to theorise social relations.

Theorising Heterosexuality will be of interest to a wide range of students in the social sciences and humanities, especially in sociology, cultural studies, lesbian and gay studies, social psychology and women's studies.

Contents
Heterosexuality and social theory – Heterosexuality and feminist theory – Heterosexuality and domestic life – Heterosexuality and social policy – Heterosexuality and the desire for gender – Recognition and heterosexual desire – Heterosexuality and masculinity – Which one's the man? The heterosexualization of lesbian sex – In the same boat? The gendered (in)experience of first heterosex – Collusion, collaboration and confession – References – Index.

Contributors
Jean Carabine, Janet Holland, Wendy Hollway, Stevi Jackson, Sheila Jeffreys, Caroline Ramazanoglu, Diane Richardson, Victoria Robinson, Carol Smart, Rachel Thomson, Jo VanEvery, Tamsin Wilton

224pp   0 335 19503 2 (Paperback)   0 335 19504 0 (Hardback)

MAKING VIOLENCE SEXY
FEMINIST VIEWS ON PORNOGRAPHY

Diana E. H. Russell (ed.)

A crucially important collection of feminist voices challenging the pornocrats.
Even if you read nothing else on the subject, read this.

(Robin Morgan)

Making Violence Sexy is a courageous book that chronicles women's resistance to
pornography over the last twenty years. It does this in a collection of feminist
articles, including testimonies by victims/survivors of pornography that together
make a convincing case for the view that pornography (as distinct from erotica)
causes harm to women, including acts of violence.

This book will appeal to students and lecturers of women's studies and sociology,
political activists, public officials, social scientists, legal and medical professionals
– those who consider it a form of discrimination against women. Women's studies
teachers will find it a welcome addition to their required reading lists, and those
working against sexual violence will appreciate it as a primary, up-to-date, and
comprehensive source and inspiration.

Contents
Introduction – Part I: Survivors of pornography – Part II: Overview – Part III:
Feminist research on pornography – Part IV: Feminist strategies and actions against
pornography – Notes – References – Index.

320pp   0 335 19200 9 (Paperback)